Structuralism in Literature

Structuralism
in
Literature

AN INTRODUCTION

Robert Scholes

New Haven and London, Yale University Press

Library of Congress catalog card number: 73-90578
International standard book number: 0-300-01750-2 (cloth)
International standard book number: 0-300-01850-9 (paper)

Designed by Sally Sullivan
and set in Garamond type.
Printed in the United States of America by
Vail-Ballou Press, Inc., Binghamton, N.Y.

19   18   17

For all my family—official and unofficial, living and unliving

Contents

Preface

In attempting to present an introduction to structuralism in literature, I have found it necessary to make certain choices which should be acknowledged at this point. In emphasizing the literary aspects of structuralism I have necessarily deemphasized other aspects. The reader will not find here any discussion of structuralism in philosophy, in psychology, in history, in the physical sciences or mathematics. There are books in existence in which such discussions may be found, and they will be mentioned in the Bibliographical Appendix. But in this book the emphasis will be on literature, and only the most essential concepts from linguistics and the other sciences of man and nature will be presented. Some famous names frequently associated with structuralism—Derrida, Lacan, Foucault—will not be discussed. Nor will phenomenology be mentioned except to be distinguished from structuralism.

The reasons for this intense and somewhat exclusive focus on structuralism in literature stem from my own interests and from my sense of what is needed by other students of literature whose first language is English. I hope in particular to stimulate an awareness of certain French critics whose work is not yet sufficiently known outside of Europe but whose achievements are already impressive and still growing. In attempting this I have been led to emphasize narrative literature at the expense of poetry, drama, and other forms of literary discourse. I have not entirely ignored the other major forms (poetry is considered in chapter 2 and drama in chapter 3), but it is only fair to admit at the outset that

fiction receives far more attention here than any other kind of literature. There are a number of reasons for this. Since I am mainly
concerned with the presentation of European critical thinking to
an English-speaking audience, the treatment of poetry presents special difficulties. As we all know, it does not translate, for reasons
the structuralists can demonstrate at length. But I must add to this
my feeling that poetry has also proved (thus far, at least) less amenable to structuralist criticism than fiction, for reasons that I will
explain more fully in chapter 2.

The situation of drama is rather different. Some interesting and
clearly structuralist criticism of drama has appeared (such as the
books of Barthes and Goldmann on Racine, and Jacques Ehrmann's brilliant essay on *Cinna*). In deciding to elaborate my
treatment of fiction at the expense of drama, I may simply have
erred—but my intention was to present as exhaustively as space
permitted a discussion of that aspect of literature which the structuralists have treated most extensively and thoroughly. Of course, I
have also been guided here by my own interests and limitations.
The poetics of fiction has been my major theoretical concern in literary study, and I have taken my previous work in this field as a
kind of license to enter the structuralist discussions of narrative and
offer my own alternatives to certain structuralist formulations, as
well as to develop certain positions beyond the points presented by
structuralist poeticians. My hope is that the final value of this book
will lie both in its presentation of the major figures and ideas of
this European critical movement to an English-speaking audience,
and in the elaboration of certain principles of literary theory which
emerge from this presentation.

One other omission must be apologized for if not explained before we turn to the business at hand. This book includes no treatment of the structuralist poetics of film—and that is a serious
omission for a number of reasons. One of the major developments
of structuralism is a related but distinct discipline called semiology
(or semeiology, or semiotics) which is the general study of signifying systems. Human language is one system of signification, the
most elaborate that we have, but there are others, which often take

the form of some iconography of images or some patterning of so-cial behavior which can be approached as a form of communica-tion. Human beings communicate by body language, by styles of clothing, and in many other ways besides speech and writing. Se-miology, as the study which includes these extralinguistic forms of communication, has proved ideally suited to the discussion of sig-nification in the cinema, which uses visual images, language, music, other sounds to convey its meanings. For a student of film these days, to be ignorant of semiology is to be simply illiterate. In set-ting the achievements of the semiologists of cinema to one side, then, I have certainly not meant to diminish them. But the prob-lems of this polysemous medium are so complex, and the semiology of cinema so involved, that rather than treat it sketchily in the amount of space that could be allotted here, I have decided to ex-pand my treatment of fiction as much as possible, and confine the semiology of film to some entries in the Bibliographical Appendix. In my own experience, I should add, students of film often find it easier to approach this subject by way of formalism and literary structuralism than to attempt it without such knowledge. Thus, it is my hope that there will be useful material here even for the ded-icated cinéaste who regards written literature as a mildly interest-ing historical phenomenon but not a matter of present interest.

In mentioning the aspects of structuralism not covered in this book, I have sought only to be fair to my reader by not promising or implying that he might find here more than there is. But I have not meant to be apologetic about those things which are in fact treated in this volume. In structuralism I have found a body of ideas and methods which has contributed powerfully to my own thinking about literature and about life as well. If it is the function of man in this world to raise his consciousness of himself and his situation, then structuralism has much to teach us. And I have not hesitated to push the conclusions of structuralist thought beyond the confines of art and apply them to other aspects of the human situation. For this, I make no apologies.

In the writing of this book I have had the assistance and encour-agement of many people, whose contributions I wish to acknowledge here. This project was undertaken at the suggestion of Whitney Blake, of the Yale University Press. Without his advice and encouragement this book would never have been written. Some chapters, or parts of chapters, have been read or heard by students and faculty of colleges and universities from California to Massachusetts, whose responses have often been critical and always stimulating and useful to me in revision. To them and to my own colleagues, students—friends—I am grateful, as I am to the editors of three journals, who first printed material which in altered form is included here, and who now have given their permission for this recycling: *Novel* (Edward Bloom and Mark Spilka), *The James Joyce Quarterly* (Thomas F. Staley), and *New Literary History* (Ralph Cohen). I also wish to note, with pleasure and gratitude, the contributions of Khachig Tololyan, who took time from his own dissertation to read this entire manuscript; Jane Lewin, who made a similar sacrifice to help with proofreading; and Jo Ann S. Putnam-Scholes, whose presence made it all possible.

Finally, some technical matters. For works not included in my bibliographical checklist, I give a full citation at first mention in the text. In every case the paperback edition is cited if one is available. Translations from the French, unless otherwise indicated, are my own, as are any errors of fact or judgment that still remain herein.

September 1973   R. S.

1   What Is Structuralism?

A. Structuralism as a Movement of Mind

The last half of the nineteenth century and the first half of the twentieth were characterized by the fragmentation of knowledge into isolated disciplines so formidable in their specialization as to seem beyond all synthesis. Even philosophy, the queen of the human sciences, came down from her throne to play solitary word games. Both the language-philosophy of Wittgenstein and the existentialism of the Continental thinkers are philosophies of retreat. The language-philosophers insisted that there is no possible correspondence between our language and the world beyond it. The existentialists spoke of isolated man, cut off from objects and even from other men, in an absurd condition of being. From the logical atomism of Russell to the nausea of Sartre, fragmentation ruled the intellectual world during the first part of this century. And the only concerted opposition to this posture came from the philosophers of Marxism: from Georg Lukács, for instance, a traditional humanist whose Marxist attacks on "modernist" philosophy had much to do with the various attempts of existentialists to adapt their philosophy to Marxism. (Of Sartre, that most adept adapter, more later.) One of the most penetrating of these attacks came from the scientifically oriented Marxist, Christopher Caudwell, who opposed the "coherent system" of dialectical materialism to the

chaotic confusion of "discoveries"—relativity physics, quantum physics, Freudism, anthropology, genetics, psycho-physiology, which are based on exclusive assumptions and contradict or ignore each other. [*Reality: A Study in Bourgeois Philosophy,* New York, 1970, p. 31]

Structuralism, I am suggesting, is a response to the need expressed here by Caudwell for a "coherent system" that would unite the modern sciences and make the world habitable for man again. This is a religious need, of course. Man can be defined by his insistence on a believable belief, whatever his standards of believability. For Caudwell, Marxism filled that need. For many of us now, there is simply too much of the arbitrary in the Marxian dialectic: too much faith in history, not enough knowledge of man and nature. As a social scientist, Marx, like Freud, has made a great contribution to our knowledge of human behavior. But as a religious thinker his faith is neither comprehensive enough nor scientific enough to satisfy us now.

Marxism is an ideology. Structuralism is at present only a methodology with ideological implications. But it is a methodology which is seeking nothing less than the unification of all the sciences into a new system of belief. This is why its ideological implications, incomplete as they are at present, strike us forcibly. In chapter 6, I shall try to draw out some of these implications, especially as they relate to the values that inform contemporary fiction. But here it will be useful to return to the precursors and origins of structuralist thought. Marxism and structuralism share certain values which can be seen very clearly in their response to the problems of epistemology—specifically to the problem of the relationship of the human subject with his own perceptual and linguistic systems, and with the objective world.

Caudwell himself, who died in Spain before his thirtieth birthday and remains undervalued as a thinker, had an appropriately dialectical response to the problems of mind/matter dualism. For him both thought and matter had "real" status:

Thought is a relation of matter; but the relation is real; it is not only real but determining. It is real *because* it is determining. Mind is a determining set of relations between the matter in my body and in the rest of the Universe. [*Reality,* p. 24]

In a remarkably similar fashion we find Jean Piaget considering the same problem from the perspective of modern physics and mathematics. He points out the "amazing" and "steady agreement between physical reality and the mathematical theories employed in its description," and he concludes,

> This harmony between mathematics and physical reality cannot, in positivist fashion, be written off as simply the correspondence of a language with the objects it designates. Languages are not in the habit of forecasting the events they describe; rather, it is a correspondence of human operations with those of object-operators, a harmony, then, between this particular operator—the human being as body and mind —and the innumerable operators in nature—physical objects at their several levels. [*Structuralism,* pp. 40–41]

From his anthropological perspective, Claude Lévi-Strauss has offered us another version of this view:

> The laws of thought, primitive or civilized, are the same as those which find expression in physical reality and in social reality, which is simply one of their aspects. [*Les Structures élémentaires de la parenté,* p. 591, quoted in Auzias, *Clefs pour le structuralisme,* p. 25]

Thus, from a certain perspective both Marxism and structuralism can be seen as reactions to "modernist" alienation and despair. They are opposed to one another in many ways, some of which will be considered later, but they share a "scientific" view of the world as both real in itself and intelligible to man. Both Marxism and structuralism are integrative, holistic ways of looking at the world, including man. The search for such views in this century has been one of its main intellectual currents. Even in Wittgenstein himself, who was so pessimistic about the possibilities of knowledge, we can discover an essentially structural if not structuralist view of the world. For, in its broadest sense, structuralism is a way of looking for reality not in individual things but in the relationships among them. As Wittgenstein insisted, "The world is the totality of facts, not of things." And "facts" are "states of affairs":

2.03	In a state of affairs objects fit into one another like the links of a chain.
2.031	In a state of affairs objects stand in a determinate relationship to one another.
2.032	The determinate way in which objects are connected in a state of affairs is the structure of the state of affairs.
2.033	Form is the possibility of structure.
2.034	The structure of a fact consists of the structures of states of affairs.
2.04	The totality of existing states of affairs is the world.

[*Tractatus Logico-Philosophicus,* London, 1953]

And states of affairs must each be expressed by a sentence, not a word. The study of sentences, which lies at the heart of modern linguistics, has led such linguists as Noam Chomsky to the conclusion that all men share an innate predisposition to organize their linguistic possibilities in a certain way. Thus all men participate in knowledge of some "universal grammar" that enables each one to learn his own language creatively, generating new grammatical sentences to suit his own communicative ends. In semantic study, I. A. Richards, moving beyond the atomism of *The Meaning of Meaning,* has developed a related view of language:

Things, in brief, are instances of laws. As Bradley said, association marries only universals, and out of these laws, these recurrent likenesses of behavior, in our minds and in the world—not out of revived duplicates of individual past impressions—the fabric of our meanings, which is the world, is composed. [*Philosophy of Rhetoric,* New York, 1965, p. 36]

In epistemology, Susanne Langer has summarized the achievement of the Kant-Cassirer tradition as a recognition of "the part which symbolization, or symbolic expression, plays in the formulation of things and events, and the natural ordering of our ambient as a 'world' " (*Philosophical Sketches,* New York, 1964, p. 59). In psychology the Gestalt psychologists led a revolution in our understanding of perception and thought, which emphasized the primacy of the whole over the parts in our mental processes. And in his book, *The Task of Gestalt Psychology* (Princeton, 1969), Wolfgang Köhler quotes the physicists Maxwell, Planck, and Eddington to support his contention that natural science, too, in the twentieth century, has learned of the necessity for thinking in a holistic way:

> I next read a book of Max Planck's lectures delivered in 1909 in New York City. In one of these lectures, Planck discusses the concept of irreversible processes, a concept which plays a central role in what the physicists call the Second Principle of Thermodynamics. In this connection, the author makes the following statement:
>
>> In physics, it is our habit to try to approach the explanation of a physical process by splitting this process into elements. We regard all complicated processes as combinations of simple elementary processes, . . . that is, we think of the wholes before us as the sums of their parts. But this procedure presupposes that the splitting of a whole does not affect the character of this whole. . . . Now, when we deal with irreversible processes in this fashion, the irreversibility is simply lost. One cannot understand such processes on the assumption that all properties of a whole may be approached by a study of its parts.
>
> Planck adds the following extraordinary sentence: "It seems to me that the same difficulty arises when we consider most problems of mental life." [pp. 61–62]

The very physiological processes of our brains must be, Köhler tells us, "in Maxwell's, in Planck's, and in my own sense, structured functional wholes" (p. 93).

In anthropology Claude Lévi-Strauss has insisted that "the true constituent units of a myth are not the isolated relations but *bundles of such relations* and it is only as bundles that these relations can be put to use and combined so as to produce a meaning" *(Structural Anthropology,* Garden City, N.Y., 1967, p. 207). Anthropology itself he sees as "a general theory of relationships" (p. 95). All human mental process, he describes as governed by universal laws which manifest themselves most clearly in man's symbolic function. Even the unconscious as defined by psychoanalysis, Lévi-Strauss asserts, now

> ceases to be the ultimate haven of individual peculiarities—the repository of a unique history which makes each of us an irreplaceable being. It is reducible to a function—the symbolic function, which no doubt is specifically human, and which is carried out according to the same laws among all men, and actually corresponds to the aggregate of these laws. [p. 198]

In literary criticism the Russian formalists and their structuralist descendants have worked toward discovering the universal principles that govern the literary use of language, from the syntax of fictional construction to the paradigms of poetry. Thus structural thinking has enabled such concepts as Northrop Frye's "order of words" and Claudio Guillén's "system of literature." But structuralist activity has found its center in linguistic study, and taken much of its impetus from the achievements of Saussure, Jakobson, and other scholars like the Russian phonologist N. S. Trubetzkoy, who in 1933 summed up the achievement of his discipline in this way:

> Present-day phonology is characterized above all by its structuralism and by its systematic universalism. . . . The age in which we live is characterized by the tendency in all the scientific disciplines to replace atomism by structuralism and individualism by universalism (in the philosophical sense of these terms of course). This tendency can be observed in physics, in chemistry, in biology, in psychology, in economics, etc.

Present-day phonology is thus not isolated. It has a place in a broader scientific movement. [Quoted in Emile Benveniste, *Problems in General Linguistics,* p. 82]

The movement Trubetzkoy referred to has not been merely scientific but has affected the arts as well, for it is a general movement of mind—one of those currents of thought that from time to time sweep through a culture and move its most disparate elements in the same direction. The impact of this movement on literature and literary study will be our concerns throughout this book.

B. *Structuralism as a Method*

Let us consider the following two critical statements:

Like everyone, I believe that the end of criticism is to arrive at an intimate knowledge of critical reality. However, it seems to me that such an intimacy is only possible to the extent that critical thought *becomes* the thought criticized, which it can succeed in doing only by re-feeling, re-thinking, re-imagining this thought from the inside. Nothing could be less objective than such a movement of mind. Contrary to what one might expect, criticism must prevent itself from seeing some sort of *object* (whether it is the person of the author seen as an Other, or his work considered as a Thing); for what must be arrived at is a *subject,* which is to say a spiritual activity that one cannot understand except by putting oneself in its place and causing it to play again within us its role as subject. [Georges Poulet, *Les Lettres nouvelles,* 24 June 1959; quoted in Gérard Genette, *Figures,* p. 158]

This intersubjective criticism, which the work of Georges Poulet itself illustrates admirably, belongs to the type of interpretation that Paul Ricoeur, following Dilthey and some others (including Spitzer), calls *hermeneutics.* The sense of a work is not conceived through a series of intellectual operations, it is received, "recovered," as a message at once old and totally renewed. On the other hand, it is clear that structural criticism resorts to that objectivism which Poulet condemns, because structures are not *lived,* either by the creative or the critical consciousness. [*Figures,* p. 158]

In the second of these two statements, Gérard Genette begins a discussion of the ideas raised in the quotation from Poulet. He goes on to point out that Poulet would accuse structuralism of treating literary texts reductively, X-raying them in search of their bone structure while missing their substance. From the point of view of Poulet, of Ricoeur, of hermeneutic criticism in general, "everywhere that the hermeneutic recovery of meaning is possible and desirable, through the intuitive agreement of two consciousnesses, structural analysis would be (at least partially) illegitimate or impertinent" (p. 159). Following this line of thought one could divide literary study into two domains, two bodies of works upon which each kind of criticism might legitimately operate. The hermeneutic critic would treat "living" literature, and the structuralist would treat

    literatures distant in time or space, infantile and popular literatures, including recent forms like melodrama and the serial novel, which criticism has always neglected, not only because of academic prejudice but also because intersubjective participation can neither animate nor guide in this study, whereas structural criticism can treat this material anthropologically, studying its large masses and recurrent functions, following the way traced by folklorists like Propp or Skaftymov. [pp. 159–60]

Genette accepts provisionally this gambit, but he then proceeds to point out that many of the great "literary" texts are themselves more remote from us than critics sometimes admit, and may respond more satisfyingly to a structural approach than to one which achieves an intimacy that falsifies the work. And he suggests that what we really have here is not a choice of approaches to be dictated by the nature of particular texts, but of methods to be adopted according to our relationship to a particular text and what we wish to know about it. To this end he quotes Merleau-Ponty on the subject of ethnology as a discipline, suggesting that Merleau-Ponty's words can also be applied to structuralism as a method:

> It is not a specialty defined by a particular object, "primitive" societies; it is a manner of thinking which imposes itself when the object is "other" and requires that we transform ourselves. Thus we become ethnologists of our own society if we distance ourselves from it. [*Signes,* p. 151; *Figures,* p. 161]

Seen in this way, structuralism and hermeneutics are not in a relation of opposition, dividing the world into objects belonging exclusively to each group, but are in a relation of complementarity, capable of profitably approaching the same work and disengaging from it complementary significations. Thus literary criticism should not refuse to learn what structuralism can tell it, even about the works that seem nearest to us, precisely by distancing them and examining objectively their functioning. Genette concludes this part of his discussion (which I have been summarizing here) by reminding us that we cannot in fact appreciate the particular quality of, for example, the Stendhalian novel, without some grasp of the novelistic imagination as a general historical and trans-historical entity. He does not add, as I should myself, that the "subjectivity" of hermeneutic criticism can never be entirely subjective. The critic who "recovers" the meaning of any given work always does so by establishing a relationship between the work and some system of ideas outside it. This may be a theory of man, or as with Poulet a theory of "human time," but the theory must be there in order to justify the critic's presence. Merely to recreate the work would be, as Tzvetan Todorov suggests in his essay on poetics in *Qu'est-ce que le structuralisme?,* to repeat its own words in their own order. Interpretation, however subjective, must justify itself by bringing something external to the work, if only the subjectivity of the critic, which is different from that of the artist. Which is why interpretations of their own work by artists are rarely attempted and seldom valuable. The hermeneutic "recovery" of meaning is often just the story of the critic's struggle to recover it. This activity can be interesting, intelligent, sensitive, illuminating, and even produce a minor kind of literature in itself. But it need have no privileged place among the possible activities of the critical mind.

Structuralism, on the other hand, may claim a privileged place in literary study because it seeks to establish a model of the system of literature itself as the external reference for the individual works it considers. By moving from the study of language to the study of literature, and seeking to define the principles of structuration that operate not only through individual works but through the relationships among works over the whole field of literature, structuralism has tried—and is trying—to establish for literary studies a basis that is as scientific as possible. This does not mean that there should be no place in literary studies for the personal and subjective. Even the physical sciences can show us example after example of subjective genius at work. But for such work to be most fruitful, an intellectual framework must be established on which the work can be based. At the heart of the idea of structuralism is the idea of system: a complete, self-regulating entity that adapts to new conditions by transforming its features while retaining its systematic structure. Every literary unit from the individual sentence to the whole order of words can be seen in relation to the concept of system. In particular, we can look at individual works, literary genres, and the whole of literature as related systems, and at literature as a system within the larger system of human culture. The relationships that obtain between any of these systematic units may be studied, and that study will be, in some sense, structuralist. The danger in all this—which structuralists like Genette are well aware of—is to assume a systematic completeness where it does not exist. For literary structuralism one of the great challenges is to discriminate accurately between the tendency toward system—especially at the level of the individual work—and the failure to achieve it. Genette, in particular, has been eloquent in pointing out the danger of regarding literary works as "closed" and "finished" objects in order to treat them systematically.

Another danger for structuralism has been what we might call the "formalistic fallacy"—for it is related to a reproach usually leveled against formalism, and which the Russian formalists, especially in their earliest enthusiasm, sometimes deserved. The formalistic fallacy is a lack of concern for the "meaning" or "content" of literary works, and it is a charge frequently brought against that criticism which refuses to acknowledge the presence of a cultural world beyond the literary work and a cultural system beyond the literary system. It must be acknowledged that the purely formal description of literary works and literary systems is an important part of the structuralist methodology. But the fallacy does not lie in this necessary isolation of certain aspects of the material being studied, it lies in the refusal to acknowledge that these are not the only aspects, or in the insistence that these aspects function in an entirely closed system without influence from the world beyond literature. Structuralism, properly understood, far from being cut off from the world in a formal prison, approaches it directly at several different levels of investigation.

In particular, structuralism seeks to explore the relationship between the system of literature and the culture of which it is a part. We cannot even define "literariness" without setting it against "non-literariness"—and we must recognize that these two functions are in an unstable relationship which changes along with other functions of a given culture. A culture, observes Genette, "manifests itself as much in what it reads as in what it writes" (p. 169). And he quotes Borges to the effect that "If it was given to me to read any page written today—even this one—as it would be read in the year 2000, I would know the literature of the year 2000" (*Enquêtes*, p. 224; *Figures*, p. 169). Borges, as always, delightfully exaggerates. But the notion behind this exaggeration is precisely the structuralist idea of a system in which all the elements are interrelated and therefore mutually inferable from any significant sample. That a single page is not a significant sample is simply a Borgesian joke, a stretching of the idea. And one might stretch it further to suggest that much more than the literature of a particular culture could be inferred from its way of reading a particular text—without parting company with structuralism.

On the level of the individual text, structuralism approaches the world again whenever it considers the semantic aspect of any textual feature. In some investigations, individual critics may choose to ignore this aspect as much as possible in order to isolate other features. And indeed, in my view some formalist and structuralist critics have on occasion pretended that the semantics of literature could be ignored to a greater extent than it is really possible to do—with the result that semantic meanings and values often creep back into analyses unnoticed or unannounced. But since linguistics, the mother of structuralist literary theory, is still very much uncertain about the role of semantics in linguistic description, it is not surprising that literary structuralism evidences some uncertainty in handling it as well. Still, this has been something of a weak point in structuralist criticism, and it would be a mistake to ignore it. For this is precisely the place where literary criticism has something to teach linguistics about the functioning of language. We shall be returning to this point in the later chapters, especially chapter 5. But now we must begin a more systematic investigation of the roots of structuralist literary theory and its development, beginning with its heritage from the study of language.

2 From Linguistics to Poetics

In this book we are concerned with the relevance of structuralism to literature and literary criticism. Thus we must face the fact that the structural methodology is not the exclusive property of literary study—far from it—that its roots are in the social sciences (linguistics, anthropology), and that its very application to literature depends upon the relationship between the language of literature and the whole of language. Both the virtues and the limitations of structuralism stem from its linguistic roots. In this chapter, then, we shall consider two aspects of the relationship between linguistics and the theory of literature. First, it will be necessary to present those concepts of modern linguistics which have been most influential on literary studies, and then it will be appropriate to investigate the most important attempt to move from linguistics to poetics in order to establish a theory of literature. In considering these two aspects of structuralism, we shall inevitably concentrate on the work of those two linguists who have been most influential on literary studies: Ferdinand de Saussure and Roman Jakobson.

A. Linguistic Background: Saussure to Jakobson

The basic conceptual tools of structural analysis were developed by the Swiss linguist Ferdinand de Saussure in the early part of this century. His *Cours de linguistique générale,* reconstructed from the notes of devoted students, was first published in 1915 and quickly became a major influence in modern linguistic studies.

(The late date of its translation into English, 1959, is a testimony to the continuing relevance of Saussure's views as well as to the growing interest in linguistic matters in the English-speaking world.) In it Saussure developed a number of concepts that have influenced all later structural thought.

In the *Cours* Saussure begins by defining language itself. His definition is unusual in that it distinguishes three levels of linguistic activity: *langage, langue,* and *parole. Langage* is the broadest aspect, for it includes the entire human potential for speech, both physical and mental. As such, it is simply too broad and undefined an area to be studied systematically. *Langue,* however, is defined precisely by virtue of its systematic qualities. For *langue* is "language" as we use the word in speaking of the English "language" or the French "language." *Langue* is the language-system which each of us uses to generate discourse that is intelligible to others. Our individual utterances are what Saussure calls *parole.* Thus *langage* is linguistic potential, *langue* is a language-system, and *parole* is individual utterance. For Saussure, the central object of linguistic study must be the language-system. Language-systems, because they are social products, are conventional. In speaking English we have an infinite number of potential utterances at our command, but these are based on a finite number of words and grammatical relationships. And these words and relationships are aspects of a single system.

A language-system, it must be emphasized, has no tangible existence. The English language is not *in* the world any more than the laws of motion are *in* the world. In order to become an object of study a language, or a model of it, must be *constructed* from the evidence of individual utterances. The importance of this principle for other structural studies cannot be overemphasized. In order to become a science any human discipline must move from the phenomena it recognizes to the system that governs them, from *parole* to *langue.* In language, of course, no utterance is intelligible to a speaker who lacks the language-system that governs its meaning. The implications of this for literature are striking. No literary utterance, no "work" of literature, can be meaningful if we lack a sense of the literary system into which it fits. This is why Roman Jakobson insists that the proper object of literary study is "literariness"; and why Northrop Frye argues that we must teach literature not as a collection of autonomous "works" but as "an order of words"; and why Claudio Guillén, specifically acknowledging Saussure's contribution to his thinking, maintains that

> the theoretical orders of poetics should be viewed, at any moment in their history, as essentially mental codes—with which the practicing writer (the writer as individual, as *hombre de carne y hueso*) comes to terms through his writing. The structures of this order are no more alien to the poems he produces than the linguistic code is to the actual utterances in his speech. [*Literature as System,* p. 390]

After establishing the need to emphasize the language-system, Saussure proceeded to devise conceptual tools for the description of that system and its elements. First, he redefined the basic element of linguistic structures: the sign. A sign, he declared, is not simply the name for a thing but a complex whole which links a sound-image and a concept. (By "sound-image" he designates both what we actually hear in listening to speech and what we imagine we hear in the mind's ear when we read or think in language.) Attending to this dual aspect of the sign enables us, for instance, to speak of those things which the English word "tree" and the Latin word "arbor" have in common as well as those things which differentiate them. The concepts are essentially the same, in this case, though the sound-images are different. Refining his terminology, Saussure then called these two aspects of the sign the *signifiant* ("signifier" is the usual English rendition) and the *signifié* (signified). The relationship between the signifying sound and the signified concept, he insisted, is arbitrary.

From this arbitrariness many things follow; therefore, it may be well to pause and consider it. What it means is that in all (or nearly all) signs the sound-image is in no way dictated by the concept. The concept "tree" may be signified by dozens of quite different sound-images in different languages. In fact, if the sign were not arbitrary, we would all speak the same language, no other being possible. The connection between sound and concept is arbitrary with respect to nature, of course, but not to culture. We who grow up in English must call a tree a tree if we wish to be understood. It is possible to be offended by this state of affairs, to see in it an existential absurdity, but this would be an un-Saussurean and unstructuralistic response. The arbitrariness of the sign in no way need imply the arbitrariness of the concept or its inadequacy as an image of reality. And, in fact, the study of signs and sign-systems can lead to a deeper knowledge of human beings and the systems in which they live. Saussure posited such a study himself:

> Language is a system of signs that express ideas, and is therefore comparable to a system of writing, the alphabet of deaf-mutes, symbolic rites, polite formulas, military signals, etc. But it is the most important of all these systems.
>
> *A science that studies the life of signs within society* is conceivable; it would be a part of social psychology and consequently of general psychology; I shall call it *semiology* (from Greek *sēmeîon* "sign"). Semiology would show what constitutes signs, what laws govern them. Since the science does not yet exist, no one can say what it would be; but it has a right to existence, a place staked out in advance. Linguistics is only a part of the general science of semiology; the laws discovered by semiology will be applicable to linguistics, and the latter will circumscribe a well-defined area within the mass of anthropological facts. [*Course in General Linguistics,* p. 16]

Semiology is duly coming into being as an aspect of structuralist thought. But the conclusions of such investigators as Claude Lévi-Strauss and Roland Barthes are that language is so central to human communication that no other meaning-system can manage without its aid.

Another of Saussure's crucial observations about the nature of the sign is that "the signifier, being auditory, is unfolded in time . . . ; it is a line." And, of course, not only is each sign linear, each utterance is even more obviously so. Unlike the picture, which can display various significant elements simultaneously, the elements of a verbal utterance must be delivered in an order which is itself significant. The sign, then, as well as the sentence and all larger units of discourse, is primarily narrative, and from this it follows that the larger structures of narrative will ultimately receive close attention from students of literature initially influenced by Saussurean linguistics. We shall continue with the linear aspect of the utterance, but first it will be useful to pause here and examine a larger aspect of language. Perhaps the most generally influential idea of Saussure's is his distinction between the synchronic and diachronic approaches to the study of language, and his consequent emphasis on the synchronic at the expense of the diachronic.

Any particular phenomenon in language (and in many other studies) can be examined in either of two ways. It may be seen as part of a total system simultaneous with itself, or as part of a historical sequence of related phenomena. Thus the use of a particular word or even a particular sound can be examined synchronically, as related to the other words or sounds in use at the same time by speakers of the same language; or that same word or sound may be examined diachronically, as related to its etymological or phonological antecedents and successors. In synchronic linguistics, then, one examines the whole state of a language at a given time, while in diachronic linguistics one examines a particular element of language over a span of time. From this it follows that only synchronic linguistics can provide an adequate treatment of any given language-system as a whole. Since the great successes of nineteenth-century linguistics had come in the area of diachronic studies (such as Grimm's and Werner's discoveries of the laws governing pronunciation changes in the Indo-European languages) Saussure's view was iconoclastic in the extreme. It also led the followers of Saussure, which means structuralists in general, into repeated conflicts with thinkers influenced by Hegel—especially the Marxists. These conflicts have two aspects, both traceable to Saussure's emphases. First, by insisting on the arbitrariness of language, Saussure made extralinguistic influences on language apparently irrelevant. Since for Marxists the economic aspect of a culture is seen as a prime determinant of all other cultural elements, the idea of something as influential as language being self-determined posed a considerable problem. But even more of an affront than the arbitrariness of language was the relegation of historical considerations to a minor role. For the Marxists, of course, history is purposeful, and the only way for man to recognize its purpose is through diachronic study (accompanied by actual engagement in its processes). But for the Saussurean linguist, each language is complete and adequate at every stage of its historical development. There is no progress in languages, only change. The purposefulness or ordering principles that are accessible to linguistic study lie not in the history of language so much as in the logic of relations and oppositions among the signs of any given language-system at a particular time. This logic has been studied in depth by Jakobson, Trubetzkoy, and many other linguists after Saussure, and is far too complex to be summarized here, even if my powers were adequate to the task. But this summary statement by Emile Benveniste can serve as a representative view of structuralism in linguistics:

> Granting that language is system, it is then a matter of analyzing its *structure*. Each system, being formed of units that mutually affect one another, is distinguished from the other systems by the internal arrangements of these units, an arrangement which constitutes its structure. Certain combinations are frequent, others fairly rare, and still others, while theoretically possible, are never realized. To envisage a language (or each part of a language, such as its phonetics, morphology, etc.) as a system organized by a structure to be revealed and described is to adopt the "structuralist" point of view. [*Problems in General Linguistics,* p. 82]

Saussure himself developed one other distinction that has become crucial for later students of language and has important applications for literary study as well (which we shall return to later in this chapter and in chapter 6.B). This is the distinction between the syntagmatic and paradigmatic relations among signs. The syntagmatic element of language has to do with the positioning of a sign in any particular utterance. In a given sentence, for example, the meaning of a single word is determined partly by its position in the sentence and its relation to the other words and grammatical units of that sentence. This is the word's syntagmatic (linear, diachronic) aspect, often conceptualized as a horizontal axis along which the sentence is spread out in its necessary order. The meaning of a single word in a sentence is also determined by its relation to some groups of words *not* in the actual sentence but present in a paradigmatic (or "vertical," synchronic) relationship to the actual word. A word is thus defined partly by all the words which might have filled its place but have been displaced by it. These displaced words may be conceived as belonging to several paradigmatic sets: other words with the same grammatical function, other words with related meanings (synonyms and antonyms), other words with similar sound patterns—these are three obvious paradigmatic sets. Our actual selection of a word in a sentence involves something like a rapid scanning of paradigmatic possibilities until we find one that will play the appropriate role in the syntax we are constructing. In attending to paradigmatic meaning we are aware of the synchronic aspect of this word's relationship to its language-system.

Another conceptual tool bequeathed to literary analysis by linguistics was added to the Saussurean developments by Roman Jakobson. Firmly grounded in study of language acquisition among children and language loss among aphasiacs, Jakobson's concept of a polarity in linguistic performance is crucial to structuralist poetics. Beginning with the observation that all types of language disorder in aphasia "oscillate between two polar types," Jakobson moves toward a view of traditional poetics as characterized by "an amputated, unipolar scheme which, strikingly enough, coincides with one of the two aphasic patterns, namely with the contiguity disorder." How he reached this conclusion is worth examining.

The two poles of linguistic performance described by Jakobson are connected to the syntagmatic and paradigmatic relations of the sign as Saussure understood them. Jakobson's contribution, then, is partly that he found empirical support for Saussure's logical and theoretical terminology. But he went further than this in relating the Saussurean distinction to traditional rhetorical theory and finally to poetics. Jakobson observed that the two disorders he found in studying the symptoms of aphasia (similarity disorder and contiguity disorder) were strikingly related to two basic rhetorical figures: metaphor and metonymy.

Since we are frequently so careless about theoretical terms in our criticism, it may be well to pause and examine these two with respect to both their traditional meanings and Jakobson's application of these meanings. In our usage "metaphor" often serves to indicate *all* substitutions of a figurative word for a literal one in any context. The reasons for this are related to Jakobson's major argument about an imbalance in poetics, and I will return to them later on. But for the moment let it suffice to remember that metaphorical substitution is based on a likeness or *analogy* between the literal word and its metaphorical replacement (as when we substitute *den* or *burrow* for *hut*), while metonymical substitution is based on an *association* between the literal word and its substitute. Things which are logically related by cause and effect (*poverty* and *hut*) or whole and part (*hut* and *thatch*), as well as things that are habitually found together in familiar contexts (*hut* and *peasant*), are all in metonymic relationship to one another. (Metonymy may be broken down into subfigures such as synecdoche, just as metaphor may be subdivided into simile and other figures of analogy. Jakobson here takes the two figures as generic matrices for all the others.) Jakobson finds this distinction between metaphoric and metonymic processes in language discernible not only at the level of individual expressions in language but at the level of larger patterns of discourse as well. Thus in any work of literature the discourse may move from topic to topic according to relationships of similarity or of contiguity, which is to say according to metaphorical or metonymic thought processes. Different literary styles, adds Jakobson, may be distinguished according to their preference for one or another process. Illustrating the distinction, he writes:

> The primacy of the metaphoric process in the literary schools
> of romanticism and symbolism has been repeatedly acknowl-

edged, but it is still insufficiently realized that it is the pre-
dominance of metonymy which underlies and actually prede-
termines the so-called "realistic" trend, which belongs to an
intermediary stage between the decline of romanticism and
the rise of symbolism and is opposed to both. Following the
path of contiguous relationships, the realistic author meto-
nymically digresses from the plot to the atmosphere and from
the characters to the setting in space and time. [*Fundamentals of Language,* pp. 91–92]

Jakobson makes powerful claims for the basic dichotomy between metaphor and metonymy, asserting its "primal significance
and consequence" in all human endeavor. The alternation in ascen-
dancy between the metaphoric and the metonymic processes extends to sign systems other than the verbal: in painting, Jakobson
points out, cubism is manifestly metonymic, the object being transformed into a set of synecdoches; in surrealism the painter's attitude is "patently metaphorical." Competition between the processes

is manifest in any symbolic process, either intrapersonal or social. Thus in an inquiry into the structures of dreams, the
decisive question is whether the symbols and the temporal sequences used are based on contiguity (Freud's metonymic
"displacement" and synecdochic "condensation") or on similarity (Freud's "identification and symbolism"). The principles
underlying magic rites have been resolved by Frazer into two
types: charms based on the law of similarity and those
founded on association by contiguity. The first of these two
great branches of sympathetic magic has been called "homeo-
pathic" or "imitative," and the second, "contagious magic."
[p. 95]

Jakobson raises the question of why this dichotomy, for all its
importance, has been neglected in the study of symbolic behavior,
and he suggests that the reason is twofold. First, metaphor is easier
to grasp conceptually than metonymy. Second, metaphor predominates in poetry, which has been the main object of rhetorical study

for centuries. "For poetry, metaphor, and for prose, metonymy is
the line of least resistance and, consequently, the study of poetical
tropes is directed chiefly toward metaphor" (p. 96). Jakobson powerfully suggests that we need a poetics of both poetry and prose,
which will attend to the functioning of metaphor and metonymy
at all levels and in all kinds of discourse. In chapter 5.C we shall
find Gérard Genette doing just that, considering the way that
Proustian "metaphors" are actually combinations of metaphorical
and metonymical strategy, in which metonymy often predominates.
But for the moment we must return to a more fundamental consideration and explore, in the next section, some of the possible relationships between linguistics and poetics, in particular some notable attempts to unite these disciplines by Jakobson himself, and
some reactions to them.

B. Poetic Theory: Jakobson and Lévi-Strauss versus Riffaterre's Superreader

The "poetic theory" in this section heading means poetics with
an emphasis on poetry. The poetics of drama and of fiction will be
attended to later on—drama briefly and fiction at length—
but here we are mainly concerned with the poetics of poetry itself. This comes first for a very good reason. Poetry has almost always been defined by its special use of language—usually in
terms of its "difference" from "ordinary language." Clearly this
kind of definition is linguistic in nature, thus opening the door to
investigations of poetry by theorists who are linguists first and literary critics second (sometimes a very distant second). The idea of
linguists putting poetry on the rack and forcing it to yield up its
secrets, or even worse to confess falsely, has horrified a sizable por-
tion of the literary world. And the actual results of literary criticism by linguists have often been horrible enough. For many
tender spirits who in their undergraduate days fled from the sciences into the humanities, the spectacle of linguistic science pursuing them into their refuge like Grendel's mother, jaws dripping
with pieces of broken poems, is indeed a nightmare. This book is

intended to confront that nightmare with a certain amount of calm, daylight reasoning. I personally agree with Roman Jakobson's view of the matter, which can serve as an epigraph for the rest of this chapter:

> If there are some critics who still doubt the competence of linguistics to embrace the field of poetics, I privately believe that the poetic incompetence of some bigoted linguists has been mistaken for an inadequacy of the linguistic science itself. All of us here, however, definitely realize that a linguist deaf to the poetic function of language and a literary scholar indifferent to linguistic problems and unconversant with linguistic methods are equally flagrant anachronisms. ["Linguistics and Poetics," in Sebeok, ed., *Style in Language,* Cambridge, Mass., 1960, p. 377]

The first problem in poetics is the one we keep coming back to again and again: What is poetry? This problem and its big brother (What is literature?) continue to haunt all our attempts to regularize literary study. At a section of the MLA meeting of December 1972 devoted to structuralism, the participants got well off the track for a long time, arguing about the nature of poetic language —while at an earlier session the same day the leading paper on "poetics and literary theory" had been a cogent attack on the thesis that poetic language can be defined as a deviation from something called "ordinary language." Similarly, at a very different conference, in the summer of 1972, where the participants were trying to establish guidelines for a nationwide survey of literary competence at several age levels from preteen to young adult, the same problem bogged down every participating group: What is literature? I, for one, am convinced that we have to go to the linguists for help with this problem, though we must still solve it ourselves. Jakobson is very helpful here, because he has provided a clear and systematic way of talking about the relationship between the "poetic function" of language and its various other functions. Jakobson's method, as developed in the well-known essay just quoted from, is certainly not complete, but it is the most useful point of departure that I know. In the pages that follow, I will outline this method (with a few changes in terminology) and then show some ways in which it may be adapted to do more than Jakobson does with it.

Jakobson's communication theory provides us with a handy way of analyzing the six constitutive elements in any speech event. Whether we are considering ordinary conversation, a public speech, a letter, or a poem, we always find a *message* which proceeds from a *sender* to a *receiver.* These are the most obvious aspects of communication. But a successful communication depends on three other aspects of the event as well: the message must be delivered through a *contact,* physical and/or psychological; it must be framed in a *code;* and it must refer to a *context.* In the area of context, we find what a message is about. But to get there we must understand the code in which the message is framed—as in the present case my messages reach you through the medium of an academic/literary subcode of the English language. And even if we have the code, we understand nothing until we make contact with the utterance; in the present case, until you see the printed words on this page (or hear them read aloud) they do not exist as a message for you. The message itself, uniting sender and receiver in the quintessentially human act of communication, is simply a verbal form, which depends on all the other elements of a speech event to convey its meaning. *The message is not the meaning.* Meaning lies at the end of the entire speech event, which gives the verbal formula of the message its life and color. (And of course certain kinds of meaning can be conveyed without verbal messages, as by a glance, a touch, a picture—but these are not our concern here.) These six elements of a speech event can be schematized in the following way:

The message, of course, is at the heart of every speech event, and in a rough and ready way we think of every message as being referential, as being aimed at some context, at some object or idea outside of itself. In fact this is usually the case. But not all of every message is aimed at an outside context. Consider the following:

> Listen! I'll put it in plain English, dammit. Do you hear me? Well, once upon a time there was a man . . .

Different parts of this message can be related very directly to different elements within the speech event. An outside context only begins to enter in the last words of the utterance. And before that we have had "Listen!"—an imperative, directed at the receiver; we have had a sentence about the code itself ("plain English"); we have had two interjections ("dammit," "Well") which communicate only the sender's attitude; and we have had "once upon a time there was a man"—which introduces a "man" as the context toward which all this has been leading, but does some other things which need considering as well. By adopting a standard phrase from a subcode (that might be called "fairy-tale English") this message has succeeded in calling attention to itself, to its own composition. The sudden appearance of a pronounced rhythm (a repetition of iambs) in this last sentence has a similar function. The rhythm draws attention away from the context toward the message itself, so that the "man," by the time he appears, has a dubious ontological status.

Thus within the message itself the different elements of the speech event reappear as "functions," which shape the nature and the structure of the utterance. Jakobson presents these functions in a schema which parallels the schema of elements presented above:

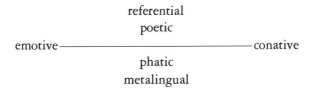

referential
poetic
emotive————————————————————conative
phatic
metalingual

Every message is framed in terms of these six functions, and some messages (or parts of messages, as in the above example) are dominated by one function or another. Most messages are *referential,* oriented to context. Some are *emotive,* oriented to sender, as in the interjections used in the example, which express the sender's attitudes. Some are *conative,* aimed at the receiver primarily, as in imperative locutions. Some are *phatic,* concerned with the contact itself. Jakobson quotes an amusing passage from Dorothy Parker, in which a dialogue proceeds in almost purely phatic terms: " 'Well!' the young man said. 'Well!' she said. 'Well, here we are,' he said. 'Here we are,' she said, 'Aren't we?' 'I should say we were,' he said. 'Eeyop! Here we are.' 'Well!' she said. 'Well!' he said, 'well'." An orientation to the code itself, as in questions about meanings of words and so on, is *metalingual.* Naturally, the speech of young children, or others in the process of language-learning, is highly metalingual.

For our purposes, the most important kind of emphasis in utterance is what we find when the message emphasizes itself, drawing attention to its own sound patterns, diction, and syntax. This is the *poetic* function, which appears in all language. It is by no means confined to "art." Nor is the language of literary art ever entirely and exclusively poetic. As Jakobson puts it,

> Poetic function is not the sole function of verbal art but only its dominant, determining function, whereas in all other verbal activities it acts as a subsidiary, accessory constituent. This function, by promoting the palpability of signs, deepens the fundamental dichotomy of signs and objects. [In Sebeok, *Style in Language,* p. 356]

The principal way in which the poetic function manifests itself in poetry is by a projection of the paradigmatic and metaphoric dimension of language onto the syntagmatic. By emphasizing resemblances of sound, rhythm, image, poetry thickens language, drawing attention to its formal properties and away from its referential significance.

Jakobson's formulation strikes me as at once immensely fruitful and seriously inadequate. It is fruitful because it both suggests much and clarifies much about the nature of poetic language. It is in no sense "wrong," and can be used perfectly well as a point of departure for further developments in poetics. But it is inadequate in a number of respects which must be noted before it can be so used. Some of the inadequacies are in the terminology and the use of it. The term "message" itself is used by Jakobson in two different senses. At times "message" seems to equal "meaning" and at other times to equal "verbal form." In my own summary I have tried to reserve the term "meaning" for the import of the total communication and use "message" to refer only to the verbal formula itself. The problem is that we have a whole system of significations working in any utterance. The message may be described as a sign with its signifying verbal formula and its signified content. And this little message/sign may be seen as a part of the larger sign which is the whole utterance—the whole again being analyzable into its signifying and signified aspects.

There are other problems as well. In trying to present a single universal description of communication acts, Jakobson has necessarily ignored the difference between written and oral communications. But in the oral act, all of the Jakobsonian elements of communication may be at hand: context, sender, and receiver may be physically present when the message is delivered through an oral contact in a code such as English. The sender may hand the receiver a cup of contextual hemlock, for instance, and deliver the message, "Drink this!" But in a written act the message itself is frequently all we have. In particular, the sender is not likely to be present, and very frequently, even though you or I may read the message, it may not be addressed to us.

Poetry, in fact, was shrewdly defined by John Stuart Mill as an utterance which is not heard but overheard. The point of this is that poetry may be definable precisely in terms of our having to supply the missing elements in an act of communication. The "fictional" element in literature, including poetry, is definable as an absent context, or perhaps as a distant context. Insofar as a literary work is mimetic it refers to the "real" world by interposing an "imaginary" world between its audience and reality. It gives us, in effect, a double context, and frequently, as in allegory, a multiple context. Similarly, in poetry or fiction we have almost invariably to consider duplicity of sender and of receiver as well. There is a sense in which a poem is a message sent to a reader, perhaps you or me, by the poet, a person like ourselves. But almost invariably this message is presented in the form of someone not the poet addressing someone not ourselves, as in "To His Coy Mistress," when someone not Marvell speaks to someone not you or me about things which make our participation distinctly voyeuristic.

I am suggesting that the visible signs of literature are to be found at least as frequently in this multiplicity of the nonverbal elements of communication as they are in any special qualities in the grammar and syntax of the message itself. And furthermore, that this duplicity often manifests itself in the message in the form of irony, paradox, and other devices which require for their analysis extended consideration of the full semantic range of the poetic utterance. This duplicity, which is a kind of playfulness, is at the root of any purely aesthetic experiences that literature may bring us. Granted, it brings us experiences that are very impure, very rich, and all the more valuable for their mixture of qualities; nevertheless, it is artfulness or literariness which distinguishes literature from other forms of discourse, and these qualities are always associated with linguistic duplicity. To the extent that an author resolves the elements of his utterance into unequivocal units, speaking to us in his own voice about referents immediately perceivable, he approaches the lower limits of verbal art. The poem approaches the essay as the poet himself becomes recognizably the speaker. And the essay moves toward fiction as the speaker becomes distinguishable from the author. All the specific linguistic strategies of verse, which distinguish it from speech and prose, serve, among other things, to distinguish the person who utters this poetic language from the poet's own prosaic existence.

There is also in poetic language itself a dimension which structuralism enables us to describe readily but that structuralists have not always been anxious to consider. Jakobson has identified poetry as projecting its language from the metaphoric or paradigmatic axis of verbalization onto the metonymic or syntagmatic. Thus poetry deliberately opposes the linear, ongoing, diachronic qualities of speech with spatial, obstructive, synchronic qualities. I believe that this insight is substantially valid, but it, too, needs some amplification and qualification. In doing this we shall have to return also to the question of context in the Jakobsonian communication model. In the model Jakobson uses "context" to mean something like "referent": the state of affairs which the utterance is "about." I have already indicated that fictional utterances can be defined by duplicity of context, in that they present an imaginary world which stands in some potentially discoverable relationship to our experiential world. But there is another aspect of contextual duplicity, more specifically related to poetic language and to the poem as an utterance that is not necessarily mimetic or fictional but is nonetheless different from most other kinds of speech act.

The poet, I wish to suggest, works out of a paradigmatic system different from that of the ordinary speaker. By this I mean that when a poet selects a word for use in a poem, he brings into play a set of possibilities which is radically different from that used in our ordinary discourse. Let me be more precise. By "the poet" I mean the person making a poem, who is not, in this sense, the same as the man of the same name, who pays the poet's bills, sleeps with his wife, and uses language in lots of ordinary ways, even perhaps to make some ordinary and unpoetical things called poems as well as the works recognized as his true poetry. It is as if the poet in the process of making a true poem turns on some additional neural circuitry which enables him to produce these peculiarly high-powered verbal objects called poems. The result, in Saussurean terms, is that the poet's utterance (*parole*) comes from a different sign-system (*langue*) than that employed by an ordinary speaker.

What I am suggesting here must be distinguished from the common formalist notion of a "poetic diction" as the distinguishing mark of poetry. A poetic diction which acts as a kind of screening or censoring device to eliminate "unpoetical" language from poems may indeed be an aspect of much poetry—perhaps all poetry.

But it is notoriously an aspect shared by poets whose works are of very unequal values. The eighteenth century was full of little poet-asters who could avoid all the unpoetical locutions that Alexander Pope avoided but could not produce a single couplet worthy of inclusion in "The Rape of the Lock." The kind of poetic language I want to speak of here is defined in quite the opposite way: it is not exclusive, but inclusive; and it is not so much the property of any single poetical school as a characteristic of all serious poets at all times.

When a poet is working with all his neural circuitry functioning well, he has at his disposal a paradigmatic word-hoard which is different from the ordinary man's in its organization as well as in its scope. We recognize this as an attribute of the oral-formulaic poet, who composes as he recites, drawing upon certain fixed combinations of metrically matched phrases, but I am suggesting that in a modified form it is an attribute of every poet. Among other things, the poet's paradigmatic system is paradoxically diachronic. To stick to the case of Pope, for the moment, his verbal resources included not only a command of the English language of his own time but also in a very precise manner a command of certain poetic languages of the past. He knew Dryden, Milton, and Shakespeare, among others, superlatively well, and had in his mind not only their words but countless contexts in which they used these words. Thus he could produce words of his own in contexts of his own, which nonetheless reverberated and took on meaning from their previous incarnations in the utterances of his great predecessors. It is precisely this diachronic context which enables poetic utterances to survive the temporal decay of any merely poetic diction and remain contemporary far beyond their own time. The poet's paradigms are, then, diachronic in the obvious sense that they extend well into the poetic past and supply words with an awareness of that past. But they are also diachronic in the less obvious sense that by operating freely over the past, and not being confined to their immediate synchronic language, they become more open to the future as well. It is as if there were a level of poetical language which through its own diachronic awareness can achieve a true synchronicity, enabling all poets, past and present, to speak to one another. And in the teaching of poetry, it is this higher level of linguistic potency which we wish to make available to our students.

We must now consider the question of what this high-powered use of language may be about. Jakobson, as I have indicated, uses the word "context" primarily to mean something like the subject or referent of an utterance. But in the case of poetry we encounter duplicity here as well. I suppose the context of "Lycidas" in the referential sense is the death of Milton's friend Edward King. But, as has frequently been observed, there are some other contexts that overwhelm this one in the poem. There is first of all a literary context in which the whole poem can be said to mean something like, "This is the way to write a pastoral elegy." This literary context, it may be argued, is the major one, but it is in turn overwhelmed, or at least interrupted, by an ethical context with fairly specific reference to pastoral behavior among the clergy of Milton's own time. Contexts in poetry (and again I would assert that this is true to a greater extent than in other verbal forms) are multiple, and are so managed that what is background at some times is foregrounded at others. And often we find in poems the gestalt perspective trick in which background and foreground exchange perceptual roles.

Here, of course, we are running into difficulties in the use of the word "context." To the extent that the context of a poem is verbal we may say that the code is itself the context of the poem. And when the code becomes the context we have that situation which Jakobson described as a growing palpability of message, what we might call a thickening into poetry. In drawing attention to its own verbal structure, poetry inevitably draws attention to the code in which it is framed. Thus it shares a certain metalinguistic perspective with linguistics itself. Poems, to a greater or lesser extent, are messages about poetry, and thus about language, as well as about love, death, and other concerns of human existence. The very fact that poetry and linguistics share an interest in codes as their subject matter, while approaching this subject matter through utterly different codes of their own, accounts for some of the hostility between them. But it also accounts for the extraordinary achievements of certain metapoets in their critical discussions of poetic language.

Having thus enlarged upon the Jakobsonian formulation, I must now return to the heart of it and to its development in critical practice. Jakobson locates the essence of poetry in its verbal formulas as they emerge in poetic syntax. Together with Claude Lévi-Strauss he has given us a demonstration of poetic analysis at this level—a description and explication of a sonnet, "Charles Baudelaire's 'Les Chats'"—and this in turn has been severely criticized by another structuralist, Michael Riffaterre, in his essay, "Describing Poetic Structures: Two Approaches to Baudelaire's 'Les Chats'." Taken together these two essays not only indicate the extent to which there is serious intellectual debate about premises and methods among structuralist literary critics, but perhaps they can also serve to illustrate the problems and limitations inherent in any structuralist approach to the practical criticism of individual literary texts.

From my perspective, and that of most of the critics I have discussed the matter with, what we have in these two critical studies is not so much a debate as a case in which the second contribution largely supersedes the first. Most of what is fruitful in the approach of Jakobson and Lévi-Strauss is preserved by Riffaterre, and much that is needed is added. The earlier formulation, I might add, has about it much of the energy and oversimplification characteristic of formalism and early structuralism. Riffaterre, though he writes only a few years later, writes with no less arrogance but with a good deal more wariness of the pitfalls of practical criticism. And one thing that emerges clearly from this confrontation is that no mechanical formula for the interpretation of poems is to be envisioned as a product of structuralist activity. Riffaterre's superiority as an interpreter comes as much as anything else from his superior command of the French literary tradition and his ability to read sensitively in the "new critical" manner. But I anticipate.

Jakobson and Lévi-Strauss set out to determine "what a Baudelaire sonnet is made of." The ensuing analysis of "Les Chats" seeks the rules determining the rhyme scheme, the syntactical patterns, and various other patterns in the choice and placement of words. It seeks, and finds, "relations of equivalence" of a remarkable number and variety, all of which are indisputably "there." The analysis also offers a reading or interpretation of the poem which is not especially dependent on the extensive grammatical analyses. It does not distinguish very well between elements which are characteristic of sonnets as a class and those which are unique to this particular poem or belong to some intermediate category. (Obviously, comparative analysis of many more texts would be required to generate such distinctions.) Riffaterre's objections to this proceeding are many and cogent. He begins by raising the thorny question of how we are "to pass from description to judgment." Then, he raises an even more pointed question:

> Far more important, however, is the question as to whether unmodified structural linguistics is relevant at all to the analysis of poetry. The authors' method is based on the assumption that any structural system they are able to define in the poem is necessarily a poetic structure. Can we not suppose, on the contrary, that the poem may contain certain structures that play no part in its function and effect as a literary work of art, and that there may be no way for structural linguistics to distinguish between those unmarked structures and those that are literarily active? Conversely, there may well be strictly poetic structures that cannot be recognized as such by an analysis not geared to the specificity of poetic language.
> [In J. Ehrmann, ed., *Structuralism,* Garden City, N.Y., 1970, p. 191]

Riffaterre's answer to this rhetorical question is plain. Structural linguistics must be modified in order to deal adequately with poetry. And he sets about demonstrating the reasons for modification and indicating the directions in which it must go. He begins by allowing that Jakobson and Lévi-Strauss present "an absolutely convincing demonstration of the extraordinary concatenation of correspondences that holds together the parts of speech" in the poem.

But he adds that "there is no telling which of these systems of correspondence contribute to the poetry of the text." And I would further add that Jakobson and Lévi-Strauss do not convey an effective method for distinguishing between systems which merely signify "this is a poem"—like the rhyme scheme and other fairly mechanical processes—as opposed to systems which convince us that this is not only a poem but poetry as well—as in a particular *use* of the rhyme scheme. Yet it is precisely this distinction we have to make in order to get from description to judgment.

Riffaterre's critique is too long to quote and too tight to summarize, but the thrust of it can be captured in a few crucial quotations from his essay in Ehrmann's *Structuralism:*

> [Certain structural divisions detected by the critics] make use of constituents that cannot possibly be perceived by the reader; these constituents must therefore remain alien to the poetic structure, which is supposed to emphasize the form of the message, to make it more 'visible,' more compelling. [p. 195]

> . . . homologue-collecting [is] an unreliable tool. Extensive similarities at one level are no proof of correspondence. . . . [p. 196]

> No segmentation can be pertinent that yields, indifferently, units which *are* part of the poetic structure, and neutral ones that are not. The weak point of the method is indeed the categories used. [p. 197]

> . . . metalinguistic rationalization of this sort betrays how easily the wariest of analysts slips into a belief in the intrinsic explanatory worth of purely descriptive terms. [p. 198]

> . . . the analytic categories applied can pull together under one label phenomena which are in fact totally different from one another in poetic structure. [p. 199]

> The sonnet is rebuilt by the two critics into a 'Superpoem,' inaccessible to the normal reader, and yet the structures described do not explain what establishes contact between po-

etry and the reader. No grammatical analysis of a poem can give us more than the grammar of the poem. [pp. 201–02]

Having found the Jakobson/Lévi-Strauss reading seriously wanting and resulting in the fraudulent construction of a "superpoem," Riffaterre then presents his own alternative version, answering the "superpoem" with a "superreader." He generates this monster by first returning to Jakobson's model of a speech act. In considering the six aspects of communication he alters Jakobson's definition of the poetic in a significant way. Jakobson had said that concentration on the message itself was the distinguishing characteristic of poetry. Earlier I tried to indicate the inadequacy of this formulation and to suggest a definition along the lines of duplicity in the treatment of all the elements of utterance. Riffaterre also finds the formulation inadequate, but his response is not the global one of looking for poetic function in some change in the status of all six elements. He seeks merely to shift the emphasis from the message to the receiver. Pointing out that the message and the receiver are "the only factors involved in this communication whose presence is necessary," he goes on to reduce all the other factors to aspects of the message/receiver relationship:

As for the other factors—language (code), non-verbal context, means of keeping open the channel—, the appropriate language of reference is selected from the message, the context is reconstituted from the message, contact is assumed by the control the message has over the reader's attention, and depends upon the degree of that control. These special duties, and the esthetic emphasis characteristic of poetry demand that the message possess certain features corresponding to those functions. The characteristic common to such devices must be that they are designed to draw responses from the reader. . . . [pp. 202–03]

Here, it seems to me, all the splendid rigor that animated Riffaterre's critique is totally abandoned. Of course, everything must be

conjectured from the message, but codes and contexts are by definition entities beyond the message itself, which must be apprehended
for the message to be meaningful. There is a danger here of reduction to a simple stimulus/response model, which we all know
won't work, precisely because it ignores the processes by which poetic stimulus is transformed in order to produce poetic response.
We can take as an example of this reductive error the treatment
Riffaterre gives irony in the poem. (Let me say in passing that his
understanding of the poem's irony is far superior to Jakobson and
Lévi-Strauss's, but this is because he does not attend to the limitations of his own theory.) His crucial generalization about irony
reads as follows: "Irony in literature must be a verbal structure,
lest it vary with different readers' opinions as to what is exagger-
ated or 'not really meant' " (p. 211).

If it were that simple the linguists would have solved the problem of irony long ago. But of course it is not that simple. Irony in
literature takes many forms, but often it is not to be detected from
the verbal structure alone. To take a small illustration, when E. B.
White tells us, in a literary essay, of the "majesty" of New York
City's ginko trees, we know he is being ironic only if we have some
command of the context. That is, we must know something about
ginkos in general, interesting trees but rarely monumental, and
New York ginkos in particular—just beyond flowerpot size—
before we can detect a gentle irony in the word "majesty." The
word is the stimulus but the response must wait until we have
matched the word against our mental context. The amount of
irony, in this case, may be said to be inversely proportional to our
apprehension of the actual size of the trees. An identical structure
which spoke of the majesty of sequoias would be devoid of irony.
Often irony is a matter of delicate interaction between code and
context. It may draw upon the private language or the special experience of an intimate group. One of its primary qualities is that
it divides its audience into an elite group who "get" the irony and
a subordinate group who miss it. (Allegory, it may be pointed out,
is similarly divisive.) Ironic use of a language is the last thing the
child or the foreigner understands. It is precisely the thing that

varies with different readers and frequently distinguishes the "good" reader from the "bad." But Riffaterre cannot allow this. His stimulus/response model results in a notion of message controlling response, when all message can really do is invite an appropriate response.

This behaviorist orientation leads him into another difficulty as well, which is central to his critical position. He develops the concept of a "superreader," which is at once so unsystematic and so lightly abandoned that one might take it for irony—except that it is not framed in an ironic verbal structure. Riffaterre's superreader is not (like that of Stanley Fish) simply a modest extension of himself. No, it is an attempt at quantification of responses in order to move from those responses really stimulated by the poem back to the verbal structures responsible for them. Superreader has two aspects. He is multiple and he is void. Like Lévi-Strauss surveying the versions of a myth, Riffaterre will survey the versions of response to the chosen text—in this case "Les Chats." Then, "each point of the text that holds up the superreader is tentatively considered a component of the poetic structure." What Superreader makes of each crux is unimportant. His response is to be "emptied of content" so that his idiosyncratic interpretations will not interfere with the scientific work going on. Riffaterre will note what has drawn the attention of students, friends, critics, translators, other poets, and literary encyclopaedias in this particular sonnet —and from that he will arrive at a true notion of its effective poetic structure, which he will then explain according to his own interpretation of the poem. The fact that his interpretation is truly excellent obscures somewhat the difficulties of his methodology. For if Jakobson and Lévi-Strauss could not tell whether a bit of structure was poetic or not, neither can Superreader tell whether a response is poetic or not.

Nor—and this is at least as important—can he deal with responses which do not rise to the level of consciousness. The earlier analysis of "Les Chats" assumed that we respond to *all* the structures that are in the poem and therefore tried to identify them all. Riffaterre assumes that response *always* reaches consciousness, and he therefore denies poetical status to verbal structures which have stimulated no response in Superreader. Obviously, neither of these methods is entirely satisfactory, nor can any entirely satisfactory method exist without some way of determining the relationships among *all* structures in the poem and *all* responses, conscious and unconscious, in the reader. The impossibility of detecting and evaluating such responses sets limits to the ability of any methodology to settle the value or the meaning of any single poem. The pretense that such limits do not exist is responsible for much of the nonsense uttered by literary critics, whatever their persuasion.

In practice, Riffaterre simply explicates "Les Chats," supporting his discussion with some beautifully chosen details dredged up by Superreader. These details, taken from critics and translators mainly, coupled with an excellent discussion of Baudelaire's own poetic code, are what make Riffaterre if not a superreader at least a superior reader of the poem. But these details are *not* in the poetic structure, they must be brought to the poetic structure from outside it, by attention to the code and the context. Even the knowledge of grammar, which Jakobson and Lévi-Strauss as well as Riffaterre use expertly in describing the structure of the text, is something brought to the text by the critic, based on his understanding of the code as a system, not something found only in the message itself. When Riffaterre says, for instance, that "the last two lines owe their effectiveness to their structure as a suspense narrative (the enjambement, and the severance of the verb *étoilent* from its subject)," he is making an observation that depends on his knowledge of French and his knowledge of literature as well as on his response to the poem. And his own response to the poem is the primary element in his comment. His certainty that the last two lines are effective is not attributed to his "informants." The only supperreader invoked here is Riffaterre himself.

The confrontation I have just described suggests a number of considerations that are important for an understanding of the possibilities and limitations of structuralist literary criticism. The structuralists are quite right in suggesting that critics should borrow descriptive terminology from linguistics, simply because it is the best we have. But linguistic description will not solve the problem of literary response. Nor can we solve this problem in any neat operational or quantitative way. If poetry offered us only messages framed in special poetic structures, the problem would be easy, and attention to the specifics of grammar and syntax in the poetic message would lead to a true understanding of poetic achievement. But since, as Riffaterre insists, poetry is a matter of response, and since, though Riffaterre ignores it, this response often depends upon an awareness of poetic duplicity in the situation of sender and receiver, or in the code employed or the context invoked, any commentary on a particular poem *must* attend to more than is present in the verbal structure itself. Nor can we depend upon some quantification of responses to a particular poem to do our work for us—simply because not all responses are of equal value. In linguistics it may be perfectly reasonable to rely on native informants for "competence" with respect to the grammar of their language. This works because "competence" is a minimal function. Everybody has it, or nearly everybody. In poetics, we cannot do this, because poetry starts where mere "competence" leaves off. A person who could not read music but wished to know what a certain Chopin prelude sounded like might ask a hundred randomly selected people to play it for him, and then reconstruct the "true Prelude" from the result. But he might come closer by asking one expert pianist to perform the piece for him a single time. Ideally, he might ask several experts to play several times. But even then, without more knowledge of Chopin's musical code he would never really "hear" the piece adequately.

I am suggesting that in the criticism of particular poetic texts, as in their creation, a certain individual expertise and ability is an indispensable feature. E. D. Hirsch has argued powerfully that poetic theory can never lead us to a methodology which will work for the interpretation of all poems. The examples of Jakobson/Lévi-Strauss and Riffaterre seem to confirm this. What, then, has structuralism to offer us that will help in the practical criticism of poetic texts? I believe it has much to offer, but only in an indirect manner. In the preparation for reading a poem, structuralism can play a powerful educational role. Properly developed, it can help us to have a clear sense of poetic discourse and its relations to other forms of discourse. It can refine our descriptive terminology and our sense of linguistic process. Because it aims at describing the whole world of poetic possibilities, it can provide us with the best framework available to aid in the perception of an actual poetic text. In our instructional programs it can give new life to the oldest aspects of our discipline by aiding in the creation of a new philology and a new literary history. In our approach to specific literary texts it can make us keenly aware of the communicative aspects of the entire poetic process. But it will not read the poem for us. That we shall always have to do for ourselves.

3 The Simplification of Form

The perception of order or structure where only undifferentiated phenomena had seemed to exist before is the distinguishing characteristic of structuralist thought. In this mental operation we give up our general sense of all the observable data in exchange for a heightened sense of some specific items. These fewer items, which we now see as related, forming a system or structure, give us a greater conceptual power over the material under scrutiny. From one point of view, all such operations are reductive. But from this point of view all rational thought is reductive: we give up a sense of some "whole" in order to perceive some formal relation of "parts." But this operation can also be considered in quite another way: what is lost in mass here is gained in energy. In fact, when we discover structures we find "wholes" where only "parts" existed before. Knowing the structure of an atom gives us a certain power over whole masses of matter. A major motive behind structuralist investigations of literary phenomena is the desire to obtain a similar exchange of mass for energy. But the only explosions to be obtained here are mental ones: flashes of literary understanding that come from a thorough grasp of fundamental literary structures.

The desire to look for simple structures behind or within complex literary phenomena has led to some interesting experiments in criticism undertaken by scholars unconnected with any "school" of formalism or structuralism. In this chapter we shall be concerned with two such experiments, isolated, almost eccentric in nature, which have proved stimulating to later writers and have remained very interesting in themselves, both for their insights into literary structures and for the light they shed on the opportunities and difficulties involved in approaching literature systematically.

The critics André Jolles and Étienne Souriau undertook to do two quite different things, but both projects are clearly structuralist—or protostructuralist—in nature. Étienne Souriau's work is based on a large but relatively settled corpus of literature: the drama from Aeschylus to Anouilh. Souriau's project was to arrive at an understanding of the universal structural features of drama, to simplify dramatic forms to a system of functions and combinations that would illuminate the structure of any play and even suggest ideas for new ones. This is ambitious enough, but André Jolles attempted something even bolder. He set out to name and describe all the simple forms of literature that underlie the actual works man has produced. Grandiose undertakings, one may well observe, and no doubt doomed to failure, but fascinating all the same—perhaps because they share some simple form that lies behind all intellectual endeavor carried to its limits, some Faustian archetype to which all scholars cannot help but respond.

A. *The Simple Forms of André Jolles*

André Jolles was born in Holland in 1874 and died in 1946 in Germany, where he had taught art history and literature. His *Einfache Formen,* first published in 1930, was reissued in both Germanies after the war—at Halle in 1956 and at Tübingen in 1958, 1965, and 1968. A French translation (which I have used) appeared in 1972. An American translation may soon appear.

What is this work which has demonstrated such vitality decades after its first appearance? What, in fact, is a simple form?

A simple form, for Jolles, is a kind of structuring principle of human thought as it takes shape in language. He suggests that there are relatively few such forms, that they are as universal as human language and are intimately connected with the human process of organizing the world linguistically. Simple forms exist in the same world in which ideal linguistic entities like noun and verb exist. And just as man learns to speak a language, using the nouns and verbs it provides, man learns to "actualize" the simple forms. An "actualized simple form" is a verbal object like a folktale or any other popular or folk linguistic construct of a certain aesthetic order. These are to be distinguished from "literary" forms, which are the deliberate and unique verbal constructions of individual men. In the beginning is the simple form, an unfilled but specific possibility of structure which we may call "myth" or "joke" or "riddle," etc. These formal possibilities become concrete when a culture develops a particular myth or joke, etc. These actualizations of simple form may then be used consciously by writers to produce literary forms, some of which will combine many of the simple forms, modifying them accordingly.

The scholar interested in the formal essences that precede the actualized forms must necessarily work with existing forms in order to discover their essential qualities. Just as a linguist must derive his grammar of a language from the specific utterances he finds, the student of simple forms must work with the actual forms he finds in the world around him in order to approach the ideal simple forms that underlie these actual things. The Platonic thrust of this process is inescapable. But the simple forms themselves are not attributed by Jolles to any heaven of ideas. The forms are in the mind of man, of verbal man, that is, and emerge as his various ways of charging the world with meaning and value. They are necessary and ubiquitous forms of mental activity. Each form emerges from what Jolles calls a "mental disposition," a particular frame of mind, with certain requirements which, given linguistic solidity, result in a particular formal structure.

The universality of forms like myth, joke, and riddle argues powerfully for Jolles's postulation of universal structuring entities. It suggests the possibility of some grammar or logic of simple forms which accounts systematically for their nature and interrelationships. This, Jolles does not give us. He discusses nine forms but nowhere faces the problem of the completeness of this grouping. Why these nine and not others, is a question he never answers. This is a great problem in his work, and there are other related problems—all of which must be considered here. But we will need a better sense of the actual accomplishment of Jolles before approaching the limitations of this accomplishment. We can begin by considering his discussions of the nine forms themselves, taking them in the order of his presentation.

1. *The Legend.* The legend is a response to man's desire for ideals of conduct. Jolles shows how certain historical conditions in the Roman Empire led the persecuted Christians to need a model of heroic sacrifice and superhuman fidelity. The soldier of Christ, St. George, as presented in the early legends associated with his name, was a response to this need. Before the embellishments of the story, such as its conflation with the myth of Perseus, this legend simply presented to the early Christians a model of heroic fidelity under torture, which led to miraculous demonstrations of the new religion's potency. As such, it embodied a superhuman ideal which was nonetheless imitable, approachable, perhaps even attainable by other humans. In this form, the legend, man makes concrete his aspirations and his values. This form also manifests itself as its double, its opposite, the *anti*-form of *anti*-legend. In this antiform we find the horrible examples. The man who, when Christ sought to rest for a moment the burden of his cross, shouted "keep moving" becomes for Christians an antisaint, the Wandering Jew, cursed to keep moving himself for ever. Faust, Don Juan, and others perform the same negative function as the Wandering Jew. They are, in their heroic evil, negative examples of virtue—until, in time, values become transvalued and heroic evil takes on a romantic air of glamor.

2. *The Saga.* As the legend is based on an ideal which serves a real need, the saga is based on a reality, the tie of blood, which has its own ideals: the community of blood, vengeance in blood, the vendetta, marriage, kinship, heritage, patrimony, heredity. Around these concepts the saga gravitates. It is actualized in the Icelandic family sagas, in biblical genealogies, in song and story everywhere. It is rooted in the past, in family history and heritage, and its values are as powerful as those of the legend, though less idealistic. Both the saga and the legend go into the making of great and complex literary structures like the epic.

3. *The Myth.* For Jolles, myth implies a greater seriousness than either saga or legend. It has *dignitas* and *auctoritas*. It is a revelation of the way things are, of the cosmos seen as unchanging, world without end, as it is now and ever shall be. A myth, Jolles suggests, is the answer to an unspoken question about a matter of great import. How was the world made? Why is man unhappy with it? In myth all objects are seen as created, and the world has purpose and meaning because of the divinity of its creator (or creators). A myth tells us how and why things which will never change came to be as they are. Mythic consciousness is related to oracular or prophetic consciousness, but where an oracle may concern itself with a specific event in time, myths deal only with the eternal. The tales that come to us as myths are actualizations of the pure mythic form, often mixed with saga, legend, and other simple forms as well.

4. *The Riddle.* The consciousness that underlies riddling is closely related to mythic consciousness. Riddles assume mythic knowledge and present themselves as tests or initiations based on that knowledge. To answer a riddle is to gain admission to a circle of initiates: those who know the myth. Riddling also focuses on the ability of the riddler to veil his knowledge and of the decipherer to unravel this linguistic veil. Often, in stories *about* riddles, to fail in decipherment leads to death; to succeed is to live. More than any of the forms considered thus far, the riddle directs attention to language itself, its potential for semantic duplicity, its ability to convey meaning and to hide it, simultaneously.

5. *The Proverb.* Like the riddle, the proverb is a form that pays close attention to its own verbal structure—in this case not to conceal meaning but to compress it into a memorable formula. Proverbs, maxims, sayings—all of these are forms that compress worldly wisdom, the experience of the past, into little captions that may be consulted in the present. For Jolles, the proverb is a highly empirical form, rooted in practical observation of human behavior. But to my way of thinking there is more of the oracular and unfathomable in proverbs than he seems to allow. Brought together, "Look before you leap" and "He who hesitates is lost" can hardly function as guides to conduct. They suggest, in fact, that empiri-

cism itself cannot advise us very helpfully about our actions. The behaviorists can tell us everything except how to behave.

6. *The Case.* This is a form not usually recognized in literary studies, but it makes an essential part of what Jolles calls his "closed system of simple forms." Just how closed and how systematic this set of forms may be is a question that we will consider later on. But the "case" is certainly a useful addition to the list. A case is a hypothetical narrative that relates some possible human action to some set of norms and values. When we begin an utterance by saying, like Dickens's Mr. Jaggers, "Put the case that . . . ," we are in the hypothetical realm of the case. There is, Jolles says, a mental disposition to see the world as an object which can be evaluated and judged according to norms. A case, then, is a specific instance which may be set against these norms —not to illustrate a particular value but to test the norms themselves. A case is a problem in judgment, an exercise in casuistry, which may raise questions about such problems as the relationship between the letter of the law and its spirit. Historically, the form has manifested itself widely, not only in law but in theology, in courtly love, and in the areas of taste and sentiment. A perfect case is one in which conflicting sets of norms are brought into relief, preventing any easy solution. This form is an important ancestor and ingredient of the short story—as the "painful cases" of Joyce's *Dubliners* may easily remind us.

7. *The Memoir.* A second simple form that is not usually recognized as a form in its own right is the memoir. Our failure to recognize it is in part a measure of its power, for it has been the dominant simple form for over a century. The memoir is that form which seeks to record in concrete detail the unique features of a typical event—or the typical features of a unique event. This form is as old as the *Apomnemoneumata* of Xenophon, in which the old Corinthian recorded his impressions of Socrates—or the Gospels themselves, which have more of the memoir in them than of the legend. Often the memoir, as in both of these cases, presents itself in opposition to other versions of the same events and personalities, raising questions of validity and authenticity and using

vivid concrete details to substantiate its own claims to truth. The rise of the memoir to a position of dominance was coincidental with the rise of historical consciousness and the rise of the novel as a complex literary form. The movement of mind reflected in these developments effectively displaced myth, legend, and saga from their central position in human consciousness by opening the question of historicity and imposing the memoir's standards of validity on the other forms. The complex forms of realistic writing, then, have drawn upon the memoir for techniques and values in establishing their own dominance in the world of letters. All this has tended to obscure the fact that the memoir is only one form among others rather than *the* form upon which all narrative art must be based.

8. *The Tale.* This is an ancient and familiar form: the folk or fairy tale, which takes its place easily in Jolles's set of forms. But his discussion of it is exceptionally rich and perceptive. Unlike legend or myth, the tale takes place in a world which is deliberately set against our own world as other, different, better. The tale is a progress toward justice through potentially tragic obstacles. It is ethical in its orientation, firmly insisting that the world it presents is different from ours—long ago and far away—and better than ours, for in it justice is done. Jolles develops his presentation of the tale by comparing it closely to a related form which is not simple but learned, sophisticated: the Boccaccian *novello.* Some of the same motifs appear in both forms, but always what was general, unspecific, and ideal in the tale becomes more particular, specific, and real in the *novello.* One has only to think of the difference between a fairy-tale princess and a princess in Boccaccio to sense this difference. An *anti*-tale also exists, in which a malign universe turns life toward the tragic. Pyramus and Thisbe, or any pair of star-crossed lovers, may serve to illustrate the antitale. But this is a much less frequent form than the tale proper—in which disasters threaten regularly but are always avoided in the end. The neoclassical happy ending for *King Lear* can be seen as more than a mere desecration of Shakespearean art. It is also the simple form of the tale reasserting its power over the human imagination.

9. *The Joke.* The last form is appropriately the joke, which is essentially antiformal in its operation. The joke attacks inadequacies in language, in logic, in ethics. It revels in duplicity, giving us not the paradoxes of wisdom but the double-meanings of foolishness. Jokes are constructed on two parameters: mockery and pleasantry. They attack what is inadequate, whether merely annoying or absolutely unbearable, and by the effectiveness of these attacks they relieve our tensions and make life pleasanter. By mocking what troubles us the joke provides us with a very human form of consolation.

Jolles's discussions of the nine forms are learned, humane, and full of insights. His illustrations, which I have virtually ignored here, are shrewdly chosen and effectively illustrative of the forms he considers. Every form he treats is illuminated by his treatment. These qualities undoubtedly account for the survival of *Simple Forms*. But as a "closed system of simple forms" the book fails— because it is neither closed nor systematic. It provides us with no vision of a whole, of which these nine forms compose the parts. Nor does it even confront the question of other possible simple forms. Why not the song? the prayer? the character? and so on. These questions do not seem to have occurred to Jolles. But there are signs that he was not entirely satisfied with the book as it stands. The edition published at Halle in 1956 includes an afterword by Alfred Schossig, who states that he has a letter from Henrik Becker, a professor at the University of Iena, asserting that in his last years Jolles thought of adding a tenth form and arranging the forms in a systematic fashion. (His widow denies that he ever thought of this tenth form—the fable—or at any rate she asserts that she never heard him mention it.) In this proposed "system," the ten forms would be divided into five pairs corresponding to five modes of discourse: the "interrogative, indicative, imperative, optative [modes] and silence." And each pair would be again divided into "realistic" and "idealitic" forms. A list of modes of discourse which includes silence is troublesome enough; one need only add something like "recounted with a cryptic smile on the face" to turn the whole "system" into a Borgesian Chinese catalogue. But the division into realistic and idealistic poses even greater problems, and in the process does violence to Jolles's own conceptual apparatus. Becker's table, which has been reprinted in the editorial note to the French translation, looks like this:

	Interroga-tive	Indica-tive	Silence	Impera-tive	Opta-tive
Realistic	Case	Saga	Riddle	Proverb	Fable
Idealistic	Myth	Memoir	Joke	Legend	Tale

This places the most empirical of Jolles's forms, the memoir, which he relates to the rise of realism, in the "idealistic" category. And there are other problems, nearly as grave, which could be noted if it were worth the effort. The very distinction between realistic and idealistic is based upon a modern view of the world, precisely the view associated with the rise of the memoir, which Jolles has deliberately refused to adopt as his own perspective on the simple forms. Clearly it is better to have no system at all than to have this travesty of the systematic, which itself seems almost like a joke at the expense of structuralism. For what Becker's chart reveals is a malfunctioning of the structuralist rage for system, and in particular of the structuralist notion that all literary forms must be rooted in linguistic forms. This notion may or may not be valid, but it certainly cannot be validated by putting elementary fictional genres into grammatical boxes. The problem of completing and systematizing Jolles's collection of simple forms is still very much an open problem. If it can be solved, if a system can be established that accounts for all the actualizations of simple form that exist in the universe of discourse and explains the relationships among them, that will be a major success for structuralist criticism. For what is in question here is precisely whether the forms of verbal discourse are united in a systematic way or not. And if they are not, the whole structuralist enterprise is seriously called into question.

In addition to the questions raised by the inadequacies of Jolles's treatment of simple forms, we must consider before concluding some questions raised deliberately by Jolles about certain critical procedures that have come to be adopted by formalists and structuralists. In his discussion of the tale as a simple form, Jolles digresses briefly to criticize certain folklorists who treat the tale as a collection of motifs that can be arranged in any way, like the pieces of a mosaic. To treat the tale in this purely formal way, he insists, is to reduce it to "a skeleton deprived of sense, which cannot bestow any moral satisfaction" on its auditors or readers. To separate the tale as a structure from the mental disposition that brings it into being is to mistake the skeleton for the person, the bones for the whole sentient organism. For Jolles, the simple forms come into being as a response to certain human needs and must be seen in relation to those needs. The tale, for instance, must be seen as an experience, a struggle through tragic obstacles toward justice, however naive its concepts of tragedy and justice may be. Unlike the forms of grammar, the simple forms of literature come into being as a response to ethical and interpretive needs. Thus, when we lose sight of their semantic dimension we lose sight of their very reason for being. This warning by Jolles should be kept in mind as we consider the progress of structuralist thought from the work of his contemporary, Vladimir Propp, to that of our own contemporaries. The survival of his work, despite its structural shortcomings, suggests that his views have not been superseded.

B. The Dramatic Situations of Étienne Souriau

In 1950 Étienne Souriau, a professor at the Sorbonne who had been writing on aesthetics for twenty-five years, published a little book with a strange title: *Les deux cent mille situations dramatiques*. In recent years this book has been frequently cited by structuralist literary theorists and has taken a place, along with the earlier work of Vladimir Propp, among the influential precursors of structuralism. Perhaps because the structuralists have somewhat neglected dramatic literature as a whole, Souriau's work, while acknowledged, has yet to receive all the recognition that it deserves; for it manages to be genuinely systematic without destroying the life of the material that it considers. The title itself is perhaps to blame for the book's relative neglect. It sounds cranky. And Souriau's decision to give the various functions of drama names and symbols drawn from astrology exhibits a similar tendency toward eccentricity. But the book itself is admirably clear and lively and is based upon a wide and thorough knowledge of drama, especially continental European drama.

With his title Souriau is mocking the attempts of earlier critics to reduce the possibilities of drama to a few basic situations. He proposes instead of some fixed list of dramatic possibilities a system of functions which may be arranged in all their mathematical combinations to produce dramatic situations. And he calculates that there are precisely 210,141 situations derived from a simple set of six functions and five methods of combination. It is hard to tell how serious he is about his mathematics, but I have checked it extensively and found it totally unreliable. Given his functions and the combinations and variations he mentions, it is impossible to derive a figure anywhere near his own for the total or for many of the subtotals that he indicates. At times, I suspect that he has confused combination with permutation—at other times it appears that he is pulling numbers out of the air. This, combined with his insistence on an astrological terminology, has no doubt made him suspect to his structuralist successors. But his thinking about dramatic functions is as rigorous and consistent as any similar formulations that I have seen, and as informed by a real sense of theater as one could wish.

Souriau begins by suggesting that we think of the stage as a little space or box in which selected elements of a theatrical world are displayed to us. What we see on any given stage implies that complete world beyond the backdrop by focusing on some aspect of it dramatically, making severe selections in time, space, and character from that larger world. And that larger theatrical world may be assumed to stand in some intelligible relation to the experiential world to which the audience will return when the play is over. What interests Souriau in his present study is not the interconnection between these worlds, though he acknowledges its importance, but the play of forces within that little box: the stage. Because of the rigorous limitations of the dramatic form it is ideal for this kind of study. Since the Greeks, the length of plays has not altered greatly. The terrible brevity of the drama has always been a crucial aspect of its structure. Only a limited number of characters can be developed on the stage. And the presence of that live audience makes action essential to the theater. These and other limitations have forced the drama into a mold that is simple in its elements but rich in its configurations, and it is precisely this basic structure that Souriau sets out to investigate. Ignoring aspects of characterization which are devices of the dramatist rather than components of the action (such as choral commentators, messengers, confidants, and the like), he seeks the minimal configuration of dramatic "functions," which, when assigned to a set of characters, will make a dramatic situation. His use of the word "function" is rather different from that of Vladimir Propp, as we shall see in the following chapter, but it is easy enough to grasp and apply. A function is a dramatic role conceived apart from any particular characterization of it. A dramatic situation consists of a particular arrangement of functions. A play involves the fleshing out of these functions and the working out of the possibilities in the initial situation, through as many intermediate situations as are necessary.

Because a play requires action and conflict in order to exist at all, the primary function is that of a force, a desire around which the whole play will be oriented. Souriau calls this function the Lion and designates it by the symbol Ω. It is the desire or Will of the Lion which precipitates the action of a play. This action, to become dramatic, requires opposition. Hence Mars, δ, the rival or Opponent is essential also. The opposition of these two functions establishes the principal dramatic axis of a play. The desire of the Lion, his Will, must also have an object and a destination. He wills something for somebody. Thus we have $\odot$, the Sun or Desired Good, and δ, the Earth or Destined Recipient of the Good. To these functions Souriau adds two more: $\simeq$, the Balance or Arbiter; and $\mathbb{C}$, the Moon or Helper. This latter, the Moon or Helper,

may in fact be the assistant or ally of any of the other five functions, thus yielding ten possible roles for any dramatic situation
— ♌, ♂, ☉, ♄, ♎, ☾ (♌), ☾ (♂), ☾ (☉), ☾ (♄), and ☾ (♎) —
the five basic functions and the possible Moon or Helper of
each. But in practice Souriau does not discuss situations with more
than one Moon, or with more than the basic total of six functions,
though it is theoretically possible to have larger groups. One feature of dramatic intensity of focus is that we seldom encounter
more than six characters of consequence in a play, and when we do
they are frequently simple doublings of function in multiple plots.

A dramatic situation takes shape when the six basic functions
are assigned to characters and their interrelationships established.
But not all six need be assigned human shape. In particular, the
Desired Object may be simply that, an object, a status or position
which may or may not be symbolized in a physical shape such as a
throne, sceptor, or crown and may or may not be represented by a
character on stage. Nor need each function be embodied in a separate character. Some functions may even be suppressed or kept off-
stage, but in most plays all six functions may be discerned in operation. Let us consider an example. Suppose a simple drama of love,
in which Peter, our Lion, desires to win Mary and is opposed by
Paul, a rival for her affections. This is a situation of three characters. How may the functions be assigned? If Peter seeks Mary for
himself, then his role includes the function of Earth as well as
Lion: ♌♄ . Which gives us three characters, using four functions,
like this: ♌♄ + ☉ + ♂. But the function of arbiter will be vital in
this situation. Whose decision is it? Can Mary make her own
choice? If so, the Balance is an aspect of her role, giving us this situation: ♌♄ + ☉≎ + ♂. With no Moon in the picture this is the
simplest and most banal of situations. But we can make it interesting simply by shifting the Balance to either Mars or Lion, producing either of these two situations: ♌♄ + ☉ + ♂≎ , or
♌♄≎ + ☉ + ♂.

If the Lion's rival is in a position to decide the fate of his beloved, either legally or morally (as a father or trusted advisor) this

complicates and enriches dramatic potential. Or if the Lion himself is the legal guardian or trusted advisor of the woman whose love he seeks, a similar enrichment takes place. As we say, the plot thickens. The introduction of the Moon or Helper in this three-character situation yields further complications of the sort that drama delights in. Still confining the action to three characters, Mary may have some commitment that allies her either with Peter or Paul, giving us such possibilities as ♌♂ + ☉≏ ☾(♌) + ♂, or ♌♂ + ☉≏ ☾(♂) + ♂, assuming in each case that Mary is the Arbiter. Another interesting complication results from situations in which one of the two antagonists is under some obligation to help his rival (as in the situation of Tristan, Iseult, and Mark, or dramatic variations of it), yielding ♌♂ ☾(♂)+ ☉≏ + ♂, or ♌♂ + ☉≏ + ♂ ☾(♌). Working with this pattern Souriau discusses thirty-six distinct situations for a three-character plot of love: twelve in which the Lion desires the Sun for himself, twelve in which he desires to see her united with his apparent rival, and twelve in which he wishes only to see her in command of herself. In all these cases Souriau seeks to find a plausible semantic content for the abstract structure generated by simply listing all the possible variations on an unchanging base of three functions. He can cite actual plays that have employed many of the configurations he discusses. And though he makes it very clear that he knows playwrights do not sit down and work out plays according to symbolic formulas, he suggests very convincingly that this shorthand notation does reveal a great deal about the fundamentals of dramaturgy, and that the generative grammar he has described plays a role at some level—conscious or unconscious—in the actual construction of plays.

To his set of functions and combinations Souriau adds another important concept, which has become a commonplace in fictional theory but is seldom encountered in the criticism of drama: the concept of point-of-view. Let me illustrate briefly. The simplest dramatic situation involves six characters, each assigned a single function. There are, because of the varieties of Moon, five possible versions of this situation:

1. $\Omega + \odot + \delta + \delta + \simeq + \mathbb{C}(\Omega)$.

2. $\Omega + \odot + \delta + \delta + \simeq + \mathbb{C}(\odot)$.

3. $\Omega + \odot + \delta + \delta + \simeq + \mathbb{C}(\delta)$.

4. $\Omega + \odot + \delta + \delta + \simeq + \mathbb{C}(\delta)$.

5. $\Omega + \odot + \delta + \delta + \simeq + \mathbb{C}(\simeq)$.

But the working out of any one of these five situations will strike us differently according to the point of view from which we see it. In any scene of mixed emotions we share the feelings of a particular character or linked set of characters more fully than those of the others. There is a kind of emotional law operating in this. If the dramatist wants us engaged in the scene, he must encourage us to focus our interest narrowly enough so that it can become intense. In the same play this interest may change as the scene changes or the situation changes. But the great playwrights invariably guide our interest in directions of their own choosing. Thus, if we assume that in our symbolic notation the first role designated will indicate the character from whose point of view the situation is perceived, all five of the above situations are designated as being from the Lion's point of view. This is, of course, the usual situation. We tend to line up with the orienting force in a drama. We empathize with the Lion. But such scenes as the murder of Macduff's family or Desdemona at prayer function to separate us from the Lion and to force us to see him from a different point of view. Theoretically, at least, each of these five situations could be presented from any point of view, giving us thirty possibilities in all, though the original five are the most likely to be used— because they are the easiest.

In the three-character love story the Lion is also the most likely character for us to empathize with, and the thirty-six versions of this situation that Souriau discusses all assume the Lion's point of view. But it is quite possible to present any of these from the point of view of Mary, for instance, the Sun or Desired Object, which changes the situation entirely. A shift from Peter the Lion to Paul the Opponent seems less likely, because it might simply result in Paul becoming the Lion himself and Peter assuming the role of Mars. But it is possible for the less forceful, less passionate, of two rivals in love to gain and hold our empathy. The Lion is not necessarily the "hero" of any given scene or of an entire play. Consider *Tartuffe,* for instance, in which the title character is clearly the Lion of the play but is not allowed a hint of our sympathy. In this play Molière even delays his Lion's entrance for two acts, so that we may look upon his works without being persuaded to his point of view. In the *Misanthrope,* on the other hand, there are problems in the managing of point of view, which each director must solve for himself.

In the process of constructing a play, the bare situations envisaged by Souriau are of course varied and enriched in many other ways as well. As we consider assigning such qualities as age, sex, position, temperament, beauty, strength, weakness, ugliness, and so on, to an abstract situational formula, we can see the possibilities of theater come alive before our eyes. And if we think of all the possible variations each one of these changes may work in a situation we may be persuaded that Souriau's absurdly specific figure is if anything too low rather than too high a limit for the possibilities of dramatic construction. Which is probably what he wanted us to think when he established the number. At any rate, throughout his discussion of dramatic situations, he attends to the specifics of drama as well as the generalities, citing nearly two hundred different plays by way of illustration, some of them ten times or more. His book, then, is an astonishing and provocative blend of abstract reasoning about the drama and empirical knowledge of plays and playwrights. Yet, for a final evaluation of this unique achievement, we should ask two interrelated questions—hard questions that must also be asked of every similar structuralist endeavor. How true is it? What good is it?

How true is it? how accurate a representation of dramatic functions and situations? how complete? To answer this we must rec-

ognize some of the limits, both deliberate and inadvertent, of Souriau's procedure. First of all, he has deliberately set aside much that
is important in the theater. He is interested here in the essence of
theatrical action as it may be represented in stasis, synchronically,
in the form of situations. He is well aware that in a play situations
lead to actions and actions to new situations, but he is concerned
here only with situations. And only with fundamental building
blocks, not with the incidental devices and tactics of the theater
but with the essence of the dramatic as a configuration of potential
objects and forces. To my way of thinking what he presents is
what is really there—as far as he goes. He has given us the essences of dramatic situation about as clearly, simply, and logically
as this can be done. The real question, then, is not whether it is
valid but how much of drama it includes. Obviously, more functions would cover more possibilities, but I think he has known
well when to stop. Here his material helped him. The theater is
much more focused and limited than fiction, for instance. And it is
by no means certain that fiction demands that crucial orienting
character, the Lion, whose will shapes a play, in the same way that
drama does. But it is fair to say that even within the realm of theater, Souriau's formulas seem more applicable to the classical tragedy of Greece and France, for instance, than to our less formally
perfect but somewhat richer English theater. Shakespeare is much
farther from these basic structures than Aeschylus, Sophocles, Cor-
neille, or Racine.

This brings us to the question, What good is it? In answer I
would say that though it will never serve as an adequate description of actual dramatic situations, it can certainly function as a
structural grid to help us perceive the actualities of any work of
dramaturgy. If modern playwrights give us Cowardly Lions, wait-
ing for Godot instead of seeking him, Souriau's pattern may seem
strange applied to them, but that very strangeness should sharpen
our perception. And if Shakespeare has enriched and complicated
the basic configurations almost to the point of making them imperceptible, this, then, is a measurable aspect of his genius. And finally, it would surprise me if any playwright, toying with this sym-

bolic logic of the stage, did not find himself challenged, stimulated, and perhaps even inspired by this world of abstractions which claims to hold the essence of the one form of literary art which is incomplete unless enacted by flesh-and-blood human beings. Like Pirandello's six characters, Souriau's six functions will continue to seek and find their authors as long as the drama survives.

4 Toward a Structuralist Poetics of Fiction

The virtues and limitations of structuralism as an approach to literary study can be seen more clearly in its treatment of narrative literature than in any other aspect of literary theory or criticism. This is so for a number of reasons, which resolve themselves finally to the "fit" between narrative literature as a subject matter and structuralism as a discipline. Because the field of narrative extends from myth on the one hand (simple, short, popular, oral, prehistoric) to the modern novel on the other (complex, long, individual, written, historical), while preserving certain structural features (character, situation, action, resolution), it offers a superb field of study to the structuralist, and the field has been well cultivated. The structural study of fiction, despite a heritage going back to Aristotle, may almost be said to begin with Vladimir Propp's work on the Russian fairy tale. Propp provided for fiction that kind of "simplification of form" which has been such an important impetus to structuralist thinking. The difference between Propp's approach to simple narrative forms and that of Lévi-Strauss, which we shall explore in the following section of this chapter, suggests a range within structuralism which is so great as almost to amount to a schism. Though much simpler, much less ingenious—or perhaps *because* much simpler and less ingenious—Propp's work has proved thus far much more important for literary theory than that of Lévi-Strauss. If there is a schism, Propp is the first pope of the orthodox sect.

Vladimir Propp was a formalist, of course, and may be said to represent the formalist position within literary structuralism. This has been and still is the central structuralist literary attitude. Formalism has developed, grown in subtlety and richness in the past half-century; it has abandoned some extreme positions and qualified others; but throughout this period it has proved remarkably vigorous, attracting scholars of great learning and intellectual vigor. Thus, instead of representing a mere episode in the history of taste, it has continued to flourish at the heart of the structuralist movement which supplanted it. For this reason, as well as for its intrinsic interest, a consideration of the formalist movement's contribution to fictional poetics is an essential part of the present chapter.

The last two sections of this chapter treat contemporary microstructuralism and macrostructuralism. In section C, I inquire into some efforts to refine the functionalism of Propp and apply these refinements to some elementary narrative forms. And in the last section I consider some attempts to systematize the whole order of fiction, especially through the consideration of fictional modes and genres. These attempts, admittedly imperfect, are nonetheless tantalizingly close to being satisfactory. Above all, they encourage refinement and development themselves—and even in their tentative, imperfect condition they are usable and useful. But if they were not, and if we were to discard the structuralist poetics of fiction sketched in this chapter—where should we turn for another? Structuralism and formalism have given us virtually all the poetics of fiction that we have.

A. The Mythographers: Propp and Lévi-Strauss

Much of the structuralist achievement and many of its limitations are implicit in the two approaches to folk narratives taken by Vladimir Propp and Claude Lévi-Strauss. This is so because of the extraordinary insight and ingenuity of these two men but also because of the nature of the mythic materials they chose to investigate. Myths, folktales, fairy tales—these are the prototypes of all narrative, the ancestors and the models of later fictional developments. In studying the history of narrative, we find that in modern times forms have developed which elaborate and transform the basic constituents of primitive fiction almost beyond recognition, but we also find that modern fictional forms have never lost touch with the primitive entirely and have frequently returned to their sources to draw upon the almost magical power they possess. The universality of myth is an important aspect of this heritage, which Lévi-Strauss has emphasized in one of his most insightful paragraphs:

A remark can be introduced at this point which will help to show the originality of myth in relation to other linguistic phenomena. Myth is the part of language where the formula *traduttore, tradittore* [translator equals traitor] reaches its lowest truth value. From that point of view it should be placed in the gamut of linguistic expressions at the end opposite to that of poetry, in spite of all the claims which have been made to prove the contrary. Poetry is a kind of speech which cannot be translated except at the cost of serious distortions; whereas the mythical value of the myth is preserved even through the worst translation. Whatever our ignorance of the language and the culture of the people where it originated, a myth is still felt as a myth by any reader anywhere in the world. Its substance does not lie in its style, its original music, or its syntax, but in the *story* which it tells. Myth is language, functioning on an especially high level where meaning succeeds practically at "taking off" from the linguistic ground on which it keeps on rolling. [*Structural Anthropology,* p. 206]

Because they share so little in the way of ideas and attitudes, it is worth pointing out that C. S. Lewis has made almost the same observation about mythic forms as the French anthropologist has. "It is true," he says, "that such a story can hardly reach us except in words. But this is logically accidental. If some perfected art of mime or silent film or serial pictures could make it clear with no words at all, it would still affect us the same way" (*Experiment in Criticism,* Cambridge, England, 1965, p. 41).

Let us pause and examine the implications of these statements for a moment. We are invited to consider a continuum of literary possibilities, in which myth and poetry represent polar opposites. In poetry the lexical and paradigmatic side of language dominates—the reverberations of a given word in its own linguistic heritage. Naturally, this is, as Robert Frost said, "what gets lost in translation." Poetry celebrates the unique in a culture, a language, a man's way of using his language. In myth, however, the structural and syntagmatic side of language dominates, and at this level languages have much in common. Linguistic structures, and hence myths, have a universality which linguistic units, being arbitrary, do not have.

This is why Propp and Lévi-Strauss concentrate on the structures of myth, and why mythic materials have such a "privileged" place in structuralist activities. But the different directions taken by Propp and Lévi-Strauss lead to activities so dissimilar as to suggest a fundamental division within structuralism—one of a number of such divisions which make defining "structuralism" almost impossible while accounting in part for the vitality and versatility of structural criticism. Propp, working in the 1920s, may be considered a member of the Russian formalist group. Certainly his work influenced other formalists and an important segment of the French structuralists as well.

Propp begins with the problem of classifying and organizing folktales. Building on work done by Veselóvsky and Bédier, he notes that most attempts to classify tales according to "motifs" or "elements" result in unsystematic and arbitrary groupings. Attempting to distinguish between constant and variable elements in a collection of a hundred Russian fairy tales, Propp arrives at the principle that though the personages of a tale are variable, their functions in the tales are constant and limited. Describing function as "an act of a character, defined from the point of view of its significance for the course of the action," Propp developed inductively four laws which put the study of folk literature and of fiction itself on a new footing. In their baldness and universality, laws 3 and 4 have the shocking effect of certain scientific discoveries:

1. Functions of characters serve as stable, constant elements in a tale, independent of how and by whom they are fulfilled. They constitute the fundamental components of a tale.
2. The number of functions known to the fairy-tale is limited.
3. The sequence of functions is always identical.
4. All fairy tales are of one type in regard to their structure.
   [*Morphology of the Folktale,* pp. 21, 22, 23]

In comparing the functions of tale after tale, Propp discovered that his total number of functions never surpassed thirty-one, and that however many of the thirty-one functions a tale had (none has every one) those that it had always appeared in the same order. (So that the reader may have some sense of the concrete aspects of this formulation I will list the functions, but must refer those interested to Propp's own text for their explanation and illustration.) After the initial situation, in which the members of a family are enumerated or the future hero is introduced, a tale begins, consisting of some selection of the following functions in the following order:

1. One of the members of a family absents himself from home.
2. An interdiction is addressed to the hero.
3. The interdiction is violated.
4. The villain makes an attempt at reconnaissance.
5. The villain receives information about his victim.
6. The villain attempts to deceive his victim in order to take possession of him or of his belongings.
7. The victim submits to deception and thereby unwittingly helps his enemy.
8. The villain causes harm or injury to a member of a family.
8a. One member of a family either lacks something or desires to have something.
9. Misfortune or lack is made known: the hero is approached with a request or a command; he is allowed to go or is dispatched.

10. The seeker agrees to or decides upon counteraction.
11. The hero leaves home.
12. The hero is tested, interrogated, attacked, etc., which prepares the way for his receiving either a magical agent or helper.
13. The hero reacts to the actions of the future donor.
14. The hero acquires the use of a magical agent.
15. The hero is transferred, delivered, or led to the whereabouts of an object of search.
16. The hero and the villain join in direct combat.
17. The hero is branded.
18. The villain is defeated.
19. The initial misfortune or lack is liquidated.
20. The hero returns.
21. The hero is pursued.
22. Rescue of the hero from pursuit.
23. The hero, unrecognized, arrives home or in another country.
24. A false hero presents unfounded claims.
25. A difficult task is proposed to the hero.
26. The task is resolved.
27. The hero is recognized.
28. The false hero or villain is exposed.
29. The false hero is given a new appearance.
30. The villain is punished.
31. The hero is married and ascends the throne.

Propp calls the first seven functions as a unit the "preparation," and it is possible to distinguish other groups of motifs with such general designations. Thus we have the complication, ending with number 10, followed by transference, struggle, return, and recognition. As later commentators were quick to point out, all this is not perfectly logical, yet the structure abstracted here by Propp is clearly something that we have all encountered in our reading of fiction, from tales to novels.

In addition to the thirty-one functions, Propp locates seven "spheres of action," which involve the eight character roles of the fairy tale:

1. the villain
2. the donor (provider)
3. the helper
4. the princess (a sought-for person) and her father
5. the dispatcher
6. the hero (seeker or victim)
7. the false hero

One character may play more than one of these roles in any given tale (e.g., villain may also be false hero, donor may also be dispatcher); or one role may employ several characters (multiple villains, for instance); but these are all the roles that this sort of narrative requires, and they are basic to much fiction which is far removed from fairy tales in other respects.

We might note in passing that Propp's formulation is similar in certain respects to the independently conceived project of Lord Raglan (*The Hero,* London, 1936) of listing the events in the life of a typical mythic hero. Raglan's heroic tales are quite different from the fairy tales Propp investigated, and his methodology is far less systematic. He simply wished to show how mythic forms had certain persistent and recurring features which distinguished the lives of mythic heroes from those of historical beings. Like Frazer, Cornford, Weston, Gaster, and others, Raglan belongs to a school of primarily British protostructuralists, who are among the important theoretical predecessors of Northrop Frye, and who argued persuasively for the dependence of mythic narrative structures on certain primitive religious rituals. Disputes about cause-and-effect among myth and ritual may continue for some time, but the close association of the two, their answering to similar and fundamental human needs, are now an accepted premise in human studies. Raglan's heroic pattern has twenty-two features, not all of which are functions in Propp's sense of the word—perhaps because these hero-myths are not functioning so purely as narrative structures but still have significant elements of a ritualistic kind. But here is the pattern:

1. The hero's mother is a royal virgin;
2. His father is a king, and
3. Often a near relative of his mother, but
4. The circumstances of his conception are unusual, and
5. He is also reputed to be the son of a god.
6. At birth an attempt is made, usually by his father or his maternal grandfather, to kill him, but
7. He is spirited away, and
8. Reared by foster-parents in a far country.
9. We are told nothing of his childhood, but
10. On reaching manhood he returns or goes to his future kingdom.
11. After a victory over the king and/or a giant, dragon, or wild beast,
12. He marries a princess, often the daughter of his predecessor, and
13. Becomes king.
14. For a time he reigns uneventfully, and
15. Prescribes laws, but
16. Later he loses favour with the gods and/or his subjects, and
17. Is driven from the throne and city, after which
18. He meets with a mysterious death,
19. Often at the top of a hill.
20. His children, if any, do not succeed him.
21. His body is not buried, but nevertheless
22. He has one or more holy sepulchres.

Raglan then uses this pattern to "score" certain famous heroes. Theseus, for instance, gets twenty points, Heracles seventeen. Jesus, rather pointedly omitted, would obviously score well. Culture heroes from widely diverse parts of the world are credited with lives that resemble this pattern significantly. Raglan's point is to suggest a basis in ritual for all these similarities, but with or without ritual the similarities suggest the existence of some fundamental grammar of narrative over a wide range of humanity. Neither Raglan nor Propp is concerned with the reasons for this. Propp himself is content to describe what he sees. He speculates occasionally that the fairy tale must be derived from myth and that certain chivalric romances must in turn be developments of the tale. And he is ready to point out that the aesthetic interest of any given tale may well be a function not of its invariant structure but of its variable attributes: "By attributes we mean the totality of all the external qualities of the characters: their age, sex, status, external appearance, peculiarities of this appearance, and so forth. These attributes provide the tale with its brilliancy, charm, and beauty" (p. 87). It is obvious from this that Propp is aware of aesthetic considerations (brilliancy, charm, beauty) but not really concerned with them. If the structure of a tale has any aesthetic quality in itself he is content to ignore it, though it seems clear that he would attribute aesthetic effects to some kind of quality in the realization of a tale rather than to its structure. To get from this limited structural view of texts which have been filtered through the medium of folk transmission to a genuinely structuralist view of truly literary texts—this is one of the great problems that structural literary theorists are still trying to solve. But Propp has taught us all something fundamental about the nature of narrative literature. He has taught us to look at plot-functions and character-roles with an eye for their rigorous and narrowly delimited interconnections. Thus his work has become a point of departure for a number of later theorists, particularly the group of Greimas, Bremond, and Todorov, whose work will be discussed in section C below.

For Propp, the unit of structural analysis was the individual tale as a unique construction. From a set of one hundred tales of similar configuration he worked on deriving the structure of a master-tale, whose thirty-one functions include all of the structural possibilities found in the entire set. Though his interest, as I have indicated, was not primarily aesthetic, he was concerned nonetheless with the formal qualities of the tale, its basic units and the rules governing their combination. Essentially, he was constructing a grammar and syntax for a certain kind of narrative, which later theorists have modified in order to extend its application to other kinds of narrative forms. For Claude Lévi-Strauss, on the other hand, the form of individual narratives is not an important consideration. For him the unit is not the tale but the myth, which finds expression in any number of tales, finished or fragmentary. A myth in this sense is a body of materials, mainly narrative, which deal with a particular aspect of a given culture. Or, more precisely, the myth stands behind these materials, which always reach us in some modified form, and must be reconstructed from them.

Propp was concerned with an aesthetic form, the fairy tale, which is itself a modification of mythic materials for aesthetic ends. In seeking the master form of a group of these tales Propp may be said to have sought for the bases of a dynamics of human response to narrative. He never pursued his search to the point of asking what reaction a given function may have produced in the audience of a tale. But he isolated a structure which must itself have come into being in order to satisfy a common human desire for certain formal narrative pleasures. Lévi-Strauss, on the other hand, is concerned not with an aesthetic form but with a logical form: the system of ideas embodied, however obscurely, in primitive mythology. The aesthetic restructuring of a myth, which shapes it into a folktale or fairy tale, is for him a form of transformation which obscures the original logic of the myth. But this is almost inevitable since myths take on a pleasing narrative form precisely in order to make palatable certain truths about the human situation which men have always found it difficult to contemplate. Where Propp seeks the process by which an oyster constructs its pearl, Lévi-Strauss wants to explain the significance of the structure found in the original grain of sand.

In its procedures, the method of Lévi-Strauss bears a superficial resemblance to those of Propp and Raglan. He begins by breaking down the mythic narrative under consideration into units, each of which can be summarized by a short sentence. These are similar to Propp's "functions" and Raglan's "points" but not exactly the same as either. Each of the units expresses a "relation." In practice this usually means something like a Proppian function: for example, "Oedipus kills the Sphinx," which is a unit in Lévi-Strauss's analysis of the Theban mythic cycle, is equivalent to Propp's function number 18, the hero's victory over the villain in direct combat. But not all of Lévi-Strauss's units are narrative functions. Some, for instance, are simply interpretations of names: "Oedipus = swollen foot," which is an interpretive detail rather than a relation presented in the narrative. Using a term like "relations" enables Lévi-Strauss to adjust his categories to his material with an unscientific élan that dismays his professional colleagues. But the impulse behind this is the same as that which caused Raglan to include as his point 19 the item that the hero's death occurs "often at the top of a hill." There are significant elements in many myths and tales which are not functions of the narrative; they are semantic rather than syntagmatic in their working; yet they are not merely embellishments, but play some fundamental role in the narrative. In this case the hill is clearly associated with ritual and thus a part of myth which may not be preserved in the aesthetization of myth into fairy tale.

The reduction of a mythic narrative into relational units called "mythemes," however, is the least controversial part of the analytical process. The next stage, that of arrangement, is the crux of the whole operation. In Lévi-Strauss's view a myth is a kind of message in code from the whole of a culture to its individual members. As long as a culture remains homogeneous, a particular myth will continue to have validity for it, and new versions of the myth will be simply aspects of the same message. The code can be broken and the message deciphered if we arrange its mythemes in the proper way, which is not simply in the narrative order of their transmission to us. Here is the example given by Lévi-Strauss in his famous essay "The Structural Study of Myth," in *Structural Anthropology* (pp. 209–10).

> The myth will be treated as an orchestra score would be if it were unwittingly considered as a unilinear series; our task is to re-establish the correct arrangement. Say, for instance, we were confronted with a sequence of the type: 1,2,4,7,8,2,3,

4,6,8,1,4,5,7,8,1,2,5,7,3,4,5,6,8 . . . , the assignment being to put all the 1's together, all the 2's, the 3's, etc.; the result is a chart:

1	2		4			7	8
	2	3	4		6		8
1			4	5		7	8
1	2			5		7	
		3	4	5	6		8

We shall attempt to perform the same kind of operation on the Oedipus myth, trying out several arrangements of the my-themes until we find one which is in harmony with the principles enumerated above. Let us suppose, for the sake of argument, that the best arrangement is [that on page 71] (although it might certainly be improved with the help of a specialist in Greek mythology).

Let us consider the numerical model first. In reading the narrative string from left to right we notice quickly that 8 is the highest number reached and that the sequence repeats itself (though always partially, never completely) five separate times. Thus we arrive at an arrangement of eight columns and five rows. This is supremely easy to do with numbers because they position themselves for us. We know where to leave gaps even when we write down the first row, so that when we finally reach a 5 in the third row, we know precisely where to put it. With the units of a myth things are not so simple (though with Propp's functions we would be on much firmer ground). The chart of the Oedipus myth makes both the method and the problems involved in using it clear. In all fairness, we should acknowledge that Lévi-Strauss says that the use of his technique is "probably not legitimate" in this instance, since "the Oedipus myth has only reached us under late forms and through literary transmutations more concerned with esthetic and moral preoccupations than with religious or ritual ones" (p. 209). But a few pages later he asserts that a myth consists of "all its versions," and he is quite ready to include Freud's version of the Oedi-

Cadmos seeks his sister Europa, ravished by Zeus			
		Cadmos kills the dragon	
	The Spartoi kill one another		
			Labdacos (Laios' father) = *lame* (?)
	Oedipus kills his father, Laios		Laios (Oedipus' father) = *left-sided* (?)
		Oedipus kills the Sphinx	
			Oedipus = *swollen-foot* (?)
Oedipus marries his mother, Jocasta			
	Eteocles kills his brother, Polynices		
Antigone buries her brother, Polynices, despite prohibition			

pus story among the others. It is this fondness of Lévi-Strauss for eating his cake and having it too—and then maintaining that it is really pie anyway, or that cake and pie are the same thing—which disconcerts all but his most devoted admirers. But let us look at what he has done with the Oedipal cycle.

First of all, he has left out a lot, but let's grant him the right to do this, at least provisionally. As he himself puts it, this demonstration should not be conceived in terms of what scientists mean by demonstration but as what a street peddler might mean, whose aim was merely to explain "the functioning of the mechanical toy which he is trying to sell to the onlookers." How *does* this mechanical toy work, then, and will it work for anyone but the peddler himself? The first trick is in the arranging of the elements in columns. Lévi-Strauss is deliberately vague about this. The arrangement is "in harmony with the principles enumerated above"—but the principles are never really enumerated, only hinted at with metaphors and remote analogies. Later he observes that "all the relations belonging to the same column exhibit one common feature which it is our task to discover" (p. 211). But of course it is precisely this common feature which caused them to be arranged in the same columns to begin with. For some reason Lévi-Strauss is at pains here to suggest that his procedure is inductive, while it has very clearly been deductive from the beginning. He has arranged the mythemes in columns according to certain common features which he finds significant in the beliefs of all primitive men. The first column emphasizes relations in which kinship ties are overclose—actual incest in the case of Oedipus and Jocasta, and a kind of virtual incest in the two pairs of brothers and sisters who emphasize their relationship against the wishes of gods and men. The second column emphasizes relationships in which kinship ties are violated, by fratricide or patricide. Thus these two columns taken together express the two parts of a logical binary opposition: the overrating of blood relations versus the underrating of blood relations. The relationship between column 3 and column 4 is somewhat murkier. Because the monsters killed in column 3 are in some versions said to be autochthonous (self-born, sprung from the earth) this column is said to represent a "denial of the autochthonous origin of man." The lameness, or "difficulties in walking straight and standing upright," that we find in column 4 is in many mythologies a feature of men whose origin is supposed to have been autochthonous. Thus column 4 can be said to affirm the autochthonous origin of man. The meaning of the myth is then summed up in a paragraph which, if it can be understood, will take us to the heart of the method:

> Turning back to the Oedipus myth, we may now see what it means. The myth has to do with the inability, for a culture which holds the belief that mankind is autochthonous (see, for instance Pausanias, VIII, xxix, 4: plants provide a *model* for humans), to find a satisfactory transition between this theory and the knowledge that human beings are actually born from the union between man and woman. Although the problem obviously cannot be solved, the Oedipus myth provides a kind of logical tool which relates the original problem—born from one or born from two?—to the derivative problem: born from different or born from same? By a correlation of this type, the overrating of blood relations is to the underrating of blood relations as the attempt to escape autochthony is to the impossibility to succeed in it. Although experience contradicts theory, social life validates cosmology by its similarity of structure. Hence cosmology is true. [p. 212]

This is difficult to understand and perhaps even harder to believe. No one will deny that this legend has something to do with incestuous social relationships, and many will agree that the problem of autochthony is also present in the myth, but only a few disciples are ready to accept Lévi-Strauss's reading of the logical structure behind the myth. Yet he is certainly on to something in mythology. Experts find his treatment of South American Indian mythology more satisfying, and Edmund Leach's application of this methodology to Genesis (in a well-known essay called "Lévi-Strauss in the Garden of Eden") is a very persuasive deciphering of biblical mythology. There is something here, then, some fruitful grappling with the mental processes of myth-making which is of value and interest. But it leads away from the direction of literature and along a path that is far from being thoroughly charted. At the moment few can follow Lévi-Strauss through his mythical jungle, and many who have gone part of the way fear that at the end of the trail they will find not the Mind of Man but only the fertile brain of Claude Lévi-Strauss. He, of course, would say— has said—that it's the same thing.

B. *The Russian Formalists*

The achievement of the Russian formalists is only now beginning to be appreciated in the English-speaking world. Though the formalists flourished in the period 1915–1930, their ideas have been available to us only indirectly until quite recently. The revival of interest in formalism is partly the result of the present popularity of structuralism, since it is clear that some aspects of structuralism are direct, historical developments of formalist ideas and methods. But this interest is not merely historical, in my opinion. It is because the formalist poetics of fiction, in particular, has proved to have continuing validity and applicability that formalism has finally begun to be appreciated in England and especially in America. The publication of Victor Erlich's excellent *Russian Formalism: History-Doctrine* by Mouton in 1955 marked the beginning of this interest, but the first works of literary criticism by the formalists themselves did not appear in English until Lemon and Reis produced their very useful *Russian Formalist Criticism: Four Essays* in 1965 (hereafter abbreviated in this chapter as L & R). In that same year the Bulgarian structuralist Tzvetan Todorov produced a French translation of formalist critical writings called *Théorie de la littérature* (abbreviated here as *TL*), and in a later essay on the methodological heritage of formalism he explicitly drew some connections between formalist and structuralist literary thought. In 1968 Mikhail Bakhtin's *Rabelais and His World* appeared. Bakhtin, a transitional figure between the formalists and structuralists, is a critic of great subtlety and great good sense as well, who produced a book on problems in Dostoevsky's poetics in 1929, and then his book on Rabelais in 1940. Both of these books were republished in Russia in the 1960s—formalism refusing to die even in the Socialist Republic—and the Rabelais appeared in English a few years later. His book on Dostoevsky is presently scheduled for publication by the Ardis Press in late 1973. In 1971 an important collection of critical essays edited by Matejka and Pomorska under the title *Readings in Russian Poetics* (abbreviated here as *RRP*) was published by M.I.T., and in 1972 the Ardis Press published Eichenbaum's *The Young Tolstoi,* a work of 1921 which illustrates beautifully the dogmatic but perceptive quality to be found in much early formalist critical thinking. Victor Erlich's *Twentieth-Century Russian Literary Criticism* was published by Yale in 1975.

That such critical writings (a notoriously ephemeral form) should be translated into English as many as fifty years after their first publication attests to the vigor and the continuing interest of formalist criticism. Some important works, like Shklovsky's *Theory of Prose,* have yet to appear, but at the moment it seems likely that in a few years we will have in English a representative and very interesting body of Russian formalist criticism. In the pages that follow, I wish to provide an introduction to that body of work, in which I will try to trace certain concepts of special importance for the theory of fiction as they were developed in the early writings of the formalists and modified as formalism moved in the direction of structuralism. While doing this I shall be especially concerned to defend the formalists against certain charges sometimes leveled at them—and at the structuralists as well—most recently by Fredric Jameson in his book *The Prison House of Language.* Jameson criticizes formalism and structuralism from a Hegelian/Marxian perspective. His criticism is thoroughly informed and vigorously argued. It must be attended to by anyone interested in the subject. But I think it is, if not simply "wrong," at least unfair in its estimate of the formalist achievement, and I shall try to indicate why in my examination of formalist critical thinking.

Jameson's view is summed up in this paragraph, drawn from his essay on the same subject, "Metacommentary," which appeared in *PMLA* in January 1971:

> Formalism is thus, as we have suggested, the basic mode of interpretation of those who refuse interpretation: at the same time, it is important to stress the fact that this method finds its privileged objects in the smaller forms, in short stories or folk tales, poems, anecdotes, in the decorative detail of larger works. For reasons to which we cannot do justice in the present context, the Formalistic model is essentially synchronic, and cannot adequately deal with diachrony, either in literary history or in the form of the individual work, which is to say that Formalism as a method stops short at the point where the novel as a problem begins.

This statement, which is based partly on the assumption that formalism is mainly an attempt to put concern for form in the place of concern for content, seems to me wrong in a number of ways. It would be truer to say that formalism is more concerned with poetics than with interpretation, more concerned with producing useful generalizations about "literariness" than with ingenious readings of individual works—with the qualification that many formalists have produced excellent readings when this was their aim. But that formalist and structuralist criticism have proved unwilling or unable to deal with the temporal dimension of either particular works or literature in general is simply untrue. Though there was plenty of pressure in the direction of the synchronic from the model of Saussurean linguistics, it was counterbalanced very quickly by the linguistic influence of Jakobson and by the counterpressure of Hegelian and Marxist models, as found, for instance, in the literary criticism of Lukács. And finally, far from being helpless before the novel as a literary form, the formal method has given us virtually all the poetics of fiction we have. Though some of our theory seems to be homegrown in English, there is hardly anything in current Anglo-American thinking about fictional form that has not been touched on by the formalists and their structuralist descendants. Even the special problem of point-of-view in fiction, which we think of as belonging to a line of Anglo-American critics that extends from Henry James to Wayne Booth, was treated, and treated intelligently, by the formalists. Other important concepts in our critical thinking about fiction have come to us directly from formalism through the mediation of such critics as René Wellek, who came to this country from the Prague Circle.

In reading the formalists an American must be struck by the fact that they were truly a critical "school." American critics, with a few notable exceptions, have been loners. But the formalists spoke to one another, read one another's work, refined and developed one another's ideas. In fact, the way they were able to build on one another's work suggests that they were actually achieving to some extent that "science of literature" which was their aim—for our discipline is a science to the extent that it is cumulative and an art to the extent that each critical work is unique. This interaction among the formalists makes it difficult to credit individuals with the development of particular concepts, but the two critics who wrote most extensively on fiction were Victor Shklovsky and Boris Eichenbaum. Of these two Eichenbaum was the more systematic and judicious, Shklovsky the more innovative, but also more extreme and hyperbolical; it was Shklovsky, for instance, who defended *Tristram Shandy* against the charge of not being a novel by insisting that it should be recognized as "the most typical novel in world literature" (L & R, p. 57).

It is primarily the achievement of Eichenbaum and Shklovsky that I shall be examining here, after a brief discussion of a third figure, Boris Tomashevsky, whose essay "Thematics" (reprinted in L & R) summarizes and systematizes the whole formalist poetics of fiction. Tomashevsky begins by asserting that the unifying principle in a fictional structure is a general thought, or a theme. In a work of fiction, thematic materials reflect the presence of two rather different forces, one from the immediate environment of the writer, the other from the literary tradition in which he writes. They also reflect the different concerns of the writer and the reader. "The writer tries to solve the problem of artistic tradition," while the reader may simply want to be entertained—or he may want "a combination of literary interests and general cultural concerns." This latter kind of reader demands "reality—that is, themes that are 'real' in the context of contemporary cultural thought." Tomashevsky postulates a continuum of thematic materials ranging from the most local and topical themes, which will not sustain interest for long, to themes of general human interest such as love and death. "The more significant and long-lasting the theme, the better the guarantee of the life of the work." But even the enduring themes must be presented through "some kind of specific material" which must be relevant to reality if the formulation of the problem is not to "prove 'uninteresting'." (Quotations in this paragraph and the next are from L & R, pp. 64–65.)

In any given novel the major theme can be seen as composed of smaller thematic units. The irreducible units of fiction are *motifs*. Thus *story* can be defined as the sum of the motifs in their causal-chronological order, *plot* as the sum of the same motifs ordered so as to engage the emotions and develop the theme: "The esthetic function of the plot is precisely this bringing of an arrangement of motifs to the attention of the reader." Tomashevsky calls the principle of arrangement *motivation,* and he notes that motivation is always "a compromise between objective reality and literary tradition." Because readers need the illusion of lifelikeness, fiction must provide it. But, since "realistic material itself does not have artistic structure," then "the formation of an artistic structure requires that reality be reconstructed according to esthetic laws. Such laws are always, considered in relation to reality, conventional."

In connection with motivation Tomashevsky discusses various kinds of motifs (bound and free, static and dynamic), the different value of motifs with respect to plot and story, the different kinds of narrators (omniscient, limited, and mixed), the treatment of time and place, the varieties of character (static and dynamic, positive and negative), the various devices of the plot (conventional and free, obvious or imperceptible), and finally the relation of these devices to the two major fictional styles (natural and artificial). This material is too rich and too specific to be more than mentioned here, since Tomashevsky himself has presented it with close to the maximum possible compression and concentration. Despite the nearly fifty years since its publication, it can still function as a primer of fictional poetics. Tomashevsky has not been superseded; he has only been qualified and refined upon by later writers.

Before considering these refinements, it will be appropriate to look at the general question of the relationship of formalism to literary history, which was treated by Eichenbaum in an essay on "literary environment," published in 1929 (*RRP,* pp. 56–65).

Eichenbaum begins by pointing out that "without theory no historical system would be possible, because there would be no principle for selecting and conceptualizing facts." History, for Eichenbaum, is itself *in* history, and therefore must be continually revised:

> History is, in effect, a science of complex analogies, a science of double vision: the facts of the past have meanings for us that differentiate them and place them, invariably and inevitably, in a system under the sign of contemporary problems. Thus one set of problems supplants another, one set of facts overshadows another. History in this sense is a special method of studying the present with the aid of the facts of the past.
>
> The successive change of problems and conceptual signs leads to the reassortment of traditional material and the inclusion of new facts excluded from an earlier system because of the latter's innate limitations. The incorporation of a new

set of facts (under the sign of some particular correlation) strikes us as being the discovery of those facts, since their existence outside a system (their "contingent" status) had been from a scientific point of view equivalent to their nonexistence. [*RRP,* p. 56]

The passage will bear some analysis. It is typical of formal/structural thought in that it insists that truth is relative and that it is created rather than discovered. We should note that this view does not deny the reality of facts; it only maintains that there are too many to be apprehended unless they are limited and organized by a conceptual system. Content and form are inseparable, because one cannot exist without the other. Far from denying the temporal aspect of life, this view explicitly recognizes it. And it is closely related to a major aspect of the formalist theory of fictional construction. In their writings on fiction the formalists employ a distinction between two aspects of narrative: story (*fable*) and plot (*sujet*). The *story* is the raw materials of the narrative, that is, the events in their chronological sequence. The *plot* is the narrative as actually shaped. We can think of story as being analogous to the facts of history itself, always running on at the same speed, in the same direction. In a *plot,* the speed may be changed, the direction reversed, at will. Actually, a *story* already represents items selected according to some elementary law of narrative logic which eliminates irrelevancies. And a *plot* is then a further refinement which organizes these items for maximum emotional effect and thematic interest. But it is fair to say that the facts of life are to history as the story is to the plot. History selects and arranges the events of existence, and plot selects and arranges the events of story. The art of fiction is, then, most apparent in the artificial rearrangement of chronology which makes a story into a plot. Time is indeed crucial to fiction, and the formalists are aware not only of how crucial it is but of the ways in which it becomes crucial.

After establishing the necessity of theory for history in general,

Eichenbaum turns to the specific problems of literary history. He begins by raising the question of the nature of the data. What, he asks, is a "literary-historical fact"? The answer, he suggests, depends on the solution to a theoretical problem: the nature of "the relationship between the facts of literary evolution and those of literary environment."

> The traditional literary-historical system was forged without regard to the fundamental distinction between the concepts of genesis and evolution, these having been taken instead for synonyms. Likewise, it made do without attempting to establish what was meant by a literary-historical fact. The consequence was a naive theory about "lineal descent" and "influence," and an equally naive psychological biographism. [*RRP,* p. 59]

Pointing out that "it is not only literature that evolves; literary scholarship evolves with literature," Eichenbaum notes that naive influence-studies and naive psychologism have given way to an equally naive sociology of literature:

> Instead of utilizing under a new conceptual sign the earlier observations of the specific features of literary evolution (and those observations, after all, not only do not contradict but actually support an authentic sociological point of view), our literary "sociologists" have taken up the metaphysical quest for the prime principles of literary evolution and literary forms. They have had two possibilities at hand, both already applied and proved incapable of producing any literary-historical system: (1) the analysis of works of literature from the point of view of the writer's class ideology (a purely psychological approach, for which art is the least appropriate, the least characteristic material) and (2) the cause-and-effect derivation of literary forms and styles from the general socioeconomic and agricultural-industrial forms of the epoch. [*RRP,* p. 60]

Eichenbaum rejects these positions on the following grounds:

> No genetic study, however far it may go, can lead us to the prime principle (assuming that the aims envisaged are scientific, not religious). Science in the long run does not explain phenomena but rather establishes only their properties and relationships. History is incapable of answering a single "why" question; it can only answer the question, "what does this mean?"
>
> Literature, like any other specific order of things, is not generated from facts belonging to other orders and therefore *cannot be reduced* to such facts. The relations between the facts of the literary order and facts extrinsic to it cannot simply be causal relations but can only be the relations of correspondence, interaction, dependency, or conditionality. [*RRP,* p. 61]

After explaining briefly the terminology of relationship that he has just employed, Eichenbaum makes the following crucial statement:

> Since literature is not reducible to any other order of things and cannot be the simple derivative of any other order, there is no reason to believe that all its constituent elements can be genetically conditioned. Literary-historical fact is a complex construct in which the fundamental role belongs to *literariness*—an element of such specificity that its study can be productive only in immanent-evolutionary terms. [*RRP,* p. 62]

This statement is crucial because it sums up the formalist position in the face of Marxist pressure to abandon it. It compromises in a healthy way (which might properly be called dialectical) by accepting the notion that extraliterary facts condition the genesis of literary works. But it insists that the fundamental external conditioner of any work of literature is the literary tradition itself. This certainly does not end the debate between Marxists and formalists, but it clarifies the possibilities for further development. It asks of Marxist or sociological critics a comparable subtlety, such as we can find in the work of a contemporary Marxist/structuralist like Lucien Goldmann, whose *Pour une sociologie du roman* (Gallimard, 1964) has affinities with Lukács and with formalism as well. At any rate, it should be clear now that far from ignoring history, the formalists had an appropriately formal view of it. This view will be evident again when we come to examine the formalist approach to fictional genres. But before considering the problems of genre as such, we should consider some of the basic conceptual vocabulary of the formalist poetics of fiction.

One of the great problems in the theory of fiction from Aristotle to Auerbach has been the relationship between fictional art and life: the problem of *mimesis*. The formalist approach to this problem, far from being a lapse into pure aestheticism, or a denial of the mimetic component in fiction, is an attempt to discover exactly what verbal art does to life and for life. This is most apparent in Victor Shklovsky's concept of *defamiliarization*. Shklovsky's concept is grounded in a theory of perception that is essentially Gestaltist. (And behind the Gestalt psychologists are the Romantic poets and philosophers. In the English tradition, there are passages in Coleridge's *Biographia Literaria* and Shelley's *Defense of Poetry* which clearly anticipate Shklovsky's formulation, as we shall see in chapter 6.A, below). "As perception becomes habitual," Shklovsky notes, "it becomes automatic." And he adds, "We see the object as though it were enveloped in a sack. We know what it is by its configuration, but we see only its silhouette." In considering a passage from Tolstoy's *Diary,* Shklovsky reaches the following conclusion:

Habitualization devours objects, clothes, furniture, one's wife, and the fear of war. "If all the complex lives of many people go on unconsciously, then such lives are as if they had never been."

Art exists to help us recover the sensation of life; it exists to make us feel things, to make the stone *stony.* The end of art is to give a sensation of the object as seen, not as recognized. The technique of art is to make things "unfamiliar," to make forms obscure, so as to increase the difficulty and the duration of perception. The act of perception in art is an end in itself and must be prolonged. *In art, it is our experience of the process of construction that counts, not the finished product.*

Shklovsky goes on to illustrate the technique of defamiliarization extensively from the works of Tolstoy, showing us how Tolstoy, by using the point of view of a peasant, or even an animal, can make the familiar seem strange, so that we see it again. Defamiliarization is not only a fundamental technique of mimetic art, it is its principal justification as well. In fiction, defamiliarization is achieved through point of view and through style, of course, but it is also accomplished by plotting itself. Plot, by rearranging events of story, defamiliarizes them and opens them to perception. And because art itself exists in time, the specific devices of defamiliarization themselves succumb to habit and become conventions which finally obscure the very objects and events they were invented to display. Thus there can be no permanently "realistic" technique. Ultimately, the artist's reaction to the tyranny of fictional conventions or representation is a parodic one. He will, as Shklovsky says, "lay bare" the conventional techniques by exaggerating them. Thus Shklovsky analyses *Tristram Shandy* as primarily a work of fiction *about* fictional technique. Because it focuses on the devices of fiction it is also about modes of perception—about the inter-

* In quoting this passage, I initially intended simply to use the Lemon and Reis version (p. 12). But their treatment of the last sentence, in particular, seemed to me strange. Their version reads this way: *"Art is a way of experiencing the artfulness of an object; the object is not important."* This reading is too open to a narrowly "aesthetic" or art-for-art's-sake interpretation, in my judgment. Todorov's French version is more satisfactory: *"l'art est un moyen d'éprouver le devenir de l'objet, ce qui est déjà 'devenu' n'importe pas pour l'art"* (p. 83). With the aid of Professor Thomas Winner of Brown University, I consulted the Russian text, which reads as follows: *"iskusstvo jest sposob perezit' delan'e vesci, a sdelannoe v iskusstve ne vazno."* A close, literal translation would be: "art is the means for experiencing the making of the thing, but the thing made is not important in art.

penetration of art and life. The laying bare of literary devices makes *them* seem strange and unfamiliar, too, so that we are especially aware of them. Defamiliarization applied to art itself results in the exposure of literary devices. Thus art in general and fiction in particular can be seen as a dialectic of defamiliarization in which new techniques of representation ultimately generate countertechniques which expose them to ridicule. And this dialectic is at the center of the history of fiction.

The refinement of formalist poetics was begun by the formalists themselves. We can see one aspect of this refinment by considering an important essay of Victor Shklovsky's in relation to certain modifications of the formalist position developed by the formalists themselves and their structuralist descendants. In his essay "On the Construction of the Short Story and the Novel" (*TL,* pp. 170–96), Shklovsky uses these two forms of fiction to develop some common properties of all fiction and to distinguish some of the special qualities of these two distinct types. He begins by raising the basic question of what makes a story a story: "It is not enough for us to be presented with a simple image, nor a simple parallel, nor even a simple description of an event, for us to have the impression that we are confronted with a story." He concludes that the story is much more end-oriented than the novel; that is, that the story is carefully constructed so as to give us a feeling of completion at its conclusion, while the novel often concludes its main action before the end, or seems capable of indefinite extension. Thus certain kinds of novels resort to the epilogue, changing the scale of time so as to conclude matters briskly. (This is actually a notion developed by Eichenbaum, working with Shklovsky's ideas.) But in the short story, the plotting functions more neatly to lead to a conclusion that is a true dénouement. What kinds of motivation, Shklovsky then asks, give us this important sense of an ending? He distinguishes two basic types: that of opposition resolved, and that of similarity revealed. In the one case our sense of completion is more oriented to action, in the other to theme. But in both cases there is a common principle at work, a circular move-

ment which links the end with the beginning, either by comparison or by contrast.

Shklovsky also notes that collections of linked tales existed long
before the novel established itself as a form. He is careful not to insist that the novel was necessarily "caused" by these earlier forms
(as Eichenbaum points out, the novel derives from history, travel
narratives, and other marginally literary forms), but he implies
that the principles of construction found in the ancient collections
of tales anticipate those found in the novel. He distinguishes two
types of construction: linking and framing. Construction by framing leads to such things as *A Thousand and One Nights,* the *Decameron,* and the *Canterbury Tales.* Construction by linking is most
frequently found in works which present the various deeds of a single hero. Such narratives as *The Golden Ass* use a combination of
linking and framing. Both methods, Shklovsky points out, lead to a
certain enriching of these forms with matters outside the action,
which point in the direction of the novel. In the framed collection
of tales, for instance, the tellers themselves and the characters in
the tales are not really developed: "Our attention is concentrated
on the action; the agent is only a playing card which permits the
plot to be developed." This trend continues for a long time. Even
in the eighteenth century we find agents like Gil Blas, who is "not
a man; he is a thread which connects the episodes of the novel—
and this thread is gray." On the other hand, development of character can be found in earlier literatures: "In the *Canterbury Tales,*
the connection between the action and the agent is very strong."
The method of tales strung together around a single personage,
when this becomes a person traveling in search of employment, as
in *Lazarillo de Tormes* or *Gil Blas,* can lead to the enrichment of
fiction with materials of a sociological nature, as in Cervantes's ex-
emplary story of the "Glass Licentiate" and, of course, in *Don
Quixote.* And such enrichment does point the way toward the
modern novel and short story.

The evolution of these forms was taken up by Boris Eichenbaum
in some passages of critical writing brought together by Tzvetan
Todorov (*TL,* pp. 197–211) under the title "On the Theory of

Prose." (The second part of this material can be found in English in *RRP,* pp. 231–38, in Eichenbaum's essay on "O. Henry and the Theory of the Short Story.") Eichenbaum begins by considering the relationship between the oral tale and the written story. He first points out the way in which the prose genres, unlike verse, are cut off from vocal performance and develop techniques peculiar to written language. Thus written fictions orient themselves toward epistolary form, memoirs, notes, descriptive studies, journalistic sketches, and so on. Oral speech reenters fiction, however, in the form of dialogue. Eichenbaum suggests that such tales as those in the *Decameron* have a fundamental connection with oral speech: that is, they are related to the oral tale and the gossip's anecdote, in which the narrator's voice subsumes all others. Early novels, growing out of such collections of tales, kept this elementary oral quality. But by the eighteenth century a new kind of novel, derived from a bookish culture, established itself. The oral element persisted in the oratorical narrative voice of Scott, for example, or the lyrical voice of Hugo—but even these were closer to rhetorical declamation than to simple oral story-telling. In the main, however, the European novel of the eighteenth and especially the nineteenth centuries was dominated by description, psychological portraiture, and scenic presentation. "In this manner," says Eichenbaum, "the novel broke with narrative form and became a combination of dialogues, scenes, and detailed presentations of decor, gestures, and intonations." For Eichenbaum, then, the novel is a "syncretic" form, which is made up of other "elementary" forms. And in this connection he cites with approval the presence of this notion in earlier Russian literary criticism—quoting from Shevirev, who in 1843 had called the novel a new mixture of all the genres, with variant subclasses such as the epic novel (*Don Quixote*), the lyrical novel (*Werther*), and the dramatic novel (Scott).

In turning to the history of the novel as a form, Eichenbaum naturally confronted the problem of genres:

In the evolution of each genre, there are times when its use for entirely serious or elevated objectives degenerates and produces a comic or parodic form. The same phenomenon has happened to the epic poem, the adventure novel, the biographical novel, etc. Naturally, local and historical conditions create different variations, but the process itself exhibits this same pattern as an evolutionary law: the serious interpretation of a construction motivated with care and in detail gives way to irony, pleasantry, pastiche; the connections which serve to motivate a scene become weaker and more obvious; the author himself comes on stage and often destroys the illusion of authenticity and seriousness; the construction of a plot becomes a playing with the story which transforms itself into a puzzle or an anecdote. And thus is produced the regeneration of the genre: it finds new possibilities and new forms. [Translated from *TL*, pp. 208–09; another English version may be found in *RRP*, p. 236]

This is certainly diachronic thinking, and very convincing thinking, as well. It is as if, in 1925, Eichenbaum could envision Borges and Barth and a host of contemporary writers. (Nabokov, of course, emerged from an intellectual milieu closely allied to formalism.) Eichebaum's generic thinking represents an increasing sophistication within formalism, which leads directly to structuralism. This sophistication is especially apparent in the work of Roman Jakobson, as we find it, for instance, in a lecture he gave at Masaryk University in 1935 on the Russian formalists.

In this lecture, Jakobson emphasized the importance of the concept of "dominance" as a key to formalist poetics ("The Dominant," *RRP*, pp. 82–87). He defined the dominant as "the foccussing component of a work of art: it rules, determines, transforms the remaining components. It is the dominant which gurantees the integrity of the structure" (*RRP*, p. 82). And beyond the individual work, "we may seek a dominant not only in the poetic work of an individual artist and not only in the poetic canon, the set of norms of a given poetic school, but also in the art of a given epoch, viewed as a whole" (p. 83). Plastic art dominated in the Renaissance, music in the romantic period, verbal art in the aesthetics of realism. Using the concept of dominance, Jakobson is able to criticize the early tendency of formalism to insist on the purity of artistic language. A poem, he observes, does not have a merely aesthetic function: "Actually, the intentions of a poetic work are often closely related to philosophy, social dialectics, etc." And he points out that the converse is true as well—that "just as a poetic work is not exhausted by its esthetic function, similarly, esthetic function is not limited to the poetic work." In oratory, journalism, even in a scientific treatise we may expect to find words used in and for themselves, and not in a purely referential way. Thus a monistic aestheticism would obscure aspects of poetry. But a mechanistic pluralism, which sees art works only as documents of cultural history, social relations, or biography, is equally limited. Rather,

> a poetic work must be defined as a verbal message whose esthetic function is its dominant. Of course, the marks disclosing the implementation of the esthetic function are not unchangeable or always uniform. Each concrete poetic canon, every set of temporal poetic norms, however, comprises indispensable, distinctive elements without which the work cannot be identified as poetic. [*RRP,* p. 84]

In this view, poetic evolution can be seen as a matter of changes in the elements of a poetic system which are a function of a "shifting dominant":

> Within a given complex of poetic norms in general, or especially within the set of poetic norms valid for a given poetic genre, elements which were originally secondary become essential and primary. On the other hand, the elements which were originally the dominant ones become subsidiary and optional. In the earlier works of Shklovsky, a poetic work was defined as a mere sum of its artistic devices, while poetic evolution appeared nothing more than a substitution of certain devices. With the further development of formalism, there arose the accurate conception of a poetic work as a structured

system, a regularly ordered hierarchical set of artistic devices. Poetic evolution is a shift in this hierarchy. The hierarchy of artistic devices changes within the framework of a given poetic genre; the change, moreover, affects the hierarchy of poetic genres, and, simultaneously, the distribution of artistic devices among the individual genres. Genres which were originally secondary paths, subsidiary variants, now come to the fore, whereas the canonical genres are pushed toward the rear. [*RRP*, p. 85]

Armed with an awareness sharpened by the concept of dominance, the formalists rewrote Russian literary history in a way both richer and more ordered. This new awareness also directed attention to a fruitful area of investigation: the boundaries between literature and other kinds of verbal message:

Of special interest for investigators are the transitional genres. In certain periods such genres are evaluated as extraliterary and extrapoetical, while in other periods they may fulfill an important literary function because they comprise those elements which are about to be emphasized by belles lettres, whereas the canonical forms are deprived of those elements. [*RRP*, p. 86]

In his concluding paragraph, Jakobson pointed out how formalism finally encouraged the linguistic study of shifts and transformations, thus giving back to linguistics something in return for all that it had borrowed:

This aspect of formalist analysis in the field of poetic language had a pioneering significance for linguistic research in general, since it provided important impulses toward overcoming and bridging the gap between the diachronic historical method and the synchronic method of chronological cross section. It was formalist research which clearly demonstrated that shifting and change are not only historical statements (first there was A, and then A_1 arose in place of A) but that shift is also a directly experienced synchronic phenomenon, a relevant artistic value. The reader of a poem or the viewer of a painting has a vivid awareness of two orders: the traditional canon and the artistic novelty as a deviation from that canon. It is precisely against the background of that tradition that innovation is conceived. The formalist studies brought to light that this simultaneous preservation of tradition and breaking away from tradition form the essence of every new work of art. [*RRP*, p. 87]

Thus formalism, by refusing to abandon the diachronic aspect of poetics, helped structural linguistics become transformational.

C. Semantics, Logic, and Grammar: The Progeny of Propp

In this section we will be considering the work of three men, as it currently appears in four books: the *Sémantique structurale* (1966) and *Du Sens* (1970) of A. J. Greimas, the *Logique du récit* (1973) of Claude Bremond, and the *Grammaire du Décaméron* (1969) of Tzvetan Todorov. The amount of interaction and mutual criticism among these three has been such that any discussion must necessarily shift back and forth from one to another. But the parts of their work discussed here all bear essentially on one topic: the fundamental units and structures of fiction. If I find some problems to be not satisfactorily treated by these writers, it is the difficulty of the topic rather than inadequacy on the part of the critics addressing it that I wish to emphasize. My criticisms are meant to include my gratitude to all three writers for having made the issues and the difficulties so palpable.

The structuralist study of narrative is marked by a strong interest in two extreme aspects of the subject. The structuralists have sought both a micropoetics and a macropoetics of fiction. This macropoetics will be our concern in the next section of this chapter, the micropoetics in the present section. The structuralists' aim in micropoetics has been the isolation of basic fictional structures: the essential elements of fiction and their laws of combination. Their first problem has been the determination of the minimal configuration of elements that enable a competent observer to recognize a particular object as narrative. This is, of course, a problem in definition, but it is not a simple exercise in naming. Narratives exist, they are everywhere that man is, and there is widespread agreement among observers as to what is and what is not narrative. Any work of theoretical description may be quickly tested against a range of actualities. Which raises the question of why we need such theoretical descriptions in the first place. If narratives are created, recognized, and understood without any theory, what function can theory have?

The structuralists have two answers to this question, which others may or may not find satisfying. One of their aims in attempting to isolate the fundamental structures of narrative is to relate them to other fundamental structures (of logic and grammar, for instance) in an attempt to understand the configurations of human mentality itself. This may well prove ultimately fruitless, since the best logicians of our time have made it plain that we cannot expect by the actions of our own mental processes to master these same mental processes as subject matter. But before the dead end of inquiry is reached, we may well claim some further territory for human understanding. We may. But so far, the results in this direction seem to me very slender indeed.

The second answer the structuralists give to the question of why one should seek the microstructures of fiction is a much more convincing one. If we know what the universal elements of narrative are, and can agree upon a terminology for these, then it will be possible to make the comparisons and discriminations which are the basis of literary understanding, and to make them much more clearly, convincingly, and systematically than we do at present. If it is good in the first place to understand literary history and the processes at work in it, then it must be good to do this as rigorously and systematically as we can. And here the structuralists have some concrete achievements as well as some pious hopes to offer us.

Attempts to describe basic narrative structures are as old as Aristotle, and it is frequently said that little progress has been made since his time. But Vladimir Propp made a major breakthrough in this field, and his system, despite its inadequacies (and in some cases because of them), has become a major point of departure for later theorists. The speculations of Souriau on drama have also been taken over by the theorists of fiction, and even some notions of Lévi-Strauss (who has himself written a critique of Propp) have been tested by the "narratologists." But it is Propp whose work has been most fruitful, and the theorists we shall be considering in this section may properly be called the progeny of Propp. Though others have extended Propp's ideas in various directions (e.g., Alan Dundes in *The Morphology of North American Indian Tales,* Helsinki, 1964, and "On Game Morphology," *N.Y. Folklore Quarterly* 20, no. 4, 1964) we shall be concentrating here on the three theorists who have done most to adapt Propp's system to a general theory of narration, including ultimately "literary" texts as well as myths and folktales. But before considering their achievements we must inquire more closely into the difficulties they have faced.

One problem in the study of fundamental narrative structures lies in the essential duality of narrative. This duality can be expressed in a number of ways. Using Jakobson's diagram of a speech act we may see narrative as emphasizing either its relation to context or its relation to receiver. Narrative can be mainly concerned to communicate a vision of a context or to stimulate a reaction in an audience. The elements chosen in any given tale may be selected primarily for their ability to convey ideas or for their ability to evoke reactions. This is not exactly the same as a distinction between form and content. Some "content" may be present in a story mainly to evoke a reaction (the appearance of a ghost or monster, for instance), while some structural features may function mainly to evoke a context (a particular verbal structure may identify a recognizable aspect of social behavior, for example, as in dialects attributed to characters). But fiction, unlike philosophical discourse, is poised between the informative and the emotive aspects of utterance.

What we know of the history of fiction suggests that its fundamental dynamic involves a movement from an informationally ordered structure toward an emotionally ordered one. Myth, for instance, precedes fairy tale, and we can see in the fairy tale an attempt to preserve those structural elements of myth which function to please audiences, while abandoning those for which no emotive value can be discerned. It is as if, once a decision is taken to use the power of fiction as a vehicle for ideas, a certain evolutionary law begins to operate which finally leads to the loss of those very ideas. But fictions which seek to move their audiences too directly find that the formal machinery of emotive evocation loses its power when it moves too far from invocation of context. In examining the history of narrative, we see that specific fictional genres, as they become emptied of contextual value, seek to compensate for this by formal elaboration until they die either of their own weight or through parody, which often means by having forced upon them a system of contextual reference they are too fragile to sustain—as when Cervantes forces the chivalric romance to refer to contemporary Spain.

For those who seek to describe the bases of fictional structure, this poses a great problem, the problem of looking for universals in a body of material which is itself suceptible to such variant exigencies and has responded with so many formal variations. There are a number of ways of responding to this problem. One way is to ignore it—which is fatal, as we shall see. Another is to limit the material being considered to a body of homogeneous fictions, similar in purpose and form. A third is to limit the description to certain aspects of the material being considered, ignoring others. Two of the most successful seekers for fictional universals, Propp and Lévi-Strauss, have employed both of these methods of limitation. Lévi-Strauss has confined himself to certain mythic fictions and concerned himself only with the contextual information hidden in the mythic structure. Propp has confined himself to certain fairy tales and has concerned himself with the structural features which organize the emotive elaboration of the tales. Thus each of them has not only limited his material but concentrated on its most obvious qualities. In doing so they have tacitly acknowledged the distinction between informational and affective fiction—both in their selection of material and in their treatment of it. The difficulties encountered by some of Propp's followers are the result of their attempts to exceed him in universality as well as to improve upon the logic and rigor of his methods.

A related difficulty for those who seek fictional universals lies in the definition of narrative itself. I have suggested that there is widespread agreement among competent observers about what is and is not narrative. This is so—but there are problem cases, and these problems become clearer when we seek the extremes that define the limits of narration. One of these extremes, familiar in modern literature, consists of works with a narrative base (such as *Marius the Epicurean* or *Ulysses,* to name two different cases) upon which so many non-narrative elements have been erected that the work's narrative quality is severely attenuated for the sake of other qualities. But for our purposes, in considering microstructures, it is the other extreme limit of narration that is most important—not the point where narrative ends but the point at which it begins. Consider for a moment the following verbal structures:

1. The king was healthy, but he became ill, and though he tried every medicine in the kingdom, he finally died.
2. The king was healthy but then he became ill and then he died.
3. The king was healthy but then he became ill.
4. The king was healthy but then he died.
5. The king was ill and then he died.
6. The king was ill and then the queen died.
7. The king was ill and then John Smith died.

All seven of these verbal constructs mention at least two events that take place successively in time. Number 1, though not very interesting, is clearly a narrative. Number 7 (assuming there is no connection between Smith and the king), can hardly be called a narration at all, though it has some of the quality of chronicle history. But where in this graded sequence of examples do we pass from the level of narration to some inferior level? And to what

more complex level would we have to move before we felt ourselves in the presence of a "story"? If narration is simply the re-
counting of a temporal sequence of events, then a story is a special
kind of sequence, with special qualities, and it is certainly debata-
ble whether even number 1 in this sequence is of sufficient aesthetic interest to be called a story. The structuralists have not always made it clear whether they were interested in the minimal
units of narration or in the minimal units of story—both of
which hide behind the French term *récit*. And in fact two quite
different assumptions in this respect seem to animate the early
works of Greimas and Bremond.

Bremond, in his first essays in *Communications* 4 and 8, is
clearly more concerned with narration than story. In fact, his emphasis on logic suggests that he sees narration as being more
closely allied to philosophy than one might expect. Like Greimas,
who approaches narrative from the perspective of semantics, he
does not seem to acknowledge sufficiently the aesthetic dimension
of his material—a point on which the formalists might have
something to teach him. Bremond begins by noting, as Propp himself observed, that some of the functions of the fairy tale are logically linked, necessarily implying one another. Lévi-Strauss, Greimas, and others have also pointed this out. Bremond simply goes
furthest in trying to spell out the nature of this linkage and re-
trieve from it the "primary elements of fiction." The problem Bremond discerns is in part that Proppian functions which are logically linked—like number 17 (the hero is branded or marked)
and number 27 (the hero is recognized)—are often separated by
a number of intervening functions so that their structural relation
is blurred in Propp's monolinear system. Bremond sets himself the
task of devising a system of schematic representation that would
clarify the relationship of all the logical subsets in an entire narrative and would thus present a schematic picture which could serve
as a basis for comparing one specific narrative to another. As he
observes,

We escape, thus, one of the worst inconveniences of formalism, which is, that after having begun by opposing the intelli-

gibility of form to the insignificance of content, it finds itself
incapable of recovering the typological diversity of the objects
from which it has selected only the common characteristics.
This is why Propp, who has so beautifully discovered the generic form of the Russian tales, has failed completely when he
tries to differentiate them, except when he reintroduces sur-
reptitiously (for which Lévi-Strauss has reproached him) the
same crude content that he had begun by eliminating. [*Communications* 4, p. 23]

Bremond's fundamental proposition is that the basic narrative
unit is not the function but the sequence, and that a completed fiction, however long and complex, can be represented as an inter-
weaving of sequences. The atomic sequence is a triad, in which a
possibility is actualized and a result follows from this actualization.
He represents this basic scheme as shown in figure 1. At every stage
of development there is a choice: at the second, realization or not;
at the third, success or failure. But we can observe that the second
choice in the second stage is not really a narrative choice at all,
since it simply keeps us at the point of departure. Bremond com-
pares the structure of any narrative to a vector or the flight of an
arrow. Once the bow is drawn and the arrow aimed at a target, we
have the basic situation. The nonactualization of this situation
would amount to unstringing the arrow without shooting it. (We
might note in passing that James's *The Beast in the Jungle* is
based precisely on this situation. The story is *about* whether or not
the arrow has been shot, whether or not the protagonist is a man

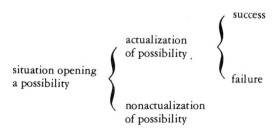

Figure 1

without a story. This is a modern antistory with a vengeance.) But once the arrow is shot, though it may be carried by the wind or ricochet off various objects, it must ultimately reach the target or miss it. Narrative simplifies communication by orienting all details to the flight of that arrow.

All this is well enough, but Bremond's attempts to actualize this scheme in specific forms leave much to be desired. There is not space enough here to treat his inadequacies at length, but they can be illustrated in a brief compass. Working with four of Propp's functions, he shows how in one of Propp's tales these functions do not actually arrange themselves in the supposedly inviolable Proppian order. His manner of displaying these matters is frequently useful, but there are other problems here which we will have to note. Bremond (see figure 2) presents Propp's functions 2 (interdiction), 3 (violation of interdiction), 6 (trickery by villain), and 7 (victim falls into trap)—first as they appear in Propp's scheme (with 4 and 5 left out as irrelevant here) and then as they appear in a particular tale. The upper section of figure 2 shows the chain-linked relationship of functions that Propp presents. But in his tale no. 148 these events are actually arranged as shown in the middle section of the figure. In this tale the villain actually tricks the victim into violating the interdiction, so that function 6 appears right after 2 and is followed by 3 and 7, which appear simultaneously rather than successively. Violation of the interdiction *is* the trap that the victim falls into. Here, Bremond has given us a useful way of schematizing these relationships. (He uses such schemata extensively and often illuminatingly.)

But what are those non-Proppian pseudo-functions called "Interdiction violated" and "Success of trickery"? They are remnants of Bremond's necessary triad, and very awkward ones. For "Interdiction violated" is in no way a result of "Violation": it is the same thing, a mere restatement cluttering up the sequential process. And the same is true for "Success of trickery." When the victim falls into the trap, the trickery has succeeded, and if there is a result it must contain something additional. In fact, in the basic Proppian system, violating the interdiction leads to a change in the status or

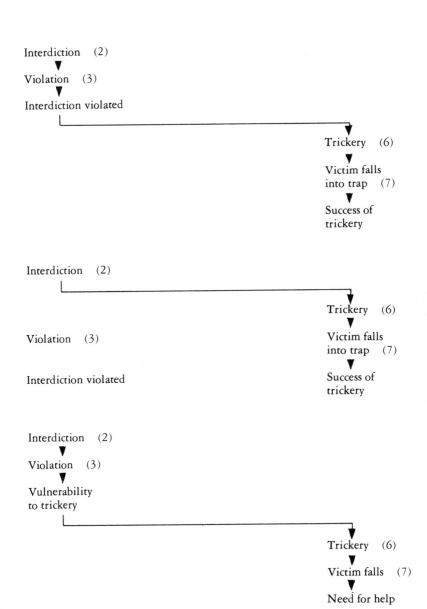

Figure 2

situation of a character. And so does falling into the villain's trap. Accepting Bremond's notion that the triad is a basic narrative structure, we could rewrite his presentation of Propp as shown in the lower section of figure 2. If we adjusted this scheme to describe tale no. 148, functions 3 and 7 would again appear simultaneously, but there would only be one result, need for help—the vulnerability sequence having been absorbed in the trickery sequence. In Propp's tales in general, however, it is often the new vulnerability resulting from the violated interdiction that facilitates the trickery. Propp does not mark elements like vulnerability and need for help, because they are not functions in his sense but situations. They are not events, though they contain events in a potential way. It is situation which provokes action, and action which changes situation. This is why Todorov, in his *Grammaire du Décaméron,* finds it necessary to emphasize equally verb and adjective, action and attribute, in order to describe narrative syntax.

But one other point must be observed here. In assigning the label "Vulnerability to trickery" to the third element in the lower section of figure 2, I have been guided by the knowledge that trickery was indeed scheduled in the narrative system of Propp. But in some other fiction, what was to come might simply have been punishment of the violator by the interdictor—or a number of other things. Similarly, my "Need for help" is not simply a view of the unfortunate victim's situation. In some stories he might already be dead and beyond help. The "Need for help" becomes a situational feature because we know that help is on the way. These situations do not simply imply verbs, they exist for the sake of the verbs to come. Which reminds us that narrative is verb-oriented, a matter of predication, and also that narrative, as an experience for the audience, is teleological. It is the target which has provoked the arrow and not the arrow which has sought the target. The writer has a range of choices among narrative possibilities, but the reader must follow a beaten track toward a preconceived end. And the end of fiction casts a long shadow before it. This teleological continuity is in fact a major attribute of narrative and a primary source of satisfaction for the reader. On finishing no matter what fiction we can say that what was intended has come to pass. This is a frequently overlooked difference between the reading of a sequence of events and living through such a sequence. Life approaches narrative art in this respect precisely to the extent that we live in accordance with a philosophy sufficiently deterministic to allow us the comforting belief that everything that happens is planned, significant, designed. This is precisely the appeal of many religions—they allow us to think of our lives as divinely planned fictions.

Having noted that Bremond himself has difficulty in delineating adequately the units of triadic series, we have only begun to encounter the problems involved in seeking the minimal units of narrative in triadic form. Consider the following example, which clearly has the required three-part structure of potential, enactment, and result:

1. The king was healthy. (Potentiality of illness.)
2. The king became ill.
3. The king died.

This, however, can be broken down into smaller triads, like this:

1. The king was healthy.
2. The king was exposed to illness.
3. The king became ill.

or this:

1. The king was healthy.
2. The king was threatened with exposure to illness.
3. The king was exposed to illness.

or this:

1. The king was healthy.
2. The king was possibly threatened with exposure to illness.
3. The king was definitely threatened with exposure to illness.

We are faced with an infinite regress here. There is no action which cannot be divided into three stages if we insist on so dividing it. Narration, from Bremond's point of view, seems to consist of precisely this structuration into triplets. Yet it seems clear that narrative potential is not merely a matter of triplification. In fact, the more we subdivide, the farther we seem to be moving from narration. There is, then, some necessary minimum of *difference* or *distance* between each of the three stages in any three-part narrative sequence which makes them narrative—a point which Bremond ignores.

A complementary difficulty exists as well. It is possible to enclose the whole of an immense fiction in the form of a single triad:

1. Marcel wants to be a writer.
2. Marcel learns how to articulate his experience.
3. Marcel becomes a writer.

But few people would find this an adequate representation of Proust's *Recherche*. The point of these extensions of triadic form to absurdity in both directions is to suggest that there is an arbitrariness in Bremond's very logic that prevents it from functioning usefully as a description of fiction. The triads of the logical mind are not necessarily the structure of any given narrative. They are simply a way of dividing preexisting structures into units of an entirely arbitrary size. All the attempts of structuralists to derive narrative form from logical categories emptied of semantic content have proved fruitless. But their attempts to work in the other direction, to examine specific forms and derive from them some inventory of basic narrative lexical and syntactic elements—these have proved much more fruitful and interesting. This is precisely what Todorov has attempted in his grammar of the *Decameron* and what Greimas has done in his best work. But before turning to that work it will be useful to consider one more ambitious failure: Greimas's attempt to describe the genesis of narrative structure from semantic process.

For Greimas, working from the linguistics of Saussure and Jakobson, signification starts with binary oppositions. Just as the elementary sounds of speech are differentiated from one another in this way, so are the elementary concepts of thought. Up and down, left and right, dark and light are defined in relation to one another by their mutual opposition. Greimas then postulates a level of thought prior to language, in which these rudimentary oppositions are given anthropomorphic shape, through which purely logical or conceptual oppositions become *actants* in a polemical situation that, when allowed to develop temporally, becomes a story. These actants, if they are given social or cultural qualities, become *rôles* in fictional actions. If they are given individuating qualities, they become *acteurs,* or, as we would say, characters. But in any case, this beginning of narrative in a semantic opposition leads to situations and actions which are characterized by this same opposition. The basic number of actants in a narrative sequence is two, and the basic actions are disjunction and conjunction: separation and union, struggle and reconciliation. Narratives consist essentially in the transfer of a value or an object from one actant to another. The typical narrative sequence consists of a descriptive utterance, characterizing a subject and his situation; followed by a "modal" utterance, in which the subject's wishes, fears, and beliefs are made known, implying an action related to them; and a transitive utterance in which some transfer of value or change of situation is effected. For example,

1. The king is healthy. (Descriptive.)
2. The king fears illness. (Modal, implying action.)
3. The king takes preventive medication. (Transitive, action accomplished.)

This is similar to Bremond's triadic division of narrative, but with the addition of descriptive features that require each element in the triad to have a specific function.

None of this is unreasonable as a description of narrative genesis. But it is, in Greimas's own presentation as well as in this brief summary, rather crabbed, cryptic, and overselective. As a description of the genesis of *all* narrative structures, it seems woefully incomplete, yet Greimas claims to be dealing with a grammar of narrative as a whole. In fact, what seems to happen to all thinkers who seek a basic narrative structure emptied of semantic content has happened here. Greimas, like the other structuralists, has certain concrete, semantically filled structures in mind, which become the invisible models for his apparently abstract manipulations. And the model he has in mind here is precisely the kind of text he has done his best work on when proceeding in the opposite direction —moving from the specifics of certain concrete structures to the common structural features behind them. He has done this in two ways, both of which are of interest to us here. He has taken the actantial categories of Propp and Souriau as a point of departure in one case; and he has also worked directly with mythic materials, seeking the structural principles that organize them. Both attempts are interesting.

In working with Propp and Souriau, Greimas begins by examining Propp's "spheres of action," which provide him with an "inventory of actants." And then he considers Souriau's list of dramatic functions. Though neither list is entirely satisfactory to Greimas and though both show some hesitation—Souriau debated between six and seven functions, Propp lists seven actantial categories but one has two separable features—still, Propp's seven and Souriau's six, when displayed together, reveal some interesting correspondences:

Propp	*Souriau (rearranged by R. S.)*
1. villain	Mars—opposition
2. donor (provider)	
3. helper	Moon—helper
4. sought-for person	Sun—desired object
and her father	Balance (scales)—arbiter, rewarder
5. dispatcher	Earth—ultimate beneficiary
6. hero	Lion—will, one who desires
7. false hero	

The two lists, even with Souriau rearranged, do not quite match, and the differences are a measure of the differences between the fairy tale and the stage play as well as of the different conceptual processes of Souriau and Propp. But, taken together, they suggest very strongly that there is a basic inventory of actants from which many of the complexities of fiction may be derived, and without which fiction would be impossible. Greimas proceeds by trying to regularize and systematize the possibilities suggested by Propp and Souriau.

He divides the actants into three sets of opposed pairs, from which all the individual actors of a story may be derived. His first category is composed of Subject and Object. The Subject corresponds to Propp's "hero" and Souriau's Lion or "will." The Object corresponds to Propp's "sought-for person" and Souriau's Sun or "desired object." This pair of actants is the most fundamental and leads to the mythic structure of quest. Greimas's second category is that of the Giver or Sender (*destinateur*) and Receiver (*destinataire*). In Souriau these categories are clearly marked: "the arbiter or rewarder" and "the ultimate beneficiary." In Propp they are less clear. The Giver is, as Greimas observes, somewhat naively presented by Propp as an aspect of the Object: the "father" of the "sought-for person." The Receiver is also hidden in Propp's system, under the title of "dispatcher," since the one who sends the hero on his quest is often the ultimate beneficiary. Greimas favors an arrangement of narrative elements into these two actantial pairs because it recapitulates the structure that he finds basic to signification in all discourse: sender/receiver and subject/object. In some narratives, he suggests, these four actants may be represented by just two actors. In a simple love story the boy may be both Subject and Receiver, the girl Object and Sender. But in more complex narratives four actors will be distinguishable. Thus in *The Quest of the Holy Grail,*

$$\frac{\text{Subject}}{\text{Object}} \simeq \frac{\text{Hero}}{\text{Grail}} \qquad \frac{\text{Sender}}{\text{Receiver}} \simeq \frac{\text{God}}{\text{Humanity}}$$

There are problems in this formulation that Bremond and Todorov are aware of and respond to in different ways. For one thing, subject and object are matters of point-of-view and are therefore reversible. In a love story, and not just a modern one, Boy and Girl may both be Subject and Object, both be Sender and Receiver.

And for another, in the Grail illustration, it is by no means clear that God and Humanity are present at the same level of action as Hero and Grail.

Greimas fills out his scheme by adding another pair: Helper and Opponent, who work for and against the successful communication and the consummation of desire. These categories are amply present in Propp and Souriau. Propp has two Helpers, the "donor" and the "helper," since these two roles are usually separate in the Russian fairy tale. He also has two Opponents: the "villain" and the "false hero." Souriau's categories are virtually identical with those of Greimas. In fact, Greimas appears to have simply taken over Souriau's categories, and with considerable loss in flexibility and subtlety. For instance, where Souriau was careful to insist that the Lion need not be the character from whose point of view a situation is presented, Greimas, by insisting on the term Subject, introduces a confusion between point of view and orienting force. This confusion is worth exploring a bit.

In even a single sentence, there may be as many as three ways of designating the "subject"—all of which are relevant to the study of fiction. Consider the following two examples:

1. John hit me.
2. I was hit by John.

In sentence 1, John is the grammatical subject, but "me" is the rhetorical subject, in that the first person is always subjective; we are pulled in the direction of the first-person's viewpoint. In sentence 2, "I" is both grammatical and rhetorical subject; the point-of-view is concentrated more intensely. But notice that in both sentences "John" is the Lion; he is the agent who performs the act described in the verb; it is his will, his passion, his desire that orient this little scene. He is the dramatic subject of both sentences. Only in such a sentence as "I hit John" are the grammatical, rhetorical, and dramatic subjects all combined into one. The use of the word Subject, then, introduces an extraordinary potential for confusion into any discussion of narrative structure. Thus Greimas's system is anything but an advance over that of Souriau. He has apparently been unsatisfied with it himself, and has continued tinkering with it in later essays, abandoning some features of his set of actants, though less explicitly than one might wish. As with a good deal of structuralist micropoetics, his efforts are more interesting than satisfying.

Perhaps the ultimate in actantial inventorying is that attempted by Claude Bremond in his *Logique du récit*. Bremond begins by a logical division of fictional roles into two fundamental types: agents and patients, those who do things and those to whom things happen. He considers patients first because in so many stories the subject or hero is first a patient and then becomes an agent, often returning to the status of patient at the end of the tale. There are, in fact, two types of action that a patient may undergo, which are in themselves typical of the beginnings and endings of stories. A patient may be acted upon subjectively or objectively. He may be *influenced* subjectively (given information, caused to feel satisfied or dissatisfied, encouraged to hope or fear). Or he may be acted upon objectively: his situation may be *modified* by improvement or degradation, or it may be maintained (for the good) by protection or (for the bad) by frustration. Each of these three categories of action on the life of the patient implies the agent necessary to enact it. Each function implies its role. Thus, among the influencers we find such roles as informer, dissimulator, seducer, intimidator, obligator, and interdictor. Among the modifiers we find the improver and the degrader; and among the maintainers, the protector and the frustrator. Bremond also finds that the introduction of the concept of merit involves agents who act as rewarder and punisher, as well as patients who are beneficiaries and victims of these agents.

The problem with this system is similar to the problem with Bremond's triadic structures. Starting with agent and patient, which are clear and intelligible enough as a binary opposition, one could make endless divisions into various kinds of subagents and subpatients. There is no true system here because there is no necessity for halting the procedure at any particular level. How many kinds of "improvers," for instance, can be conceived? And how

many is it useful to list? Nor is there any way of ascertaining
whether all the possible roles have been adequately presented. Bremond, for instance, does not designate specifically the roles of arbiter or judge, which have been found important in other investigations. There is, in fact, less logic in this presentation, less system,
than one might have wished.

Somewhat more useful, though admittedly neither exhaustive
nor systematic, is Greimas's attempt to initiate a basic list not of
actants but of syntagms. If some inventory of roles or actants could
be said to constitute a lexicon of narrative paradigms, then a comparable list of syntactic structures or principles of structuration
would be needed to complete a grammar of narration. Greimas attempts no universal list of syntactic structures, but is content to
point out that he has found three distinct types of syntagms in the
folk narratives investigated by Propp and himself:

1. performative (tests, struggles)
2. contractual (establishing and breaking of contracts)
3. disjunctional (departures and returns)

This list is obviously incomplete in some ways, but it offers opportunities for a development and correlation with the list of actants
which Greimas himself has not pursued but which it will be appropriate to develop here. We should test a bit the extent to which
narrative structures can be derived from this set of syntagms.

Beginning with the contractual syntagms, we can observe that
Greimas has not completed a description of them. Contracts are
not only established and broken in life and in art. They are also
fulfilled or completed. In the works considered by Propp and Greimas a contract is normally an affair between the hero and a superior power, the hero thus acting as *destinataire* or Receiver and the
other character (king, God, parent, priest) as *destinateur* or Giver.
This hierarchical relationship is important, and it suggests a very
interesting question about the nature of narrative: namely,
whether fictions can exist without such hierarchical relationships.
But the idea of contract needs to be developed more concretely
here. A contractual relationship of the sort we are considering in-

volves a rule or set of rules laid down by a superior power, along with the promise of reward for good behavior and punishment for bad. The rules may be explicit or implicit, laid down by heaven, by society, or by any individual, provided that he has the power to reward and to punish. Thus the fulfilment of the contract by the Subject-hero requires the fulfilment of it by the Authority-figure who established it. Similarly, failure requires punishment. In terms of total fictional structure, the contract always comes at the beginning, the reward at the end. Any testing based on this contract must come in between. Departures and arrivals, though they certainly occur in Propp's and Greimas's mythic materials, are derivative syntagms, one would say, rather than fundamental ones.

Thus, the fundamental structures of the narrative type under consideration at the moment involve three basic functions and their necessary actants. The functions are Contract, Test, and Judgment. The actants are Contractor and Contractee, Tester and Tested, Judge and Judged. But this sequence of functions with its six actants *is not a narrative.* It does not, in fact, become a narrative until we assign the roles of Contractee, Tested, and Judged to a single Subject, who becomes the Hero of a story. And we do this precisely by giving to these three actants a name or title. The hero, once named, is the subject of a narrative as a substantive may be the grammatical subject of a sentence: John receives a contract. John is tested. John is judged. In this sequence the contractor, the tester, and the judge are merely implied by their functions. In a narrative based on this scenario these functions could be embodied in various ways. John could contract with himself to climb a mountain. The mountain itself would provide the test. And success or failure would constitute reward or punishment. The roles of tester and judge, in other words, need not be embodied in any anthropomorphic form. On the other hand, these roles invite characterization. Thus we might have God, Man, and Satan as basic figures in precisely this structure of contract, test, and judgment. The invention of Satan, it might be pointed out, simply takes the onus of testing away from God, who might have done it all himself. The assignment of punishment (an aspect of the role of judge) to

Michael in the Christian story also removes some onus from God. And the similar doubling of Man into Adam and Eve complicates and enriches the testing. (Satan first fails his test, then tests Eve, who adopts the role of adversary in order to test Adam.) The characters proliferate but the functions remain the same.

A number of things should be clear from this discussion. First of all, the hero or subject is on a different footing from all the other actants in a narrative. In a very real sense he is not an actant at all. Consider this sequence:

1. John is given a contract.
     (John accepts / rejects it.)
2. John is given a test.
     (John passes / fails it.)
3. John is given a judgment—reward / punishment.
     (John enjoys / suffers it.)

John is the grammatical subject of all six sentences in this sequence, but he is passive in three of them—the three which initiate new action. This, I would suggest, is the way many narratives work. The hero is not an agent but a patient. His actions are essentially reactions. The interesting roles in fiction are those that are called into being by the predication, the active roles of contractor, judge, and especially the tester. Thus John, our hero, to be interesting and sympathetic must be given more attributes than a name. He must be young, handsome, an underdog perhaps, and so on. He must become a character, and he is the only essential character in a fiction. But he becomes a character precisely because of his actantial deficiency. The more purely functional elements of fiction, on the other hand, may never even reach actantial status. That is, such functions as contracting, testing, and rewarding may occur without ever being localized in an actant, let alone being represented by a specific character. Thus there are no actantial figures basic to all fiction. There is only that strangely passive creature, the subject / hero, and the functions that shape his existence.

All this does not mean that inventories of the actants in certain homogeneous bodies of fiction are impossible or useless. Far from it. It means only that the attempt at an absolute matrix of actants is doomed to failure for two reasons: (1) because the Subject is on a different level from all others and (2) because functions do not need to be actantualized in order to operate in narrative. But the question remains as to whether a list of essential functions of all narrative may be developed. My own speculation on this matter is that functions, too, will disappear if we follow them back far enough into the narrative matrix. But the question of what functions and actants appear in given bodies of narrative material, and how these relate to others, seems to me well worth pursuing. This is, of course, where Propp and Souriau began; this is where Greimas's most interesting work has continued (on specific tales); and it is where Todorov, in particular, has extended and clarified Propp's methodology in working on Boccaccio's *Decameron.*

Tzvetan Todorov's *Grammaire du Décaméron* is the most important step forward in basic narratology since Propp himself. It is not perfect, but taken together with the critical reactions it has provoked (especially Bremond's incisive chapter in *Logique du récit*) and with Todorov's own second thoughts and developments (especially his essay on narrative transformations in *Poétique de la prose*) it is a study fascinating in itself and a useful model for and invitation to further studies on other bodies of narrative material.

Todorov starts from the assumption of a universal grammar:

> This universal grammar is the source of all universals and it gives definition even to man himself. Not only all languages but all signifying systems obey the same grammar. It is universal not only because it informs all the languages of the universe, but because it coincides with the structure of the universe itself. [p. 15]

Whether or not to adopt this almost mystical faith in the universality of grammar is important for those who wish to see structuralism as a religion, since this is a central tenet of the faith. But the mere fellow-traveler or interested bystander can limit himself to accepting provisionally the idea that all human languages share some similar properties, and that all narratives in linguistic form exhibit remarkable structural similarities both to the grammar of our languages and to one another. For Todorov, as for Greimas and others, narrative is simply a set of linguistic possibilities focused in a particular way by a set of supragrammatical rules of structuration. Because, in the large, narrative is a severely limited selection from the total pool of grammatical possibilities, it can be described in terms simpler than those needed for description of an entire language.

Using the grammatical tradition as a source of structural possibilities, Todorov begins by distinguishing three general aspects of the narrative text or *récit*. Any work of fiction (*récit*) may be considered from the point of view of semantics (the content or world that it evokes), from the point of view of syntax (its structural features and their combination), or from the point of view of rhetoric (*aspect verbal*—including such matters as diction, point-of-view, everything that has to do with the actual words of the text). Todorov's study of the *Decameron* deals with syntax mainly, semantics slightly, and ignores the verbal aspect of the text. In fact, as he makes quite clear, his method is first to reduce each tale to a bald syntactic summary, and to operate analytically on that rather than on the language of the text itself. As he is well aware, the more "literary" a text is (as opposed to mythic or popular) the more this method will leave out, and the more important other methods of analysis will become (such as those of Barthes and Genette discussed in chapter 5, below). But by working with the *Decameron* at essentially the same level as that Propp chose for his work on the Russian tale, and examining essentially the same aspect of the text, Todorov has extended an inventory of narrative possibilities that may be developed beyond the fairy tale and the *récit Boccaccien* in the direction of other texts including those called "literary."

The structural units that Todorov investigates can be broken down as follows:

1. Stories (the one hundred tales of the *Decameron*)
2. Sequences (a sequence is a complete system of propositions, a little tale in itself; a story must contain one sequence at least

but may contain many; we recognize its completion by the modified repetition of its opening proposition)

3. Propositions (a proposition is a basic narrative sentence, and is structurally equivalent to a sentence or independent clause in a language like French or English)
4. Parts of speech
   a. the proper noun (or character)
   b. the verb (or action)
   c. the adjective (or attribute)

In this abbreviated grammar of narrative, a proposition is made from the combination of a character and either an action (which may include another character as object) or an attribute. The character or proper name is simply a blank counter to be filled in by adjective (attribute) or verb (action). All the specific attributes found in the *Decameron* can be classified under three headings:

States (*états*):
   All of these are variations on a scale that runs from happiness to unhappiness. These are unstable attributes, like love (a common one), and many tales involve their changes.

Qualities (*propriétés*):
   These are variations on a scale running from good to evil, and are relatively fixed attributes, though changes occur, as when the wicked are reformed. In the *Decameron* the evil attributes are more highly discriminated, and tend to organize themselves along the lines of the deadly sins.

Conditions (*statuts*):
   These are the most durable attributes. Religion, as in Jew or Christian; sex, male or female; or social position, from king to beggar. A social position of importance in the *Decameron* involves the difference between married and unmarried persons, especially women. This condition is changeable, of course, but not often—and in many tales it is fixed: a wife must be faithful, but if she is not, her quality and state may change but not her condition.

All the actions in the *Decameron* may be reduced to three verbs in Todorov's system. But, as Bremond has pointed out, Todorov's principal verb (to "change" or "modify" the situation) is general enough to include both the others, which are to "trangress," or "sin," and to "punish." In fact, sinning and punishing are simply the most common semantic realizations of the basic verb, "to change." But Todorov distinguishes between the first verb and the other two for a very good reason:

> There are other analogies between *a* [the verb of modification] and *b* [the verb of transgression]. In fact, *b* could equally be described as "to provoke a modification in the preceding situation"—someone commits a crime where order reigned before. But this modification has a different nature from the modification in *a*. In *a* a concrete situation is modified, an occasional configuration of attributes. The crime or sin on the other hand is a transgression of a general law, common to the whole society and acknowledged (virtually) in all the tales. *a* and *b* are opposed to one another as the individual to the social, the variable to the constant. The crimes and sins are always the same because they concern the same laws; the modifications are all different because they concern unique situations. [p. 38]

It appears that this particular grammar cannot be adequately described without recourse to the semantic level. Nor can any other, and the more subtle and "literary" the fiction, the more semantically oriented the grammars will have to be.

Todorov's grammar of propositions requires some secondary categories which must be at least mentioned here. These are categories of *negation* (when an attribute or action is significantly not present), of *comparison* (when it is present but in a different degree, as between the conditions of rich and very rich), and of various *modes* which qualify actions or conditions as feared, hoped for, predicted, renounced. It is also significant to note whether certain actions are done willingly or not, and when certain actions or situations are actual or only "believed" to exist. These categories and the various verbs and adjectives are codified by Todorov into a simple system of symbols which can be used to reproduce the scheme of any particular story. I have avoided reproducing that system here simply because it is useful only if one is going to undertake a comparative study of many tales, which we cannot attempt here, and, simple as it is, it is much more complicated than the order of Proppian functions or Bremond's linked triads. It is complicated enough, in fact, to do something like justice to the grammar of the *Decameron.*

In turning from propositions to sequences, Todorov makes a number of interesting observations. With respect to the structure of the tales in general, he notes two basic patterns related to the two verbal structures he distinguished within the propositions:

> Only the study of a whole tale can permit us to identify its structure. The initial situation in each tale can be described as composed of (1) A certain number of general laws (the violation of which is considered a crime or sin); and (2) A certain number of specific attributive propositions, which present the concrete characters in the tale. At the beginning we do not know whether we have to do with a story of law or a story of attributes. Two ways are open at that time. . . . Only a certain number of the propositions which appear at the beginning of a tale will be actualized and made relevant by integration into the structure of a sequence. [p. 60]

At this point Todorov does not say it, but he indicates elsewhere that the laws, being taken for granted by a cultural community, are not so likely to be articulated by attributive propositions as those features which must be individualized by each story. Such culture-bound codes of values are important structural elements which operate almost invisibly in the specific tales but may be construed from an examination of a number of related texts. Thus structural investigation can lead us directly to important extratextual semantic considerations. In the case of Todorov, the whole system of the *Decameron,* in which so many sins go unpunished and so many changes are effected, leads him to suggest that a connec-

tion may be made between the values of the book and other values
emerging historically in the time of Boccaccio:

> If the book has a general sense or direction, it is certainly that
> of a general liberation of exchange—of a break with the
> old system in the name of daring personal initiative. In this
> sense, it would be quite correct to say that Boccaccio is a de-
> fender of free enterprise and even, if you wish, of nascent cap-
> italism. The ideology of the new bourgeoisie consisted pre-
> cisely in attacking the old system of exchange, which had
> become too restrictive, and in its place imposing another,
> more "liberal," which could make believe, at the beginning at
> least, that it amounted to the total disappearance of system.
> This description applies, word by word, to the moral of the
> tales in the *Decameron.* Free action, un-coded (which we
> have called *a*—modifying action) is the most appreciated
> in this universe. Literature undoubtedly has more than one
> connection with political economy. [pp. 81–82]

Having observed that Todorov goes at least this far in the direction of Marxian analysis, let us return to some of his more formal
and aesthetically oriented observations. In noting that certain
propositions function in different ways in the same tale—the
same action, for instance, being a punishment from one perspective
and a crime from another, Todorov finds it necessary to allow for
different ways of symbolizing such propositions in his scheme. This
brings to light a certain ambiguity in some tales, which the reader
finds pleasing. Such ambiguity gives "an impression of peculiar
density, of a well-constructed intrigue" (p. 66). Though evaluation
was not a part of his intention in examining the tales (any more
than Marxian interpretation) Todorov's careful description has allowed an aesthetic principle to surface here. Such principles are developed much further in his description of the one tale which vio-
lates most strikingly the grammatical system that has proved
adequate to describe nearly all the others.

The ninth tale of the fifth day presents "the justly famous story
of the falcon" which Frederick cooks for his beloved, unaware that

she had come to ask for it alive as a present for her sick son. Up to a point this story can be described by the grammar devised for the other tales. But as the actions become more ambiguous, even multiple notation of propositions will fail to catch the essence of the tale. As each gesture reverberates in several systems of action and value, the central act of the tale becomes unrecordable. It is not correct to say that Frederick gives the falcon to Giovanna, nor is it right to say that he doesn't give it. And we cannot solve the problem by saying that he does from one point of view and doesn't from another. The meaning and the power of the story lie in the symbolic value of this "gift" which is and is not given. Todorov suggests that ironic symbolism of this kind belongs to another order of narrative which will require a somewhat different grammar for its notation. But by refusing to stretch his grammar of the *Decameron* to include this tale, while pointing so clearly to its qualities, he has done us a considerable service. And the grammar itself, though admittedly inadequate to this object (and to a few others that Todorov mentions) has been sufficiently adequate to identify these special cases and direct our attention to the most interesting and difficult features of them. Not the least of the virtues of the *Grammaire du Décaméron* is that it shows us where the work needs to be continued.

D. Systems and System-Builders

"The notion of structure," Jean Piaget tells us, "is comprised of three key ideas: the idea of wholeness, the idea of transformation, and the idea of self-regulation" (*Structuralism,* p. 5). We shall be returning to this notion as it may be applied to an individual literary text in chapter 6.B, but for the moment it can serve us as a point of departure for the consideration of the structure of literature as a whole. The possibility of considering literature as a self-regulating system has been a strong force in modern critical thought. It is powerfully present in the work of the Russian formalists and of the British mythographers. Its most persuasive and influential presentation in Anglo-American literary study in recent years has been that of Northrop Frye in his *Anatomy of Criticism*. I was a graduate student at Cornell when the *Anatomy* was published, and I can remember vividly the excitement the book caused, the debates it aroused (including a memorable confrontation between Frye himself, then visiting the campus briefly, and M. H. Abrams—who objected to the book's "fearful symmetry"). There is no question in my mind that Frye's book filled a deeply felt need in the academic literary community. It offered the possibility of literary study's attaining the progressive, cumulative qualities of science, and it presented specific, concrete examples of systematization which could be used—and have been used—to organize everything from freshman literature courses to anthologies of Elizabethan fiction. Frye's persuasive suggestion of an "order of words" which could be mastered and taught gave teachers of literature a powerful incentive to think about their work more systematically. And it provided some necessary formal support for men of letters during the ideological onslaught of the late sixties. Frye's system had the considerable virtue of persuading readers of the possibility of a systematic study of literature without convincing them that it had been achieved. It was a system that rang deeply true in its essence while being plainly wrong in much of its substance.

For myself, and I believe for many others, Frye's ways of organizing the possibilities of fiction in particular proved most interesting and fruitful. They have provided a major contribution to one of the most interesting critical enterprises of recent years—the attempt to organize a system of narrative genres. For our purposes, then, in this study, the attempt to arrive at a system of literature will be represented by this lesser included problem of the systematization of fictional genres, which is a problem of sufficient complexity to illustrate the difficulties as well as the potential usefulness of a generic structuralism. In addition to Frye, I will consider the work of Tzvetan Todorov and Claudio Guillén on this subject, and will include some of my own reflections on fictional genres and modes.

Frye presents two different generic systems relating to fiction—

a system of "modes" and a system of "forms." His system of modes has a diachronic thrust. He organizes it according to "the hero's power of action" in relation "both to other men and the environment of other men." He also makes a distinction between the hero superior in "kind" to other men and the hero who is merely superior in "degree." Allowing for a state of equality or equivalence, there are sufficient variables in this system to provide us with a minimum of nine modal categories and a maximum a good deal higher. The minimal system would look like this:

1. Superior in kind to both men and their environment
2. Superior in kind to either
3. Superior in degree to both
4. Superior in degree to either
5. Equal to both
6. Inferior in degree to either
7. Inferior in degree to both
8. Inferior in kind to either
9. Inferior in kind to both

But Frye actualizes only five possibilities, which are, using the above numbers,

1. Myth (superior in kind to both)
3. Romance (superior in degree to both)
4a. High mimesis (superior in degree to men but not to environment)
5. Low mimesis (superior in no way)
6. Irony (inferior)

This is, to say the least, unsystematic. And despite all these variables, there are many fictions which cannot be accurately classified according to this system. Some myths, for instance, are about animals with supernatural powers. This makes them superior to man's environment, but are they superior to man? In kind or degree? Are demons, witches, and so forth superior to man in degree or only in kind? Frye's use of the word "hero" has allowed him to ignore the myths in which the central figure is a magic animal or demon, wicked or mischievous, whose exploits are recounted with horror or pleasure. But let us ignore these complications for the moment, accepting a general category of "supernatural" as one mode of fiction, in which the "hero" can transgress natural laws. Is there, then, a comparable category of "subnatural" at the other end of the scale? This would seem impossible. If supernatural implies a power to transcend the laws of man's natural environment, then subnatural would imply an inability to function in accordance with those laws. Thus the opposite of transgression would be simply non-existence. The subnatural cannot exist in man's environment, let alone have sufficient power of action to function in a fiction. Man's creatural imagination can look in one direction only—and that direction is up. He can imagine beings, whether good or evil, with superior powers to his own, but he cannot imagine beings outside of nature with less power than himself. In the natural world he sits at the top in a kingdom pyramiding from the simplicity of particles and the inertness of stones to his own marvelous complexities. But in the world of the imagination this situation is reversed. The attempts of Samuel Beckett, for instance, to give us something like the subnatural in *The Unnameable* are close to the limit of this possibility. The subnatural is precisely unnameable; our language cannot accommodate it; we cannot conceive of it. What Beckett and some other contemporary writers give us, or try to give us, is the subhuman in human form—which is imaginable but not easy to make function in a form defined by action. But the "Unnameable" of Beckett comes close to attaining the "zero degree" of action in a recognizably fictional form. We can see, now, why Frye's categories collapse the inferior possibilities implied by his variables, and why he is right, up to a point, in allowing this collapse even though he does not account for it. There is simply not much scope for inferiority in fiction, insufficient "power of action" for the form to sustain itself.

What we have in abundance in fiction is the opposite category, the superhuman, the sphere of action of heroes who are subject to nature's laws but can triumph over other men with ease. Frye suggests that the laws of nature are "slightly suspended" for this hero.

This is a reasonable way to put it—if we remember that what we are recognizing here is often simply a historical shift in human understanding of those laws. What from our perspective may appear as a suspension of natural law may have seemed entirely possible to a classical or medieval narrator. For Frye's first two categories, then, we were provided with an overabundance of identifying variables. The terms "supernatural" and "superhuman" will serve to designate simply and accurately the qualities of protagonists in his categories of "myth" and "romance." And we can recognize these modes of fiction as actualities in the history of fictional forms—though pure myth is prehistorical and in some sense properly outside our system of fictional forms. But we run into greater problems with Frye's last three categories.

If high mimesis provides us with heroes superior in degree to other men but not to the environment, then low mimesis ought to provide us with "heroes" inferior in degree to other men. For mimesis, imitation of reality, is not bound like imagination to look upward only. Frye's high mimesis gives us the "leader" of epic and tragedy, Frye suggests, who has "authority, passions, and powers of expression far greater than ours, but what he does is subject both to social criticism and to the order of nature" (p. 34). This is reasonable, and is a useful encapsulation of kinds of fiction that we all know. The real difficulty comes in the next category: the low mimetic, which Frye presents not as a mode of inferiority but as the mode of equality, in which the characters are like "ourselves." (One problem here is in the normative concept of ourselves. Presumably there is a good deal of difference between Homer's original audience and "ourselves." But some normative concept of a persistent "human nature" is a necessary assumption for endeavors of this kind and for most other educational endeavors.) Frye thus locates together in the mode of equality both realism and comedy—strange bedfellows in a system designed to distinguish among fictional modes. The distinction between the truly equal hero of realism and the inferior figures of comedy is actually as clear and as significant as the distinction between ordinary man and "leader" or that between "leader" and "hero." There is no need to change the scale of discrimination at precisely this point. Actually, we need a "low mimetic" and a "middle mimetic," or just plain mimetic, category at this point—the category of realism. And even more than this, we need to recognize that the comic and pathetic characters of low mimesis are just that, comic and pathetic, because they are inferior to us. We look down on them in precisely the same way that we look up at the "leaders" of tragedy and epic. As Bergson and others have demonstrated, comedy reduces man to a mechanical and inferior human status. In a related way, we feel superior to pathetic characters, too, who have less control over their situations than "ourselves." High, middle, and low mimesis all exist as forms that we are familiar with. Middle mimesis may be a norm never absolutely attained by fiction, if only because our notions of the real will not stay put, but we can find plenty of examples of a realism which is neither tragic nor pathetic, neither epic nor comic.

Thus we have both comic and pathetic protagonists who exist below the line of equivalence to "ourselves." Are there also, then, characters—"heroes"—of fiction who are sufficiently subhuman to populate a fictional world distinguishably below the low mimetic? As I have suggested, some of Beckett's creatures live there, and so do some other figures from satiric, picaresque, and absurdist fiction. There is a category, therefore, like Frye's "irony" below the low mimetic as we have redefined it. In fact, if we leave out the troublesome category of myth, with its demons and gods, we can arrive at a simple set of narrative modes, much like Frye's, but representing the actualities of narrative more closely:

1. Romance (heroes)
2. High mimesis (epic and tragic leaders)
3. Realism (men like ourselves)
4. Low mimesis (comic and pathetic figures)
5. Irony (picaresque and absurdist antiheroes)

Why did this simple form elude Frye? Perhaps because of the diachronic thrust of his presentation. He wants to conclude with the following two statements:

> Looking over this table [the list of five modes], we can see that European fiction, during the last fifteen centuries, has steadily moved its center of gravity down the list. [p. 34]

> Reading forward in history, therefore, we may think of our romantic, high mimetic and low mimetic modes as a series of *displaced* myths, *mythoi* or plot-formulas progressively moving over toward the opposite pole of verisimilitude, and then, with irony, beginning to move back. [p. 52]

It is not clear whether the path from irony "back" to myth in this formulation leads through the other modes or directly to the beginning; that is, whether we are dealing with a line which must be retraced in reverse order, or with a circle which finds its beginning in its end. But all we know of Frye's views suggests that the circle is what he has in mind. And it is this eschatological hope that the mythic millennium is at hand, that darkest irony presages a new age of belief, which animates this diachronic system and has forced its violations of the logic of its own categories. Frye wants a progress which is a fall, down from myth, through romance and epic to low mimesis and irony, presaging a new rise, a new birth of myth. But once we develop the logical categories of inferiority, and put comedy in its proper place, we ruin this chronological system. And yet there *has* been a chronological process at work in the history of fiction as in other things that we can perceive historically. And Frye has caught some aspects of it accurately in his system, though at a price in distortion of the evidence that many of us may be reluctant to pay.

My own response is to seek a reformulation of fictional chronology, trying to see whatever system is implied by it rather than imposing on it some myth of eternal return. Robert Kellogg and I attempted just this in *The Nature of Narrative,* and on pages 132–38, below, I shall present a refined version of the novelistic part of our chronology—as an aspect of generic theory.

But before turning to this view of fictional modes, it will be necessary to consider briefly the other aspect of Frye's system of fiction: his theory of "continuous forms." This theory is a part of

Frye's larger system. And it should be noted in passing that some of the problems of his fictional theorizing result from his heroic attempt to systematize all literature. It is far easier to attack the parts, as I am doing here, than to replace the whole. Frye's system of genres begins with his acceptance of the basic Aristotelian division into lyric, epic, and dramatic forms. He then subdivides narrative form (Aristotle's epic) into two subcategories, "epos" and "fiction." This distinction is based on what Frye calls the "radical of presentation": "epos" is delivered orally; "fiction" is written to be read. The narrative connotations of both terms are allowed to stand as part of the definition. But this distinction is not easy to maintain. The examples Frye offers involve us in difficulties at once. *Paradise Lost,* we are told, was meant by Milton to be read in book form. But because its invocation to the muse brings it "into the genre of the spoken word" it is to be treated as epos and not fiction. A Dickens novel, on the other hand, is fiction when it appears in book form, but when Dickens reads it aloud the genre changes "wholly to epos." In Milton's case our classification rests on the way the book was written—its employment of the traditional formulations of literary epic. But in Dickens's case our classification depends not on how the book was written but on how it was treated after it was written. And of course neither *Paradise Lost* nor *Great Expectations* was composed in the oral formulaic manner used by the true singer of tales. If we take the oral versus written distinction seriously, it will involve us in considerable difficulty.

A further difficulty arises from Frye's distinction between "epos" and "epic." Epos is distinguished from other kinds of narrative by its oral radical of presentation, but it is not assigned any specific narrative forms. "Epic" is carefully separated from "epos" and its form is called "encyclopaedic." Purely narrative poems, which we would expect to be the main department of "epos" are, we are told, "fictions," which "will, if episodic, correspond to the species of drama; if continuous, to the species of prose fiction." But we began with a distinction between "epos" and "fiction," based on their both being different from drama, and distinguishing them from one another on the basis of their different radicals of presentation. How, then, can we assign narrative poems to these other species? If "epos" is "episodic" how can some narrative poems be "continuous"? And if some narrative poems are "continuous," how can "continuous" be used as a synonym for prose fiction? The natural narrative form to associate with the oral radical of presentation is the epic, but in this scheme the traditional epic is called an "encyclopaedic" form and is associated with such nonoral narratives as the Bible and Proust's *A la recherche du temps perdu*.

In practice this separation of epic from other narrative forms is not based on formal or rhetorical criteria but on certain mythical or archetypal characteristics. Throughout the *Anatomy* mythic and archetypal criticism tend to interpenetrate and sometimes to overwhelm ostensibly rhetorical or generic discussions. That may be a valid objection to Frye's method as a whole, but it is not the main point at issue here. What I am objecting to is the inconsistent or ambiguous use of terms like "episodic" and "continuous" and the rigid imposition of an arbitrary symmetry which obscures certain significant generic relationships. These objections can be illustrated in somewhat more detail if we turn to that discussion of the four forms of prose fiction which has become one of the most widely read and influential portions of the *Anatomy*. Frye defines fiction here so as to exclude encyclopaedic narrative but include all other "continuous" forms, which means in this case all narrative works of literary art written in prose to be read silently by a reader rather than recited orally to an audience. By emphasizing the "artistic" aspect of the term fiction, he seeks to rule out such noncreative forms as biography and history. He admits autobiography (or confession) as one of the four forms of fiction because "most autobiographies are inspired by a creative, and therefore fictional, impulse to select only those events and experiences in the writer's life that go to build up an integrated pattern" (p. 307). The implication is that biography and historical narrative are uncreative and therefore unfictional.

Biographers from Plutarch to Lytton Strachey are done a grave injustice by this exclusion from the realm of art, as are historians from Herodotus to Carlyle. To take Plutarch as an example, we can see that he belongs in none of the four established categories. He is not an autobiographer, a novelist, an anatomist, or a romancer. Nor can he be called inartistic by any fair standard. The whole conception of the Parallel Lives is an artistic one. And in the opening paragraph of his life of Alexander, Plutarch explains quite clearly what a "life" (*bios*) is. This explanation alone demonstrates that his intentions were artistic, even if his practice did not make this abundantly clear. Carlyle's *French Revolution* or Strachey's *Queen Victoria* could be defended as art as easily as Plutarch's *Lives*. But more important than any "injustices" done to individual authors is the fact that by leaving historical and biographical narrative out of a theory of fiction we obscure crucial lines of relationship which illuminate aspects of the epic, the saga, and the novel. A theory of prose fiction which cannot account for the artful historical or biographical narrative may be better than no theory at all, but it is obviously not the last word. It is true that history and biography can be excluded from a theory of fiction on the grounds that they are not "made-up," but we have already waived those grounds in order to admit autobiography. To define fiction as "artful narrative" in one case and as "non-factual narrative" in another is a stratagem much too arbitrary to be properly employed in generic criticism. The maximum number of literary relationships might be arrived at better by dropping the troublesome classification of "fiction" itself as it is used here and substituting a broader term such as "narrative," which would also bring biblical and Homeric narrative into the same plane of consideration as the other forms.

Still, even if we accept the limited categories of the Frye theory as necessary or useful, other problems arise. In this theory each of the four forms is allotted a pair of attributes. Each is seen as extraverted or introverted; personal or intellectual. The slipperiness of these terms makes for a good deal of difficulty in their application. Frye applies the terms in this way:

The novel: extroverted and personal
The romance: introverted and personal
The confession (or autobiography): introverted and intellectual
The anatomy (or satire): extroverted and intellectual

The difficulty with these categories is that they cannot be consistently applied. This difficulty stems partly from the fact that, despite the rigidity of this scheme, extroverted and introverted are true polar opposites, while personal and intellectual are not. But the main difficulty is that we do not know to what part of a fiction we are supposed to apply them. Do they refer primarily to plot? to characterization? to point of view? or to the relationship between the fictional world and the external world? The terms "introverted" and "extroverted" ought to refer in some way to characterization. Thus the novel and the confession ought to share the term introverted, both being concerned with a psychological approach to the inner lives of complex characters. But in the Frye system the novel is called extroverted. As employed in the *Anatomy* the term "extroverted" refers to the novelist's interest in representing "society." But if extroverted means to have an interest in the representation of the actual social world, it is clear that the novel alone of the four forms can qualify as extroverted. Lucian's *True History,* the prototype of Menippean satire or anatomy, has no such interest. Yet the whole type "anatomy" is called extroverted in this system. Actually, this interest in society is one the novelist shares with the biographer and the historian, but, since there is no place in the system for them, this relationship must remain obscured.

Frye's theory of fictional forms seems far less useful than his theory of modes. This is mainly because in dealing with modes he was frankly treating the semantic level of his material, whereas in dealing with "forms," where the structural and rhetorical levels should have been the determining characteristics, he continually resorted to semantic distinctions like factual/fictional to support his formal categories, with the result that his formal vocabulary disintegrated, and crucial terms changed their meaning with every case. This is precisely the reproach (among others) leveled at Frye by Tzvetan Todorov, in the opening chapter of his *Introduction à la littérature fantastique;* at least half of this chapter is a criticism of Frye. (I have used Todorov's critique to sharpen my own criticisms of Frye's modes in my discussion earlier.)

But our concern now is with the other part of the first chapter of *Introduction à la littérature fantastique,* a chapter addressed to the problems involved in treating literary genres. Todorov begins by pointing out that a literary genre is fundamentally different from the generic classifications of zoology and even of linguistics. In literature, he points out, "each work modifies the whole set of possibilities. Each new work changes the species." Literature is like a language in which "every speech is a-grammatical at the moment of its utterance." Every literary text is a product of a preexisting set of possibilities, and it is also a transformation of those possibilities. Therefore, literary study must operate by proceeding from the set of possibilities toward the individual work, or from the work toward the set of possibilities—which is, in fact, a generic concept. Genres are the connecting links between individual literary works and the universe of literature.

In order to be useful, Todorov points out, the concept of genre must be "nuanced and qualified." He makes a basic distinction between "theoretical genres," which are deduced from a general theory of literature, and "historical genres," which are "the fruit of an observation of the facts of literature." And he further distinguishes within theoretical genres between the elementary (defined by a single feature like the standard division into lyric, epic, and dramatic) and the complex (which are defined by the presence or absence of a combination of features). Finally, he points out that a major task of poetics is to work out the precise mesh between complex theoretical genres and the actual genres we find in the world of literature. Any generic study, he asserts,

> must satisfy constantly the exigencies of two orders: practical and theoretical, empirical and abstract. The genres that we deduce theoretically must be verified by the texts; if our deductions do not correspond to any work, we follow a false

trail. On the other hand, the genres that we encounter in literary history must be submitted to the explanation of a coherent theory; otherwise, we remain the prisoners of prejudices transmitted from century to century. . . . The definition of genres is therefore a continual coming and going between the description of facts and the abstraction of theory. [pp. 25–26]

Todorov's own treatment of the "fantastic" as a literary genre is an excellent example of his ideas in action, more satisfying in some ways than the discussion I am about to present. But I offer the following inquiry into the modes of fiction for consideration here, because it faces many of the same problems faced by Frye and offers what I believe to be better solutions, however far from perfection they may be. In the course of my discussion I shall be trying to deal with certain arguments against generic criticism in general, as well as to present a workable theory of fictional modes.

My first assumption is that we need a poetics of fiction both for its own sake—as an interesting branch of man's inquiry into his own modes of existence—and for the sake of its pedagogical value. We cannot "teach" enough individual works of literature to make our students as literate as we would like them to be. Therefore, we must help them to learn the grammar of literary forms by showing them aspects of this grammar as an abstract way of organizing individual texts—but a way which has historical validity as well as conceptual convenience. And if we accept this notion of a poetics of fiction as an indispensable tool for teachers, we are already on the way to accepting a generic criticism; for the notion of a poetics of *fiction* is itself a generic concept. In accepting it we accept the notion that fiction does not work the same way that lyric poetry does and, beyond that, that imaginative literature does not work the way that certain other verbal constructs—which are not imaginative or mimetic—do in fact work. The very pressure for a separate poetics for fiction suggests that we feel it to be a distinct genre, with attributes, problems, and possibilities all its own. I agree that this is the case. And I would go farther. I would say that this is so because the two essential things we are concerned with—the reading process and the writing process—are fundamentally generic in nature.

The writing process is generic in this sense: every writer conceives of his task in terms of writing he knows. However far he may drive his work into "things unattempted yet in prose or rhyme," like Milton himself he must take his departure from things already attempted. Every writer works in a tradition, and his achievement can be most clearly measured in terms of the tradition in which he works. The hack or journeyman—whether writing TV westerns in the 1960s or Elizabethan romances in the 1590s—takes his tradition for granted and cranks out works according to formula. The master, on the other hand, makes a new contribution to his tradition, by realizing possibilities in it which had gone unperceived, or by finding new ways to combine older traditions—or new ways to adapt a tradition to changing situations in the world around him. A writer may claim, like Sidney, to look in his heart and write, but he will actually, like Sidney, see his heart only through the formal perspectives open to him. In *Astrophel and Stella,* the Petrarchan sonnet sequence provided Sidney with the occasion to look into his heart, and it lent its coloring to the picture of Stella he found there.

If writing is bound by generic tradition, so is reading. Even a little child must come to learn what stories *are* before he likes listening to them. He has, in fact, to develop a rudimentary poetics of fiction before he learns to respond, just as he develops a grammatical sense in order to speak. In the adult world, most serious misreadings of literary texts and most instances of bad critical judgment are referable to generic misunderstandings on the part of reader or critic. In his book *Validity in Interpretation* (New Haven, 1967, p. 74), E. D. Hirsch has argued persuasively that "an interpreter's preliminary generic conception of a text is constitutive of everything that he subsequently understands, and that this remains the case unless and until that generic conception is altered." The context in which we read the language of a literary work, Hirsch insists, is generic. As we begin reading we postulate a tentative genre, which we refine upon in the course of reading, as we approach the unique nature of the work by means of its affinities with other works that use language in similar ways. Hirsch's view of the reading process finally persuades me because it squares with my own sense of what happens when I read. It also casts some light on the problems of literary evaluation.

A recurrent tendency in criticism is the establishment of false norms for the evaluation of literary works. To mention a few instances in the criticism of fiction, we can find Henry James and Co. attacking the intrusive narrator in Fielding and Thackeray; or Wayne Booth attacking the ambiguity of James Joyce; or Erich Auerbach attacking the multiple reflections of consciousness in much modern fiction. The reasons for these critical aberrations are most clearly diagnosable when we see them as failures in generic logic. Henry James set up his own kind of fiction as a norm for the novel as a whole, because he was unable or unwilling to see the term *novel* as a loose designation for a wide variety of fictional types. In a similar though opposed fashion, Wayne Booth set up eighteenth-century rhetorical-didactic fiction as *his* norm. And Erich Auerbach set up nineteenth-century European realism as his. The moral of these exempla is that unconscious monism in literary evaluation is a real danger, capable of bringing the whole enterprise of evaluation into disrepute—which is exactly where a vigorous branch of critics led by Northrop Frye would like to have it. Frye argues that all evaluative criticism is subject to distortion by personal prejudice and passing fashions in literary taste, and is therefore fraudulent or sophomoric. From the same data and premises I should prefer another conclusion: which is, that since even the very best critics of fiction—men and women of sensitivity, learning, and acumen—can go wrong when they seek evaluative principles that cross generic boundaries, we should consciously try to guard against monistic evaluation by paying really careful attention to generic types and their special qualities. Among works that have real affinities in form and content, a genuine comparative evaluation is possible.

As Todorov indicates, traditional genre theory has two facets, almost two separate methods. In one, specific works of literature are referred to certain ideal types, in which reside the essence of each genre and its potential. In the other, a notion of general types is built up from data acquired empirically, based on historical connections among specific works, and traditions that can be identified. One is essentially deductive, the other inductive. An ideal theory of fictional genres should work toward a reconciliation of these two approaches, which are equally necessary, and in fact complementary. For clarification, I wish to call my theory of ideal types a theory of modes, using the term genre in a narrower sense for the study of individual works in their relationship to specific, historically identifiable traditions.

A theory of modes should work toward a general overview of all fiction, providing a framework for discussion of literary affinities and antipathies. It should also prove amenable to historical perspectives, indicating broad relationships among the specific fictional genres which have established themselves as literary traditions. With an almost Aristotelian hubris, I will found my modal theory on the notion that all fictional works are reducible to three primary shades. These primary modes of fiction are themselves based on the three possible relations between any fictional world and the world of experience. A fictional world can be better than the world of experience, worse than it, or equal to it. These fictional worlds imply attitudes that we have learned to call romantic, satirical, and realistic. Fiction can give us the degraded world of satire, the heroic world of romance, or the mimetic world of history. We can visualize these three primary modes of fictional representation as the mid and end points of a spectrum of possibilities. Like this:

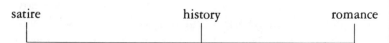

satire   history   romance

If we think of history as representing a number of fictional forms which take the presentation of actual events and real people as their province (journalism, biography, autobiography, etc.), the basic fictional forms which existed before the rise of the novel can all be located on this spectrum. But where should the novel itself be placed? Is it more satirical than history or more romantic? Clearly, it is both. Thus, the novel belongs on both sides of the fictional spectrum—a satirical novel between history and satire, and a romantic novel between history and romance. Bringing our knowledge of the actual development of fictional modes to bear on this scheme, we can make one more useful subdivision among fictional shades at this point. The satirical novel can be divided into picaresque and comic forms. And the romantic novel can be divided into tragic and sentimental forms. This more elaborate spectrum will look like this:

satire	picaresque	comedy	history	sentiment	tragedy	romance

Here a word is no doubt necessary on the arrangement of these subdivisions. In using traditional terms for the modal divisions, I run the risk of creating confusion because these terms are used in so many different ways. Let me repeat, then, that terms like tragedy and comedy here are meant to refer to the quality of the fictional world and not to any form of story customarily associated with the term. In this modal consideration, what is important is not whether a fiction ends in a death or a marriage, but what that death or marriage implies about the world. From the relationship between protagonists and their fictional surroundings we derive our sense of the dignity or baseness of the characters and the meaningfulness or absurdity of their world. Our "real" world (which we live in but never understand) is ethically neutral. Fictional worlds, on the other hand, are charged with values. They offer us a perspective on our own situation, so that by trying to place them we are engaged in seeking our own position. Romance offers us superhuman types in an ideal world; satire presents subhuman grotesques enmeshed in chaos. Tragedy offers us heroic figures in a world which makes their heroism meaningful. In picaresque fiction, the protagonists endure a world which is chaotic beyond ordinary human tolerance, but both the picaresque world and the world of tragedy offer us characters and situations which are closer to our own than those of romance and satire. In sentimental fiction, the characters have unheroic virtues, to which we may well aspire; in comedy, human failings which we, too, may strive to correct. Comedy is the lightest and brightest of the low worlds; it looks toward romance frequently, offering a limited kind of poetic justice. And sentiment is the darkest and most ordinary of the high worlds. It looks toward the chaos of satire, and it may see virtue perish without the grace of tragic ripeness. In a sense, comedy and sentiment overlap—in that comedy suggests a world somewhat superior to its protagonists and sentiment offers us characters somewhat superior to their world.

This modal scheme, crude as it is, can help us to perceive some affinities and antipathies in fiction. For example, considering a crucial century of English fiction, we could locate the names of some major figures on the spectrum in this way:

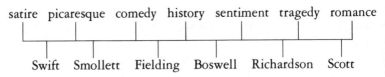

The anxieties that result from this pigeonholing are a measure of its inadequacies. They can be relieved somewhat by locating specific works more precisely. Fielding's *Jonathan Wild,* for instance, belongs well over toward satire; *Joseph Andrews,* on the picaresque side of comedy; *Tom Jones,* on the historical side of comedy, and *Amelia* well over toward the sentimental. Richardson's *Pamela* and *Clarissa* have clear affinities with sentiment and tragedy respectively. But then, what do we do with Jane Austen's blend of comedy and sentiment, or Sterne's blend of sentiment and satire? Clearly this spectrum cannot be turned into a set of pigeonholes, but must be seen as a system of shades that writers have combined in various ways.

To facilitate a consideration of fictional mixtures, and for some other reasons, I would suggest one further change in this modal system, and that is a change in its shape for graphic representation. If we bend the spectrum at its midpoint—history—we can produce a figure shaped like a piece of pie, as in figure 3. Using this scheme we can not only begin to designate more complicated fictional mixtures, like that of Cervantes in *Don Quixote,* which seems to partake of all the attributes named here; we can also trace certain interesting developments in the history of fiction. Before the novel was developed as a fictional type, both satirical and romantic fictions flourished. We can, in fact, see the rise of the novel as a result of a flow of fictional impulses from both romance and satire, attracted toward history by a growing historical consciousness in the later Renaissance and the Age of Reason. In the course of this movement, the rogues and whores of picaresque became the rakes and coquettes of comedy. The heroes and heroines of romance and tragedy became the men of feeling and women of virtue who populate sentimental fiction. (Fielding and Richardson drew from both sides of the spectrum, but in different ways.) Realism as a fictional technique, then, can be seen as the curbing of satirical and romantic attitudes in response to scientific or empirical impulses, which were also taking shape as journalistic, biographical, and full-blown historical types of narrative. In English fiction of the eighteenth century, we can see persistent traces of one or the other of the prenovelistic fictional modes. Sterne, for example,

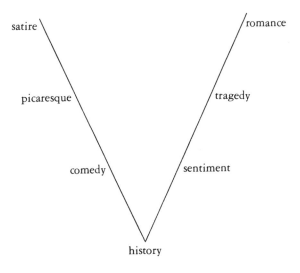

Figure 3

holds sentiment and satire in suspension; even though he mixes the
two, they never unite in a single solution. In fact, this persistence
of primitive narrative modes continues in the English novel into
the nineteenth century and beyond. In a sense, a realism which
really unites these two broad fictional traditions never establishes
itself completely in England. The difference between Stendhal and
Balzac and their predecessors in both England and France—and
their English contemporaries as well—is that Stendhal and Balzac bring these two modal lines into a much tighter fusion than
the others. We can compare Stendhal's blend of sentimental and
picaresque elements in *The Red and the Black* with Smollett's in
Roderick Random, for instance, to see the difference between
merely mixing and really fusing the two modes. There is, I think, a
value judgment implied here, but a real value judgment must take
into account many more factors than a broadly modal consideration provides.

Because the novel as a fictional form has tended to draw from
both sides of the spectrum, we can finally reintroduce it into the
scheme by representing it as a vague, dotted line slicing the center
of our piece of pie (see figure 4). This will enable us to make a fur-

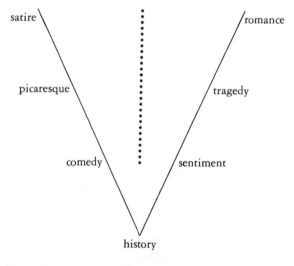

Figure 4

ther interesting refinement or two. If realistic fiction first established itself (in the form we now recognize as the novel) as a result of a movement from satire and romance in the direction of history, we can then see the subsequent development of the novel in terms of its movement away from the initial point of conjunction. If the novel began in the eighteenth century as a union of comic and sentimental impulses which we may call realistic, in the nineteenth century it moved toward a more difficult and powerful combination of picaresque and tragic impulses which we have learned to call naturalistic. The realistic novels tended toward stories of education, amelioration, integration. The naturalistic novels have been concerned with alienation and destruction. The novel reached its classic form in the nineteenth century when it was poised between realistic and naturalistic modes. We can represent the area of the classical novel by shading a segment of the graphic scheme as shown in figure 5. Stendhal, Balzac, Flaubert, Tolstoy, Turgenev, and George Eliot all work near the center of this area. Dickens, Thackeray, Meredith, and Hardy tend more toward the edges and corners.

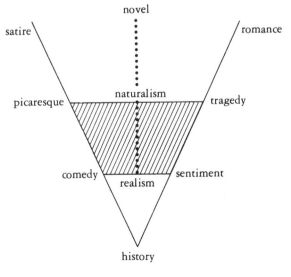

Figure 5

In the twentieth century, fiction has tended to continue moving away from realism, going beyond naturalism. In this development, the novel has had difficulty holding together as a form in the face of such extremely divergent satirical and romantic possibilities. If this scheme has any historical validity, the natural combination for our era would seem to be precisely those two divergent poles of fiction, satire and romance. Here we would expect a combination of the grotesque in characterization and the arabesque in construction. Allegory would be a likely vehicle for fiction because it traditionally has offered ways of combining satire and romance. In fiction of this sort the world and its denizens would appear fragmented and distorted, and language would be tortured in an attempt to hold the satiric and romantic views of life together. Is this, in fact, the present literary situation?

I think it is. I think the description I have just set forth represents the state of fiction as practiced by our best writers from Joyce and Faulkner to Barth and Hawkes. This modal scheme, then, can help to tell us where we are and to explain how we got there. In doing so, it should serve to make us more sympathetic and open to the varieties of fiction, old and new. It can also serve us pedagogically as a way of teaching literary history as a living and ongoing process, and as a way of putting historical learning in the service of interpretation. A theory of modes and genres is, in fact, the natural meeting place of scholarship and criticism, since both are absolutely required by it.

So much, for the moment, for fictional modes. To come down from the heady, conceptual wheeling and dealing of modal criticism to the painstaking historical study of generic traditions is a descent indeed. It is so demeaning, in fact, that many theoreticians never make it. Modal criticism, because it starts at the center of things with a limited number of ideal types, is readily demonstrable. Generic criticism, on the other hand, begins in the thick of the phenomena, trying to organize them in such a way as to make a glimpse of those ideal types possible, without doing injustice to a single individual work. In the ideal act of critical reading we pass

through insensible gradations from a modal to a generic awareness, to a final sense of the unique qualities of the individual work,
as distinguished from those most like it. Generic criticism finally
requires more learning and more diligence than modal criticism, a
deeper and more intense kind of scholarship. No student has finished a proper initiation into a generic poetics of fiction until he
has experienced the gap between generic knowledge and modal
ideas, and has some notions of his own about how to reshape
modal theory to close that disturbing space.

It is perhaps ironic that I will now present, as an example of generic criticism in the limited sense of the word, an essay by a man
who has done more to domesticate the broader concepts of structuralism in the American literary tradition than almost any other
critic. Claudio Guillén is not merely an expert in the specifics of
literary genre, especially the genre of picaresque fiction which he
may almost be said to own; he is also a critic who knows and uses
the work of Saussure, Jakobson, Lévi-Strauss, and other extraliterary structuralists in order to discuss the broadest questions of literary study. His *Literature as System* unites a great tradition of European learning with the theoretical concepts of structuralism in the
production of a number of essays of major importance for the poetics of fiction. In particular, the title essay, "Literature as System,"
and a sequence of three on the picaresque and the "uses of genre"
are especially relevant for our concerns in this chapter. Before turning to Guillén's treatment of the picaresque as an example of *genre
historique,* as Todorov calls it, we will do well to examine briefly
his notion of literature as a system.

Guillén suggests that the history of literature—as distinct
from the history of language or society—

> is characterized not so much by the operation of full systems
> as by a tendency toward system or structuration. Thus it ap-
> pears that the historian is led to evaluate, for every century or
> phase in the history of his subject, a persistent, profound "will
> to order" within the slowly but constantly changing domain
> of literature as a whole. [p. 376]

And he proposes, finally, that

> the theoretical orders of poetics should be viewed, at any mo-
> ment in their history, as essentially mental codes—with
> which the practicing writer . . . comes to terms through his
> writing. The structures of this order are no more alien to the
> poems he produces than the linguistic code is to the actual ut-
> terances in his speech. [p. 390]

For literary study, Guillén argues, the most profitable approach to
these mental codes is through the system of literary genres, and he
cites Cervantes as an example of the writer engaged in "an active
dialogue with the generic models of his time and culture" (p. 128).
The system of genres is a diachronic as well as a synchronic affair.
Genres change. And,

> As they change they affect one another and the poetics, the
> system to which they belong, as well. Although genres are
> chiefly persistent models, because they have been tested and
> found satisfactory, it has been generally known since the
> Enlightment—since Vico, since Voltaire's *Essai sur la
> poésie épique*—that they evolve, fade, or are replaced. [p.
> 121]

Thus the study of new genres, their rise and fall (like the fantastic,
which Todorov establishes as essentially a nineteenth-century
genre), is especially rewarding and significant.

The picaresque arose in the hundred-year period from mid-six-
teenth to mid-seventeenth-century Spain. In this situation it began
as a countergenre, a reaction against romance. In speaking of the
genre, Guillén distinguishes it first as a theoretical construct—a
code—and then he notes two separate groups of novels that may
be called picaresque in different senses of the word. One set, picaresque in the strict sense, follows the original Spanish pattern,
while a second set includes works which are picaresque in a
broader sense of the term, often modifying the generic concept or
blending it with some other generic code. The code itself is composed of eight features, which Guillén lists in order of importance

and discusses in greater detail than can be indicated here. The features are these:

1. The pícaro is an orphan, a "half-outsider," an unfortunate traveler, an old adolescent.
2. The novel is in form a pseudo autobiography, narrated by the pícaro.
3. The narrator's view is partial and prejudiced.
4. The narrator is a learner, observer, who puts the world to the test.
5. The material level of existence is stressed—subsistence, hunger, money.
6. The pícaro observes a number of conditions of life.
7. The pícaro moves horizontally through the geographical world and vertically through the social.
8. The episodes are loosely strung together, enchained rather than imbedded.

Guillén's characteristics are not meant to be an elaborate litmus for testing the quality of various picaresque novels but a scheme for following developments in the literary system. Other schemes set next to it, like that of the novel of education or the quest romance, will reveal interesting aspects of the system. Historical shifts in the status of a particular feature or set of features may reveal changes in the system that can be profitably correlated with extraliterary changes in the situation of man. The generic concepts enable us to do much. But, like every other feature of structuralist thought, they are merely tools to be used. They will do no more than we know how to ask them to do, and do it no better than our skill in their use will allow. But for a scholar with the mind and the learning to use them, they will augment his conceptual power like a magical gift awarded the hero of a fairy tale.

5 The Structural Analysis of Literary Texts

Perhaps the reproach most frequently addressed to structuralist literary criticism is that it fails at the level of the individual text. As I observed at the end of chapter 2, structuralism will not read the text for us. But this is only because no method will read the text for us. Reading is a personal activity, and there are as many readings of any text as there are readers of it. But all readings are not equally good. In this chapter I wish to present Tzvetan Todorov's theory of reading, as found in his essay "Comment lire?" in *Poétique de la prose,* and then to discuss the approaches to specific fictional texts of Roland Barthes and Gérard Genette as examples of structuralist practical criticism. There are some methodological problems in this latter endeavor that I wish to share with the reader at this point. Any book such as this one, which is to some extent about other books that are about still other books, is threatened with an almost vertiginous remoteness from its ultimate subject matter. The poet W. D. Snodgrass once praised himself in a poem for not having read a single book about a book for quite some time. How he might feel about books about books about books, one does not like to speculate. But that is where we are here, talking about books about books, and the problem becomes acute when we are talking about books of practical criticism.

Roland Barthes's *S/Z,* for instance, is a full-length study of a single short tale by Balzac, and I have given myself the task of saying something useful about this work in the space of a few pages. Obviously, I can do no more than sketch Barthes's method in this situation. I cannot begin to do justice to his specific analysis of passages in the work he is considering. There is the risk, then, or rather the inevitability, that my summary will bring into relief the theoretical implications of Barthes's method without demonstrating that he is, indeed, a structuralist who can read a text as closely as anybody. This I must merely assert, referring the reader finally to Barthes's text itself. In my opinion Genette is a more satisfying reader than Barthes, but there is no way to "prove" that in these pages. All I can hope to do is show what a structuralist does when he approaches a specific text, using Todorov's description and the actual works of Barthes and Genette as my examples.

A. Tzvetan Todorov's Theory of Reading

A literary text can be approached in a number of ways. In his essay "Comment lire?" Tzvetan Todorov has addressed himself to the variety of possible approaches to studying literature and writing about it. He begins by reminding us of three traditional approaches, which he names *projection, commentary,* and *poetics.* Projection is a way of reading *through* literary texts in the direction of the author, or of society, or some other object of interest to the critic. Certain kinds of psychological criticism (such as Freudian) and sociological criticism (such as Marxian) are examples of critical projection. The complement of projection is *commentary.* As projection seeks to move through and beyond the text, commentary insists on remaining within it. The most familiar form of commentary is what we usually call explication or close reading. The extreme limit of commentary is paraphrase—and the extreme of paraphrase is reiteration of the text itself. The third approach to literature is *poetics,* which seeks the general principles that manifest themselves in particular works. Poetics should not be confused with a desire to see in particular works mere instances of some general law. The poetic study of any particular work should lead to conclusions which complete or modify the initial premises of the study. A mere hunt for archetypes or any preestablished structural pattern is not an exercise in poetics but a parody of it.

Poetics itself is open to the charge that it is a kind of projection, however privileged, which does not do justice to the individual work. Thus there must be an activity which is related to poetics but concerns itself with the individual work as an end in itself. Todorov calls this critical approach simply *reading*. Reading approaches the literary work as a system and seeks to clarify the relationships among its various parts. Reading differs from projection in two ways: it accepts the autonomy of the work as well as the particularity, while projection accepts neither. Its relation to commentary is closer. Commentary is in fact an atomized reading. Reading is a systematized commentary. But one who aims at discerning the system of a work must give up hope of being literally faithful to the text. He must emphasize some features at the expense of others. And, of course, to the extent that he finds system he will be treating not the uniqueness of a text but its similarities to others. This is an aspect of the material. There can be no texts which are both intelligible and unique.

The activity of reading can be clarified by relating it to two other critical stances that are closely allied to it: *interpretation* and *description*. The *interpretation* of a text involves the substitution of another text for the one we are reading. This search for hidden meanings has a long history, from the allegorical interpretations of the ancients to certain kinds of modern hermeneutic criticism. Nor is this notion of the text as a palimpsest of layered significations alien to the idea of reading. Only, for the reader, one level of the text is not a substitute for another (e.g. the "hidden" for the "literal"); rather, the relationship among levels becomes a matter of interest, without either of them being subsumed by the other. The text is multiple. In approaching a text of any complexity, then, the reader must choose to emphasize certain aspects which seem to him crucial. This is a matter of personal judgment. There is no single "right" reading for any complex literary work. And, in fact, the variety of readings which we have for many works is a function of the selection of crucial aspects made by the variety of readers. In considering the critical readings of a work, Todorov points out, we do not speak of readings that are simply true or false, but of readings that are more or less rich, strategies that are more or less appropriate.

Reading can also be distinguished from *description,* and this is especially important because what Todorov means by description is precisely what many people believe to be structuralism at work upon individual texts. By description he means what is sometimes called "stylistics": the application of the tools of structural linguistics to literary texts. (This should not be confused with the "old" stylistics of such critics as Spitzer and Auerbach, which is simply a special kind of reading.) The approach of Jakobson and Lévi-Strauss to the text of "Les Chats" is a typical example of description in action, and, as we saw in chapter 2, this approach leaves something to be desired. Todorov lists three major assumptions behind this descriptive criticism, which distinguish it from a proper structuralist reading as he is presenting it here:

1. Description assumes that the categories of literary discourse are fixed. Only the combination is new; the matrix remains always the same.

Whereas, for reading, each literary text is at once a product of pre-existing categories and a transformation of the whole system. Only subliterary forms fail to modify their generic heritage.

2. Description holds that the linguistic categories of a text are automatically pertinent on the literary level.

Whereas, for reading, the literary work systematically short-circuits the autonomy of linguistic levels; literary works organize themselves around a pertinence which is unique to each of them, linking grammatical and thematic elements in their own unique way.

3. For description, the actual ordering of the elements in a text is not important; description tends to reduce poetic structures to spatial form.

Whereas, for reading, no part of the work, thematic or

structural, can be assumed to lack significance, including the ordering of the elements. [*Poétique de la prose,* pp. 246–47]

Todorov concludes this discussion of reading and its related activities by reminding us that they *are,* in fact, related. We should *read* interpretations and descriptions, too, and not reject them outright. Without the practice of description, however ultimately unsatisfying it may be, we should not have learned to pay enough attention to the phonic and grammatical aspects of literary texts.

In the second half of his essay Todorov attempts to demonstrate the procedures of reading, which he calls superposition and figuration. These are essentially ways of locating and analyzing relationships between one text and another, or one part of a text and another part. To my mind, the two activities that he names are not clearly distinguished from one another. They both involve relating certain formal features of a work to other features, as if one might relate the structure of a Jamesian sentence to the structure of an entire novel or to a recurring theme in the work of James. And, in fact, this is very much what Todorov has done in his excellent essay on James ("Le Secret du récit") in *Poétique de la prose.* As it happens, he is a very good reader of literary texts himself—but I think that in the kinds of texts he chooses and in the sketch of reading he presents in "Comment lire?" there is a certain formalist bias which limits somewhat the universal applicability of his notion of "reading." He tends to select for study the well-made literary object, and his treatment always remains close to if not entirely within the formalist domain of "literariness."

The issue here is a complicated one. Todorov's work seems to me extremely valuable. He is lucid, systematic, and ingenious. The range of his criticism—from reading to poetics, from the *Arabian Nights* to James—has been considerable. But he rarely emphasizes the semantic dimension of literary texts, and rarely selects for study texts in which that dimension is extensive (though when he deals with the themes of fantastic literature in his book on the fantastic, he says some very interesting things). There is a great critical issue here. The explicative criticism which he calls commentary is the dominant critical mode in our schools, for the very good reason that, given the proportion of our (American) population that we try to educate, we have reading problems at every educational level. The college student who cannot read poetry is simply the advanced version of the high school student who has difficulty with prose. But explicative commentary is not simply a pedagogical necessity for us, though it certainly is that. Nor is it entirely bound within the text, as Todorov suggests, and as some new-critical dogmatizing might seem to have implied. A poem *does* mean things. It is a message as well as an object—a multiple or duplicitous message but a message none the less. Thus one important aspect of commentary is always the semantic one. And the more mimetic a work is, the more important this aspect becomes. Meaning is never simply folded into a work (implicated) so that it can then be unfolded (explicated) by a technician of language processes. Meaning is a continual shuttling back and forth between the language of the work and a network of contexts which are not *in* the work but are essential for its realization. A good commentary sketches in this elaborate structure which forms around the work as we perceive its semantic connections with our world of meanings. In suggesting that paraphrase, and finally reiteration, represent an extreme limit of commentary, Todorov was considering one extreme only. But clearly there is another—the point at which the establishing of semantic connections turns the text into a pretext for some unliterary study, thus ceasing to be commentary and becoming projection—or the point at which the search for meaning turns toward meanings which are secret or hidden, giving us not a message to be read but a revelation to be interpreted.

For structuralism, then, the problem of reading a text must involve finding satisfactory ways of incorporating the semantic dimension within the consideration of structure. In the next two sections of this chapter, we shall be considering two quite different responses to this problem: the codes of Roland Barthes and the figures of Gérard Genette.

B. The Codes of Roland Barthes

Roland Barthes is a literary critic, an advocate of *le nouveau roman* and a practitioner of *la nouvelle critique,* a student of popular culture, a scholar of Racine, a brilliant polemicist, a formidable rhetorician, an ingenious, mercurial man of letters. He is an essentially unsystematic writer who loves system, a structuralist who dislikes structure, a literary man who despises "literature." He loves to take up the outrageous position on any question and defend it until it becomes plausible, or—better still—attack the other views until they seem inferior. In presenting one aspect of his work here, I wish to make it clear that it is merely one aspect, and that not even this one aspect will fit neatly into any little box labeled "structuralism."

In 1970 Barthes's book *S/Z* appeared in France. *S/Z* is a two-hundred-page study of a thirty-page story by Balzac, called "Sarrasine." In its procedures it is informed by every development of structuralist literary thought that we have already considered, yet it deliberately and specifically repudiates one important aspect of structuralist poetics. Here are the opening sentences of the book:

> They say that by virtue of their asceticism certain Buddhists come to see a whole country in a bean. This is just what the first analysts of the *récit* wanted to do: to see all the stories in the world . . . in one single structure. We are going, they thought, to extract from each tale its model, then from these models we will make a great narrative structure, which we will apply (for verification) to any story in existence— an exhausting task . . . and finally an undesirable one, because the text thereby loses its difference. [p. 9]

This is not exactly a fair representation of the work of Greimas, Bremond, and Todorov, which Barthes had proudly introduced in *Communications* 8, but it is close enough to be painful, and it indicates, though perhaps too starkly, too dramatically, a certain shift of emphasis within structuralism. This same shift may be seen in the difference between Todorov's early polemic against commentary (then called "description") in *Qu'est-ce que le structuralisme?*, which allowed no place for "reading," and the elaborate attention given to reading in "Comment lire?" Structural poetics has been forced, over the past ten years, to justify itself by applicability to individual texts, and this has been a healthy phenomenon. I take it as a sign of vitality that interpretive works as rich and satisfying as *S/Z* and Genette's *Figures III* have emerged from the structuralist matrix. For *S/Z is* a satisfying work in many ways though exasperating in others.

Both the satisfaction and the exasperation one feels in reading *S/Z* are related to Barthes's use of the concept of code. Most of his work as a student of popular culture has been inspired by Saussure's brief hints about a study of semiology (quoted above in chapter 2.A). Barthes has made himself into the semiologist *par excellence,* and has even produced a little book of *Elements of Semiology* in which he explains the mysteries of the discipline. More than any other scholar, Barthes has concerned himself with the pervasiviness of codes and coding in human experience. He is close to Lévi-Strauss in many respects, and is certainly the most sociologically oriented of the literary structuralists. He finds, for instance, in modern France an active codification of clothing, furniture, food, and many other aspects of ordinary life. There is a food system, for instance, in which the various possible foods are arranged paradigmatically, according to their affinities, and syntagmatically, according to the order in which we eat them at any given meal. Barthes points out that both aspects are present on a typical restaurant menu. If we read a menu horizontally, looking at all the entrees or all the deserts, for instance, we are exploring the system's paradigms. If we read vertically, from soup to nuts, we are proceeding syntagmatically. The whole menu represents the *langue* of the restaurant (and a sublanguage of the whole culture). When we select from the menu and place our order we make a statement (*parole*) in the language of food. A statement consisting of all deserts, for instance, or beginning with desert and ending with an appetizer, is theoretically possible but would be ungram-

matical. Like Propp's functions, the vertical categories of a menu
represent all the possible choices in the only possible order. We
may leave out a course but we may not rearrange. For a Frenchman, the American custom of serving salads before the main
course is simply ungrammatical.

I have been elaborating on Barthes's treatment of the food system to indicate how plausible it is, how linguistically such solid
entities as food actually may behave in a verbal culture such as
ours. Barthes makes similar demonstrations with clothing (he has
written a whole book on the system of "fashion"), with furniture,
with architecture, to the point where one is finally ready to agree
that human beings organize virtually all their experiences along
linguistic lines. These various "codes" then shape our lives into
symmetries which may be fearful or comforting, depending on
one's point of view. In turning to literature, Barthes applies the
concept of code in a slightly different but related way. In considering the codes of literature, it may be well to remember Jakobson's
communication diagram and the discussion of codes and contexts
in chapter 2.b, above. For the basic tenet of Barthes's entire approach to literature may be stated in terms of that diagram. For
Barthes, there is no such thing as a pure context. All contexts
come to man already coded, shaped, and organized by language,
and often shaped in patently silly ways. The great error of the
"realist" in literature or in criticism is to assume that he is in touch
with some ultimate context, while in reality he is simply transcrib-
ing a code. Thus in approaching the archrealist, Balzac, Barthes
will be intent on showing how Balzac's "reality" is always derived
from some preexisting code. But he will be concerned with much
more, as well. For he wishes to demonstrate how this structuralist,
semiological *nouvelle critique* can approach a "classic" text, dear to
the heart of the *ancienne critique,* and deal with it not merely
effectively but exhaustively. And he wishes also to make this analysis function as another blow in a battle not merely between the
old and new criticism but between the old and new literature as
well. For Barthes there is a great difference between literature
which is merely "readable" in our time (the classics) and that

which is "writeable." That which is writeable is indispensable for us, because it is our only defense against the old lies, the exhausted codes of our predecessors. That which is readable is then in some sense inimical, since it perpetuates all this nonsense. The writeable is a special value for Barthes, producing texts which are uncriticizable because in some way unfinished, resistant to completion, to clarification. We do not need to accept this almost mystical faith of his in order to understand his sentiments. For our purposes, it is important to note only that he approaches Balzac by way of Butor, with an attitude well this side of idolatry.

Barthes's method of interpretation differs from what we usually think of as interpretation in a number of ways. And it may be well to consider what we usually understand by that word before we examine this Barthesian version more closely. Interpretations, especially in American criticism, are usually "readings" (though not in Todorov's sense) of particular texts. Each reading is in some way a reduction of the text to a particular meaning that may be drawn out of it. I am speaking, of course, of interpretations of works of fiction, which differ markedly from interpretations of poetry in a number of respects. This difference is interesting in itself and will repay some consideration here. It is not merely a function of the different kinds of structuration and verbalization that we find in poetry and fiction; it is also a function of mere size. The average interpretation in American criticism runs to about twenty pages, whether the work being considered is a poem of twenty lines or a novel of two hundred pages. This means that our interpretation of poetry is habitually expansive, extending the significations of the poetic text in various directions, while our interpretation of fiction is habitually reductive and highly selective. Any such "reading" of a fictional text will be insufficient and hence will require other "corrective" rereadings and reinterpretations. A whole critical industry battens on this situation, culminating in anthologies which present these various and conflicting interpretations for the edification of students. All this is not criminal, of course, but it is mildly ludicrous. Barthes's answer is the two-hundred-page treatment of a thirty-page text, which attends specifically to the "plurality" of the text, its various systems of meaning and their interaction. In the hands of a man as learned and lively as Roland Barthes, the method has great value.

The two main problems of this sort of analysis are how to arrange and divide the text and how to organize the interpretive materials. Barthes chooses to simply proceed through the text, dividing it into 561 meaning-units or "lexies." He deliberately ignores the obvious "structural" divisions according to incident or episode, and even the divisions of the discourse into sentences and paragraphs. He does this to emphasize that the process of reading is linear—through the text from left to right—and also involves our movement from the text out to the various codifications of the world invoked by it. The frequent critical device of "structural" spatialization of the text, which diagrams its contours, does great violence to the process of reading that Barthes wants to enact for us, because it ignores both this linearity and this moving out of and back to the language of the text. Barthes continually insists that structuralism broaden its concept of structure and grow in flexibility:

> . . . to work on the unique text down to its least details, is to resume the structural analysis of fiction at the point where it is presently stopped—at the large structures; it is to give it the power (the time, the ease) to follow the capillaries of meaning, to leave no significant spot without presenting the code or codes that it may be connected to. . . . [*S/Z*, p. 19]

Thus Barthes will quote a few words or lines of "Sarrasine" and then stop to consider the various significations of this lexie before resuming his quotation. He will also digress from time to time, to discuss the more general implications that are raised by a particular lexie or sequence of lexies. There are ninety-three numbered digressions in *S/Z*, including the ten which actually precede the analysis, and many of them are brilliant exercises in poetic theory, though often iconoclastic of accepted critical ideas. Number LXXI is a typical example, though briefer and simpler than most. It follows lexie 414, which describes Sarrasine's embrace of Zambinella in a carriage on the way to Frascati. At this point Sarrasine thinks Zambinella is a woman, and presumably the first reader of the story knows little more than the character at this point. A second reader, however, knows that Zambinella, an operatic soprano, is actually a *castrato*. This leads Barthes to a digression on rereading:

> The second reading. Beneath that transparent cover of suspense imposed on the text by the first reader, avid and ignorant, a second reading locates a knowledge based on the anticipation of the issue of the story. This other reading—unduly censured by the commercial imperatives of our society which oblige us to squander the book, to throw it away on the pretext that it is deflowered, so that we may buy another—this retrospective reading gives to the kiss of Sarrasine a precious enormity. Sarrasine embraces passionately a *castrato* (or a boy transvestite); the castration imprints itself on the very body of Sarrasine, and we others, second readers, we receive the shock of it. It would be false, therefore, to say that if we agree to re-read a text it is for an intellectual profit (to understand better, to analyse with knowledge of the cause); it is in fact and always for an increase in pleasure; it is to multiply the signifiers, not to attain some ultimate of the signified. [p. 171]

The ease and the time are there in this method for a vigorous and well-stored mind to express itself. Obviously, the length of a text will place some limits on the method. But what this can tell us about the *récit balzacien* in general will be immensely useful in any other reading of a story by Balzac. The other problem in this method of interpretation applies to texts of any size. This is the problem of organizing the significant materials in the text. If dividing and digressing are the physical procedures, what then are the mental ones that will effect the division? What will determine where and how we interrupt the text and the kind of things we say about it? Barthes's solution, though unsatisfactory in some respects, is still a significant breakthrough in structural criticism. He recognizes five master codes in the text, under which every significant aspect of it can be considered. These codes include both the syntagmatic and the semantic aspects of the text—the way its parts are related to one another and the way they are related to the outside world. Here Barthes's emphasis on the codification of all the aspects of culture enables him to move easily from the fictional structure to the various intellectual structures invoked by it. Paraphrased, the five codes are as follows:

1. The proairetic code, or code of actions. Under this code we can consider every action in a story from the opening of a door to an orgy of musicians. Actions are syntagmatic. They begin at one point and end at another. In a story they interlock and overlap, but in the classic text they are all completed at the end.

2. The hermeneutic code, or code of puzzles. Like the code of actions, this is an aspect of narrative syntax. Whenever questions are raised (Who is that? What does this mean?) which the story will ultimately answer, we have an element of the hermeneutic code.

(*Note:* A story may be said to exist by virtue of starting actions and raising questions which it then refuses to complete for a certain period of time. A story consists of barriers to the completion of actions and various lures, feints, and equivocations which delay the answering of questions. These two levels of narration interact and relate in various ways; thus the action (proairetic) of Sarrasine in pursuing Zambinella is imbedded in the puzzle (hermeneutic) of the Lanty family and the sources of their money.)

3. The cultural codes. Under this heading Barthes groups the whole system of knowledge and values invoked by a text. These appear as nuggets of proverbial wisdom, scientific "truths," the various stereotypes of understanding which constitute human "reality."

4. The connotative codes. These are the themes of the fiction. As they organize themselves around a particular proper

name they constitute a "character," which is simply the same name accompanied by the same attributes.

5. The symbolic field. This is the field of "theme" as we usually understand the word in Anglo-American criticism: the idea or ideas around which a work is constructed. In "Sarrasine" the symbolic field is based on the human body as a source of meaning, sex, and money. Thus a rhetorical figure like antithesis is one aspect of this code, and the concept of castration is another. The two are symbolically related.

A number of criticisms can be made of this selection of codes. Such criticisms would echo many made of Lévi-Strauss. There is something too arbitrary, too personal, and too idiosyncratic about this method. The system operating here is not systematic enough to be applied easily by other analysts to other texts; yet there is a great emphasis on the process of systematization. Even in trying to rationalize the five codes for this presentation, I have had to describe them in more restricted ways than Barthes does himself. For them to be useful to me or anyone else, they would have to be tightened farther, and given more of that logic which Barthes disdains. Yet it would be a mistake to reject this kind of approach out of hand simply because of Barthes's casualness and arbitrariness. We need a systematic approach to the analysis of fiction which cuts across the traditional divisions of narrative texts into plot, character, setting, and theme. And Barthes is right about the danger of structuralism's bogging down at some ideal level of analysis and never coming to grips adequately with the materials of actual texts. It is a real danger, and he is helping the structuralists to avoid it. If at the moment we find it difficult to distinguish between connotative and symbolic codes, for instance, or between a connotation and a cultural reference, it is not because these functions do not exist or because it is not useful to separate them for analytical interpretation. It is because this method of approaching a text involves us precisely in distinguishing among things that we have been content to lump together before. It is up to us now to attempt the systematization of these codes and to see if they can be

made to work on other texts as well as Barthes makes them work
on this tale by Balzac. Five is not a magic number. It may be that
four or six would be better. But the opportunity of improving this
system awaits anyone who attempts to use it—indeed the *necessity* of improving it awaits all those who seek to use it. And it has
the great virtue of bringing the semantic dimension of narrative
into the field of structuralist criticism in a vigorous and productive
way.

It is impossible to illustrate in this sort of recapitulation
Barthes's skill as a commentator on the text. Which of the 561
lexies could serve as an example? But in order to suggest the quality of this analytical process, I will quote part of one more digression, which relates interestingly to the discussion of literariness in
chapter 2. B, above. In digression LXII Barthes considers double
meaning as a form of equivocation in the hermeneutic code. This
digression is occasioned by lexie 331 in which at the musicians'
party the tenor tells Sarrasine that he need fear no rival:

> "Vous ne risquez pas de rival," says the tenor: 1) because
> you are loved (understands Sarrasine), 2) because you are
> courting a *castrato* (understand the tenor's accomplices and
> perhaps already the reader). With respect to the first auditor
> this is a lure; for the second, an unveiling. The intertwining
> of the two meanings forms an equivocation. The equivocation
> is then the issue, in effect, of two voices, equally received;
> there is interference between two lines of communication. In
> other words, the *double entente* (well named), the foundation
> of all play on words, cannot be analysed in simple terms of
> signification (two signifieds for one signifier); it requires a dis-
> tinction between two receivers as well. And if, contrary to
> what we find here, the two auditors are not given by the
> story, if the play on words is addressed to a single person (the
> reader, for example), it is necessary to conceive of this person
> as divided into two subjects, into two cultures, into two lan-
> guages, into two hearing-spaces (from which comes the tradi-

tional association of the play on words with "foolishness": the "Fool," dressed in a bi-partite costume—divided—was once the practitioner of the *double entente*). In comparison to a message ideally pure (such as we find in mathematics), the division of listeners constitutes a "noise," it makes communication obscure, fallacious, risky: uncertain. Nevertheless, this noise, this uncertainty, are produced by the discourse as an act of communication; they are given to the reader for his nourishment. What the reader reads is a counter-communication. . . . [pp. 150–51]

Need I add that in reading Barthes we also read a countercriticism, a rich noise, on which we can nourish ourselves, and which we are meant to enjoy?

C. The Figures of Gérard Genette

In bringing together Barthes and Genette as exemplars of structural criticism, I have sought in part to illustrate two related but distinguishable approaches to structuralist activity. Barthes, along with Lévi-Strauss, Michel Foucault, Jacques Lacan, and Jacques Derrida is a star performer, an individual who must be approached as a system in himself, and understood for the sake of his own mental processes. Whatever contributions of these men are absorbed by the general culture, their texts will not suffer the same absorption but will remain—like philosophical texts, which they are, and literary texts, which some of them aspire to be—as unique objects to which later thinkers must return in order to grasp the ideas and methods that have been developed therein. This is what we may call "high structuralism"—high in its aspirations and in its current prestige.

There is also a "low structuralism," practiced by men whose intelligence and learning is considerable—often not inferior to that of the high structuralists—but whose aspirations are more humble, whose achievement is less dazzling to the contemporary eye. The works of such men may also achieve recognition, especially among their colleagues, but this sometimes comes slowly, even to the point of being posthumous. Saussure himself, Propp, the other formalists and their followers seem to me clearly in this second category. I do not mean to suggest that a man like Shklovsky, for instance, has been passive or invisible in his life and work taken as a whole—but that as a formalist critic he did a certain amount of hard analytical work which others have been able to accept, modify, and build upon. The low structuralist writes to be immediately useful, to be ultimately superseded. He makes a considerable distinction between creative and critical activity—especially if he is, like Shklovsky, also a creative writer. In a sense, formalism has lasted until now mainly because we have been so slow in assimilating it and so feeble in improving it. But in another sense the achievement of the formalists, like that of Aristotle, will be permanent because it will have to be incorporated in any later poetics of fiction. Poetics is, in fact, the discipline par excellence of low structuralism. At its worst it degenerates into mere taxonomy, as Boris Eichenbaum in 1929 feared formalism might degenerate, becoming "the work of academic second-stringers" who "devote themselves to the business of devising terminology and displaying their erudition" (*RRP,* p. 57). Interpretation, commentary, or "reading," however, if these are to be attempted by structuralism at all, seem more likely to be the work of high structuralists than low.

Thus Barthes's brilliant reading of "Sarrasine" should not surprise us. What is surprising in *S/Z* is the extent to which Barthes is able to temper his ingenuity by a concern for poetic generalizations based on the text. He is, however high, a structural not a hermeneutic critic. In Gérard Genette, on the other hand, we have a critic who is almost militantly a low structuralist, even when approaching a specific text which has often inspired the highest flights of hermeneutism. In the *après-propos* to his nearly book-length study of Proust, he makes three statements which will serve to locate provisionally for us his views on his own critical activity, on interpretation, and on literary structure:

> The categories and the procedures proposed here are certainly not faultless in my eyes. It has been a question, as it often is, of choosing among inconveniences. In a domain habitually conceded to intuition and to empiricism, this proliferation of notions and terminology will no doubt be irritating, and I do not expect "posterity" to preserve too much of what has been proposed here. This arsenal [of terminology], like every other, will inevitably disappear before too long, all the more quickly if it is taken seriously, discussed, tested, and revised with use. [*Figures III,* p. 269]

> . . . it appears to me foolish to search for "unity" at any price, and in this way to *force* the coherence of the work— which is, we know, one of the strongest temptations of criticism, one of the most banal (not to say vulgar) and also one of the easiest to satisfy, requiring only a bit of interpretive rhetoric. [p. 272]

> The "laws" of the Proustian *récit,* like the *récit* itself, are partial, defective, perhaps dangerous: common laws, entirely empirical, that should not be hypostasized into a Canon. The code, here, like the message, has its gaps, and its surprises. [p. 273]

There is, in these quotations, the humility of low structuralism, to be sure, but there is also a suspicion of excess of all kinds—of the hermeneutic zeal that forces "unity" on every literary text, and of the structuralist zeal that persists in describing as laws what are only customs, usages, habits. There is a degree of common sense in these statements, and in all Genette's work, an avoidance of hyperbole, which is not to be found among all structuralists. It is one quality among others that are going to make him, along with Todorov, a French critic whose work will "travel" like the best French wine, without losing any virtues in crossing the Atlantic.

In addition to an uncommon common sense, Genette has precisely the kind of learning which will enable Anglo-American readers to feel comfortable with his work, for he knows both the critical and the fictional traditions of our literary history well enough to be at ease with the paradigms of the English and American novel (*Tom Jones, Tristram Shandy, Wuthering Heights, Lord Jim, The Ambassadors, The Sound and the Fury,* etc.), and he is also at ease with Lubbock, with Booth, and with the whole American approach to such problems as "point of view" and "stream of consciousness" in fiction. More than any French critic I have read, he knows our critical and literary traditions and assumes us as a part of his audience. He and Todorov, in the pages of their important journal *Poétique* (of which Hélène Cixous is the third editor) have published translations of Wayne Booth and other American critics for their international readership. Structuralist criticism, it seems to me, *is* more international, more genuinely comparative, than any other kind. Genette and Todorov are simply actualizing this potentiality, which has been there since the formalists began their work.

In approaching a particular text, like Proust's *Recherche,* Genette also reassures us by having so clearly done his homework. He knows the textual variants, he knows the scholarship, he knows the criticism—the extensive American criticism of Proust as well as the French. Where Barthes gives us a structural *performance,* in which his command of ancillary materials figures only as an aspect of his rhetoric, Genette gives us a structural *dialogue,* citing the other poeticians and critics, crediting, qualifying, disagreeing, always assuming response and continuation. At the end of *Figures III* there is a three-and-a-half-page list of works cited in the text. At the end of *S/Z* there is a single quotation from Georges Bataille, which "inspired" Barthes to consider "Sarrasine." All this is helpful, I hope, in suggesting the kind of critic Genette is. But of course it does nothing to suggest his quality. And there is no way I can adequately do that in a few pages confronting the three volumes of *Figures* (*I,* published in 1966; *II* in 1969; *III* in 1972). What I hope to accomplish here is to suggest what Genette means by "figures," and how he approaches fictional texts—in particular the *Recherche,* to which he has devoted a part of the first two volumes and nearly all of *Figures III.*

His interest in figures proclaims that Genette is a rhetorician —in the opposite sense from Barthes. One uses rhetoric, the other studies it. The word "rhetorician" here threatens to become a figure, because it signifies ambiguously, requiring the addition of those two auxiliary signifiers (*uses* and *studies*) for its completion. But by bringing them into the text directly, I reduce the figurative status of the word to mere literalness. As Genette puts it,

> Every figure is translatable, and carries its translation, visible in its transparence, like a watermark or a palimpsest, under its apparent text. Rhetoric is tied to this duplicity of language. [*Figures,* p. 211]

For Genette, rhetoric is our traditional name for "the *system* of figures." And he studies the various historical attempts to fix this system with sympathy and pity. For rhetoric as a traditional discipline attempted to fix the unfixable, to codify what cannot be codified, to treat as a finite list of figures (metaphor, metonymy, synecdoche, etc., etc.) what is in actuality a self-regulating system. Traditional rhetoric was doomed, is dead, and cannot be revived. But the figures are there, and can often be usefully studied as a way into a literary text. Two of Genette's observations on figures should be considered before we turn to his approach to fiction.

> The rhetorical fact begins at the point where I can compare the form of this word or that phrase to that of another word or phrase which might have been used in their place and which the word or phrase used may be said to have displaced. [*Figures,* p. 210]

This can be related to Jakobson's view that poetic language draws attention to itself by forcing us to consider the paradigmatic aspect of language. This is precisely what we do when we are aware of the presence of a figure. We make a connection between the word

we find before us and the other word or words paradigmatically invoked by the figure. As Genette says,

> The figure is nothing more than a sense of figuration, and its
> existence depends totally on the consciousness the reader de-
> velops, or fails to develop, of the ambiguity of the discourse
> that he is offered. [*Figures,* p. 216]

In pursuing the interaction of metaphor and metonymy in Proust,
Genette may be said to bring out these latent structures by making
us aware of the configurations he perceives in the text. His insisting on the difference between metaphor and metonymy in Proust
leads him, and us with him, deep into the heart of the work's
structure and its theme. He is a rhetorician in the older sense of
one concerned with verbal figures, but he is also, as we shall see, a
rhetorician in yet a third sense, the sense Wayne Booth gives the
word in *The Rhetoric of Fiction,* a student of larger fictional structures.

What Barthes and Genette have in common, and what they
share with all good readers or interpreters of texts, is a strong sense
of how much the text depends on the reader's activity for its completion. Since this is precisely what has been missing in linguistic
structuralism and descriptive stylistics, this emphasis on the role of
the reader is of immense importance for the future of structuralist
activity. Barthes's interest in codes and Genette's in figures take
them both away from the text in order to find the meaning of its
message. But Barthes, going to the cultural codes explicitly, finds
meanings that are cultural, collective, almost involuntary as far as
the reader is concerned. While Genette, tracing the rhetorical activity involved in the perception of figures in a text, locates meanings that are closer to the reader's experience of the text than to
the cultural codes alluded to by the text. Genette's reading stays
close to the "how" of perception; Barthes moves explicitly to a
"what" which is not so much perceived as recognized.

Proust, of course, can be read in many ways. Coding the text, we
would find behavioral systems such as homosexuality and anti-Sem-
itism to be important, as well as more philosophical systems relat-

ing to perception, consciousness, memory, imagination, time, space, and so on. For Genette, the systems relating to the process of reading are more important than the cultural codes alluded to by the text. That he should choose the epistemological Proust, while Barthes chose the sociological Balzac, is certainly no accident. Because the *Recherche* is about Marcel's becoming a writer, about his learning how to see his world clearly and understand it, how to structure his vision of this world in a way that will enable him to write the book that we are reading—because of all this it is a book ideally suited to Genette's interest. In discussing this great book, he will also be able to discuss the poetics of fiction, and to locate Proust's achievement within the entire narrative tradition.

For Genette, as we shall see, it is inconceivable to treat an individual text without a literary theory, just as it is impossible to have a theory without basing it upon specific texts. He makes this view explicit on many occasions, but most thoroughly in his long study of Proust, which he calls "Discours du récit," emphasizing the general and theoretical in his title even though the *Recherche* is the main object of consideration in his text. His explanation of this is so eloquent and so characteristic that it must be quoted here at some length. He says that he has chosen this title neither "par coquetterie ni par inflation délibérée du sûjet."

> The fact is that very often, and in a manner exasperating for some readers, the *récit proustien* will seem forgotten while more general considerations are attended to; or, as we say today, criticism will give way to "literary theory," and more precisely here the theory of the *récit* or *narratology*. I might have justified or clarified this procedure in two different ways: either by frankly putting the specific object in the service of a general design, as others have done elsewhere—the *Recherche* becoming merely a pretext, a repository of examples and a place of illustration for a poetics of fiction in which specific features lose themselves in the transcendence of "generic laws"; or, by subordinating, on the contrary, poetics to criticism, and by making the concepts, the classifications and pro-

cedures proposed here mere *ad hoc* instruments, exclusively designed to allow a more correct or more precise description of the *récit proustien* in its singularity—the "theoretical" detours being imposed each time by the necessity of methodological clarification.

I admit my repugnance, or my incapacity to choose between these two apparently incompatible systems of defense. It appears to me impossible to treat the *Recherche du temps perdu* as a simple example of the *récit* in general, or the novelistic *récit,* or the *récit* in the form of autobiography, or God knows what other class, species, or variety. The specificity of Proustian narration taken as a whole is *irreducible,* and any extrapolation of it would be a mistake in method. The *Recherche* illustrates only itself. But on the other hand, this specificity is not *undecomposable,* and each one of its features disengaged by analysis lends itself to some relation, comparison, or alignment. Like every work, like every organism, the *Recherche* is composed of universal (or at least trans-individual) elements, which it holds in a specific synthesis, in a singular totality. [*Figures III,* p. 68]

Thus, in the course of discussing Proust, Genette gives us a whole system of narratology, to which the work of the Russian formalists, of Todorov, of Wayne Booth, and of many others has contributed. As my earlier quotation from his afterword indicated, he does not expect narratology to be finished or perfected by his efforts. But he has certainly improved the situation in this discipline, precisely by bringing together the Continental and Anglo-American theoretical traditions and by anchoring his discussion in a specific text. His "Discours du récit" will become a standard text in this field, the point of departure for future studies of fictional poetics. In the limited space that I have here I will try to show how his system refines and builds upon previous efforts in two obvious and important respects: the definition of fiction itself and the critical treatment of point-of-view.

Genette begins by suggesting that narrative discourse consists of three distinct levels that must be recognized in any critical approach to fictional works of literature. There is the story (*histoire*) which is recounted, the account itself (for which I will take over the essential French term, *récit*), and the way in which the account is presented (the *narration*). Thus when Odysseus tells the story of his adventures to the Phaeacians we have the situation of Odysseus as story-teller facing his audience (narration), the actual discourse he presents (*récit*), and the events represented in that discourse, in which Odysseus appears as a character (story). This is simple and logical enough. Genette's distinction between story and *récit* is similar to the Russian formalists' distinction between story and plot (*fable* and *sujet*). But there are differences. For the formalists, story and plot are both abstractions—they are simply two arrangements of the same events—one chronological and one motivated. But for Genette only story is an abstraction. The *récit* is real. It is the words on the page, from which we readers reconstruct both story and narration. The *récit* narrated by Odysseus is contained within the *Odyssey,* a *récit* narrated by Homer. In studying any work of fiction we must consider all three levels of the narrative and their various interactions:

> Story and narration would not exist for us without the mediation of the *récit.* But, reciprocally, the *récit,* the narrative discourse, can be what it is only by telling a story, without which it would not be narrative (like, let us say, the *Ethics* of Spinoza), and only in so far as it is presented by someone, without which (like a collection of archeological documents) it would not be discourse. As narrative, it lives by its relation to the story that it tells; as discourse, it lives from its relation to the narration that it offers. [*Figures III,* p. 74]

In examining the relations among these three dimensions of fiction, Genette considers three aspects of narrative discourse, which are based (loosely) on three qualities of the verb in language: tense, mood, and voice. Under the heading of *tense,* he considers the temporal relations between story and *récit*—the gaps, re-arrangements, and rhythmical devices of the *récit* through which we perceive the story. This is close to the formalist procedure with plot and story, and in fact incorporates that procedure. The *moods* of a fictional work involve questions of distance and perspective, scene and narrative. These are related to tense (scene being slower than narrative, sometimes drastically) but distinguishable. The concepts developed in this aspect of analysis are related to those of James and Lubbock in certain respects. Like tense, mood is a function of the relationship between story and *récit,* but more concerned with perspectives than with events. *Voice* involves the third level of fiction, narration, and its relationship with the other two: primarily the situation of the narrator with respect to the events narrated (story) and to the discourse, but also with respect to the audience he is addressing, which may be the "reader" if the narrator is "outside" the story, or a character if he is "inside." This consideration of voice is obviously related to Booth's rhetoric of fiction and to various studies of such experiments with voice as stream-of-consciousness and interior monologue. This is the place, also, where the New Critics' concern with "tone" might have entered the system, and if there is a weakness here it is in Genette's failure to incorporate sufficiently this important dimension of narrative art.

The analytical divisions that Genette has developed may seem too simple and obvious in this bald summary. The refinements he works within them would undoubtedly seem the reverse—fussy and pedantic—if they were to be squeezed into this space. Yet the great analytic achievement of this work is in his discussion of Proust's use of "iterative frequency" and the "pseudo-diegetic voice"—which must be followed in detail and with full examples to be appreciated. Therefore, I will content myself here with briefly exploring the implications of the major, or "simple," division of the features of fiction as they relate to our traditional approach to fictional point-of-view. Genette's separation of voice and mode breaks the question of point-of-view in half, and in a very fruitful way. There is a great difference between the question of mood (Who sees?) and the question of voice (Who speaks?), and this difference is perpetually obscured by our traditional way of designating fictional viewpoint either according to speech (first person, etc.) or according to vision (limited, omniscient, etc.). In the study of narration we need to attend to both the question of perspective (whose vision, how limited, when shifted) and the question of voice (whose expression, how adequate, how reliable). In *The Ambassadors* the eyes are the eyes of Strether but the voice is the voice of James, though sometimes modulating toward Strether's. In the *Recherche,* on the other hand, the voice is the voice of Marcel, and the eyes, too, are his, but both voice and eyes are so heightened by Proust himself that the perspective is at once limited (internally focused, Genette would say) and extended (externally focused), and the voice is both that of a character (internal) and that of an external narrator. This polymodal and polyvocal object that is the *Recherche* uses all the traditional devices of narration, but by combining them in ways that seemed forbidden by the old "generic laws" has indeed stretched the genre and enlarged the possibilities of fiction.

It would not be correct, and not even flattering, to suggest that Genette has enlarged the possibilities of criticism. Criticism is plagued by an excess of possibilities as it is. What we need in criticism are limits, guidelines, ways of focusing our work so that we avoid duplication and enlarge our knowledge of the whole system of literature. Like Todorov, Genette offers us just that possibility. And I should like to think that in the present survey and discussion of structuralist activity in literature, that invitation is being accepted and the possibilities of critical progress are being enhanced.

6 The Structuralist Imagination

The phrase "structuralist imagination" has a strange ring, even an eerie one. It suggests that device beloved of science fiction writers but abhorrent to the literati—the computer which (who?) thinks with human creativity. No matter how well disposed we are toward structuralism as a critical method, we want to keep man's creative activities in a special and safe place where our most humane achievements are enshrined. For precisely this reason, I think it appropriate in this chapter to explore briefly the roots of structuralist thinking in romanticism, especially in some of the best-known critical works of the British romantic poets. But beyond this it seems to me important that we understand structuralism as a force in modern literature, where it has had and will continue to have a powerful effect.

The influence of structuralist thought on modern literature can be considered from two quite different aspects. In a sense, structuralism is giving to literature with one hand and taking away from it with the other. It has given writers ideas in abundance, and I shall be illustrating this in some detail. But this is not, of course, a matter of something called Structuralism coming up to a writer and handing him a curiously shaped object with some such words as, "Here. I thought you might find it interesting to include this in your next book." On the contrary, writers as thinkers have often been in the forefront of this intellectual process. James Joyce became a structuralist long before the word was current, and for this reason I have included here a little essay on some structuralist fea-

tures of *Ulysses.* Contemporary writers of consequence, like Barth
and Coover, are also clearly thinking structuralist thoughts, both
about literature and about the whole situation of man in the cosmos. And this, too, has seemed worthy of illustration in this final
chapter.

The way in which structuralism may be said to take something
away from literature is less easy to illustrate, because it is simply
the way that all really good theoretical criticism takes something
away from literature. Every aspect of literature that can be reduced
to rules threatens to sink, as Coleridge said, "into a mechanical
art." It follows from this that to the extent that criticism, especially
general literary theory or poetics, is successful, it diminishes certain
poetic possibilities, precisely by making them mechanically available. As long as poetics merely codifies the prejudices of a particular age, it feeds creative art by providing rules to break, occasions
for originality. But to the extent that poetics can reach and explain
the true and permanent features of literary construction, it removes
territory from the creative writer, though leaving it for the hack.
Thus structuralism is a real danger to literature to the extent that
it is superior to previous critical practice, while it is a new opportunity to the extent that it merely organizes the particular prejudices
of our age.

Clearly, one may have mixed feelings about all this. But know-
nothingism or critical Ludditeism does not seem to be a real possibility for us. We are condemned to inquiry by our status as
humans. And it may be that by taking certain territory away from
writers, criticism simply challenges and stimulates literature to find
new ground for its own activities. Thus narrative art, for instance,
may take back from philosophy and journalism more than it loses
to criticism. But it is certainly true that some of the most aware
and intelligent writers of our time see the problem of exhaustion of
fictional possibilities as a real problem—and it is certainly a
problem to which the poetics of structuralism contributes. John
Barth's *Lost in the Funhouse* and *Chimera* are almost textbook illustrations of the writer as formalist/structuralist surveying with
excessively acute awareness his shrinking sphere of activity. Nor is

there much hope in trying to keep our writers ignorant. It is *our* knowledge as much as theirs which makes things difficult. Our suspicion matches their exhaustion. These are merely the same thing seen from different perspectives.

My own view of all this is not especially pessimistic. At the moment, particular literary forms seem more endangered than literature itself. And as for literature as a whole, to the extent that man requires it, it will survive as long as man, simply because it is a part of his system of life. Particular literary forms have always arisen and died in human history. There is no need to weep over this. Structuralism may help to accelerate this process for a time, as all processes in history are now accelerated, but it provides us finally with some ideological comfort, and some very necessary support, in facing our historical situation. If, as Lévi-Strauss suggests, myth is man's way of making the unbearable an acceptable part of life, then structuralism, as he admits, is itself a myth, perhaps *the* myth, for our time.

A. Romantic and Structuralist Theories of Poetic Language

To speak of romanticism and structuralism in the same breath may seem a little bit like looking for resemblances between an Aeolian harp and a computer. Romanticism, we all know, has to do with the "spontaneous overflow of powerful feelings" and structuralism with the reduction of literary texts to bloodless formulae. And yet we all know, too, that these stereotypes are both grossly inaccurate. "Romanticism" and "structuralism" are labels for immensely complex movements of mind, which constantly defy our attempts to keep them clearly categorized. My thesis here is a quite simple one. I wish to suggest that there are important connections between romantic and structuralist views of language, and, indeed, to note that we should not have a structuralism if we had not had a romanticism. But rather than talk abstractly about these complex matters, let me begin quickly with a familiar text—one so familiar that we have begun to lose contact with it entirely. In fact, it needs to be "defamiliarized"—to use a concept that is crucial in both romantic and structuralist poetics.

In the second paragraph of his *Defence of Poetry* we find Shelley discussing the nature of language and its relation to other human activities. He quickly invokes a familiar romantic icon— the Aeolian harp or lyre—as an image of the way man responds to nature:

> Man is an instrument over which a series of external and internal impressions are driven, like the alternations of an ever-changing wind over an Aeolian lyre, which move it by their motion to ever-changing melody. [Daniel G. Hoffman and Samuel Hynes, *English Literary Criticism: Romantic and Victorian,* New York, 1963, p. 161. All quotations from romantic critics are taken from this book, hereafter cited as *ELC.*]

Then, however, he moves to point out the inadequacy of this image as a figure of human mental process:

> But there is a principle within the human being, and perhaps all sentient beings, which acts otherwise than in the lyre, and produces not melody alone but harmony, by an internal adjustment of the sounds or motions thus excited to the impressions which excite them. [*ELC,* p. 161]

Man, unlike the lyre, has a harmonizing faculty which responds actively to the impressions received. And this is not all. Shelley insists further that man is a social being, whose activities have a vital and constructive effect on his verbal behavior:

> The social sympathies, or those laws from which, as from its elements, society results, begin to develop themselves from the moment that two human beings coexist; the future is contained within the present as the plant within the seed; and equality, diversity, unity, contrast, mutual dependence, become the principles, alone capable of affording the motives according to which the will of a social being is determined to

action, inasmuch as he is social; and constitute pleasure in sensation, virtue in sentiment, beauty in art, truth in reasoning, and love in the intercourse of kind. Hence men, even in the infancy of society, observe a certain order in their words and actions, distinct from that of the objects and the impressions represented by them, all expression being subject to the laws from which it proceeds. [*ELC,* p. 162]

In this extraordinary passage much of modern anthropology and linguistics may be said to be contained "as the plant within the seed," for Shelley has the spirit of a social scientist. He postulates "laws from which, as from its elements, society results," and he assumes that human language and human actions "observe a certain order" which springs naturally from the social interaction of human beings. At this point he declines to conduct "an inquiry into the principles of society itself," but returns his attention to imaginative forms of expression, and to poetry in particular, because, in his view, poetry is the form of art which expresses the imagination most directly. The other arts work through the mediation of such things as colors and forms which are external to man, while poetry works with language, which is internal:

And this springs from the nature itself of language, which is a more direct representation of the actions and passions of our internal being, and is susceptible of more various and delicate combinations than colour, form, or motion, and is more plastic and obedient to the control of that faculty of which it is the creation. For language is arbitrarily produced by the imagination, and has relation to thoughts alone. . . . [*ELC,* p. 164]

There is, of course, a romantic theory of the imagination operating here to enable Shelley's insights into the nature of language, but the insights remain standing even if the enabling theory should be discarded. Saussurean structural linguistics is founded on the notion of the "arbitrariness" of language, and all of structural anthropology and literary theory rests upon the primacy of language over other human products and activities. With or without a theory of the imagination, students of man must accept language as the primary characteristic of human existence.

To appreciate the importance of this romantic view of language for modern theoreticians, we need only consider the history of linguistic thought in the seventeenth and eighteenth centuries. I shall here draw upon the recent doctoral dissertation done at Brown University by Cyril Knoblauch, which is both thorough and illuminating. Knoblauch argues convincingly that a crucial shift in thinking about language took place between the middle of the seventeenth century and the end of the eighteenth. Though this shift was not total—indeed, some philosophers and other scholars have yet to accept it—it was gradual, massive, and to a great extent irreversible. Broadly speaking, it is a shift from an atomistic and ontological view of language (individual words representing things in reality) to a view that is contextual and epistemological (combinations of words representing mental processes). The latter view, of course, operates powerfully in the passages from Shelley quoted above, in romantic thought in general, and in all structuralist thinking about language. It is, in fact, the prevailing modern view of language. Such a view has deep roots in the past, and owes much to the grammarians of Port-Royal and to many unsung students of language in eighteenth-century England. But it received some of its most vigorous and effective support in the writings of the romantic poets.

One particular formulation, which is romantic in origin and which later entered structuralist poetics by way of the Russian formalists, will illustrate both the vitality of the "mentalist" view of language and the continuity between romanticism and structuralism. In Coleridge's *Biographia Literaria* we find him discussing Wordsworth's project in *Lyrical Ballads* in the following terms:

> Mr. Wordsworth, on the other hand, was to propose to himself as his object, to give the charm of novelty to things of every day, and to excite a feeling analogous to the supernatural, by awakening the mind's attention from the lethargy of

custom, and directing it to the loveliness and the wonders of the world before us; an inexhaustible treasure, but for which, in consequence of the film of familiarity and selfish solicitude we have eyes, yet see not, ears that hear not, and hearts that neither feel nor understand. [*ELC,* p. 44]

In the *Defence of Poetry* Shelley picks up this Coleridgean formulation and applies it to all poetry, suggesting that by making the mind a "receptacle of a thousand unapprehended combinations of thought" poetry "lifts the veil from the hidden beauty of the world, and makes familiar objects be as if they were not familiar" (*ELC,* p. 169). In a later passage he develops this idea further, in words that are a direct echo of Coleridge's. Poetry

strips the evil of familiarity from the world, and lays bare the naked and sleeping beauty, which is the spirit of its forms.

All things exist as they are perceived; at least in relation to the percipient. 'The mind is its own place, and of itself can make a heaven of hell, a hell of heaven.' But poetry defeats the curse which binds us to be subjected to the accident of surrounding impressions. And whether it spreads its own figured curtain, or withdraws life's dark veil from before the scene of things, it equally creates for us a being within our being. It makes us the inhabitants of a world to which the familiar world is a chaos. It reproduces the common universe of which we are portions and percipients, and it purges from our inward sight the film of familiarity which obscures from us the wonder of our being. It compels us to feel that which we perceive, and to imagine that which we know. It creates anew the universe, after it has been annihilated in our minds by the recurrence of impressions blunted by reiteration. [*ELC,* pp. 187–88]

Shelley's Platonism is visibly at work here, of course, but so was it in Descartes, in Port-Royal, and so is it in Chomsky. Platonism itself may prove to have been the indispensable scaffolding for the construction of a structuralism like that of Jean Piaget, who can comfortably chide Chomsky for reliance on innate schemata because his own structural thought is founded on principles of structuration as secure as the ideas of Plato. I have quoted Shelley at length, partly because I admire the vigor of his expression but also to demonstrate how closely he and Coleridge are followed by the Russian formalist Viktor Shklovsky on the subject of defamiliarization. I have quoted earlier (see chapter 4.B) a passage from a discussion of Tolstoy's *Diary,* in which Shklovsky says, "Habitualization devours objects, clothes, furniture, one's wife, and the fear of war. . . . Art exists to help us recover the sensation of life . . . to make things 'unfamiliar'."

For Shklovsky, as for Shelley and Coleridge, poetic language strips things of the film of familiarity and enables them to be seen afresh. But there is more to it than this. By suggesting that poetic language *orders* the world for us, giving us a view which makes the familiar world appear as "a chaos," Shelley is on the verge of a theory of entropy. This familiarity of which he speaks is a function of the way that information is lost in any process of communication—the cybernetic version of the second law of thermodynamics. The perceptual messages we receive from the world gradually turn it into stereotypes and clichés to which we do not attend. The only solution to this is an increased input of perceptual order—which is what poetry provides. Shklovsky carries the theory farther, by insisting that verbal art must achieve this increase in order by complicating its own structure. It must "make forms obscure, so as to increase the difficulty and the duration of perception." The romantics never carried the formulation far enough to reach this position or to see the difficulties that it involves. The formalists went on to observe that forms ultimately become overcomplicated, obstructed with conventions of their own, and require simplification and renewal through parody, which "lays bare" their own formal properties. Thus they generated a dialectical theory of literary change, in which forms beget antiforms, leading to new synthesis. The romantics never formulated the situation in this way, but they were certainly aware of the problem as no literary group before them. A sense of worn-out poetical forms is precisely what animated the writing of *Lyrical Ballads* and the Preface and Appendix which Wordsworth added to the second and third editions. In the interaction between Wordsworth and Coleridge on the subject of *Lyrical Ballads* we can see again how romanticism struggled with the same questions as structuralism and moved in the same direction for the answers.

Wordsworth, as a poet, faced the problem of worn-out forms, conventions degenerated into clichés, a whole poetic language which had itself hardened into a film of familiarity, obscuring both natural objects and human nature. With the instincts of a great poet, he set about to lay bare the devices of this stultifying poetic tradition. The Preface, and in particular the Appendix he added to it for the third edition of *Lyrical Ballads,* provided him with his occasion. He was not by instinct a parodist, so he made his criticisms in a straightforward way. And in his own works he began to construct new poetical forms on the basis of models such as the ballad, which had been neglected as a low species of literature. (This raising of "low" forms is noted by the formalists as a typical method of poetic regeneration.) By bringing something almost Miltonic to the simple situations and the simple forms that he adopted, Wordsworth succeeded in making a new kind of poetry. But he did this as a poet, without full critical awareness of his own procedures. (Whether it is accident or necessity that in the case of Wordsworth made a great poet and a lesser critic, and in the case of Coleridge a lesser poet and a great critic, I do not know. But I suspect that the ideal critic will often be a poet but rarely a major poet.) At any rate, Wordsworth, though he set about renewing poetical forms, offered only the most confused rationale for this renewal.

In the Preface to *Lyrical Ballads* we find a theory of language that is both untenable and inconsistent. Having uttered the thought that poetry is "the spontaneous overflow of powerful feelings," Wordsworth becomes the prisoner of his own phraseology. He complicates the situation further by assuming that the poet can produce but a shadow of the language that "is uttered by men in real life under the actual pressure of those passions" which the poet seeks to imitate. In fact, he sees the poet's task as "in some degree mechanical, compared with the freedom and power of real and substantial action and suffering" (*ELC,* pp. 22–23). We are a long way from Shelley here, and a long way from any plausible theory of language. Such confusion prevails in this Preface that before it is concluded we can even find Wordsworth quoting with approval Sir Joshua Reynolds, to the effect that "an *accurate* taste in poetry . . . is an *acquired* talent, which can only be produced by thought and a long-continued intercourse with the best models of composition" (*ELC,* p. 34; W's italics, my ellipsis). And at another point he observes, quite properly, I think, that readers should not be quick to judge poetry, since "it is not probable they will be so well acquainted with the various stages of meaning through which words have passed" (*ELC,* p. 32) as is the poet. There is simply no way that these latter two statements can be reconciled with the view of poetic language developed earlier in the same text.

In his critique of all this, Coleridge is no less devastating because he is very gentle. He shows his friend, who is by far the greater poet, as Coleridge acknowledges, to be a critical fool. It is no wonder that they quarreled. But I cite all this not so as to get embroiled in that personal history but because in the difference between the views of language held by the two men we see precisely the shift in linguistic thought which marks the beginning of structural poetics. In chapter 17 of the *Biographia,* Coleridge quotes a revealing passage in which Wordsworth stated that he chose to adopt the language of low and rustic life because of its use by men who "hourly communicate with the best objects from which the best part of language is originally derived." Before turning to Coleridge's own criticism of this view, let us explore its implications a bit. Wordsworth here subscribes to a view of language which goes back to the Renaissance and beyond, and which Cyril Knoblauch has characterized as ontological. In this view, things are the creators of words, and language is simply the total of all the words which men have derived from the things around them. Wordsworth accepts this view with almost touching simplicity, insisting that the "best objects," that is, natural objects like trees and mountains, will produce in man the best language. This view, it should also be noticed, is essentially atomistic: object produces word; language is simply a collection of words; its relational properties— crucial to the structural view of language—are ignored.

Now let us consider Coleridge's reaction. His passage on the subject, though masterful, is too long to quote entirely, so I must summarize a bit of it. First, Coleridge denies that a rustic's language will differ from that of "any other men of common-sense" except that the rustic will have "fewer and more indiscriminate" notions to convey. Second, and equally important, the rustic will be inferior to the more cultivated man linguistically, because his speech "aims almost solely to convey *insulated facts* . . . while the educated man chiefly seeks to discover and express those *connections* of things, or those relative *bearings* of fact to fact, from which some more or less general law is deducible" (*ELC,* p. 66; C's italics, my ellipsis). Coleridge thus locates the distinction between rustic and educated language precisely at the point which divides the atomic from the structural properties of language. And he develops this view in an extraordinary passage which relates the "best part of language" not to external objects but to human mental processes:

> . . . I deny that the words and combinations of words derived from objects, with which the rustic is familiar, whether with distinct or confused knowledge, can be justly said to form the *best* part of language. It is more than probable, that many classes of the brute creation possess discriminating sounds, by which they can convey to each other notices of such objects as concern their food, shelter, or safety. Yet we hesitate to call the aggregate of such sounds a language, otherwise than metaphorically. The best part of human language, properly so called, is derived from reflection of the acts of the mind itself. It is formed by a voluntary appropriation of fixed symbols to internal acts, to processes and results of imagination, the greater part of which have no place in the consciousness of uneducated man. . . . [*ELC,* p. 67]

Shelley learned from this—we have all learned from this—
how to view language in a structural way. This is not, I wish to
emphasize, a mere episode in the history of taste, but a genuine discovery about the nature of language and its workings. Coleridge's
examinations of specific passages in Wordsworth and other poets
derive their authority from the strength of his linguistic grasp.
Thus in looking at Wordsworth's practice he considers not only
the diction but the syntax as well—the "order," as he calls it, of
the words. The limitations of rustic language he relates to the inability of the uneducated "so to subordinate and arrange the different parts according to their relative importance, as to convey [an
idea] at once and as an organized whole" (*ELC.* pp. 70–71).
And he locates the difference between Wordsworth's own language
and the real language of men precisely in the poet's extraordinary
syntax, which makes his language more "compact" than ordinary
speech. In doing this Coleridge was not "inventing" a new linguistic theory from whole cloth. We know how little in the world of
thought is ever invented by anyone, and how little Coleridge in
particular liked to invent when he could borrow. What we must
credit Coleridge with is the ability to tell the difference between a
live idea and a dead one, and the ability to apply, extend, unite,
and enrich the best that was being thought and said around him.
And if this be not a kind of thought, too, and far from the least
kind, then most of us had better not lay claim to thinking at all,
for we do far less than he.

Coleridge remains the great contributor to English poetic
thought because he seized so firmly on the principles of a develop-
ing structuralism, enunciated them so clearly, and embodied them
so concretely in that discussion of actual works which he called
"practical criticism." Later writers have refined the tools, altered
the concepts, and learned to deal more or less adequately with a
range of texts he could not have envisioned. But there is little of
his thinking about poetical language which has been seriously
weakened by modern structural poetics, of which he is, indeed, if
not the father then a genial and benevolent uncle. In English poetics he first established the priority of epistemology over ontology,

giving us a theory of the imagination that both science and art
could live with, and have lived with and by, for over a century.
The last Coleridgean passage I will quote deals with his theory of
imagination, not in the familiar echoes of German idealism and
transcendentalism, but as an almost scientific instrument for controlling perception. By what rule, he has asked, does the poet determine the validity of his language. His answer will lead him to
say that no external rule can be given, for "could a rule be given
from *without,* poetry would cease to be poetry, and sink into a mechanical art." And as for the internal rule, he asks,

> Is it obtained by wandering about in search of angry or jeal-
> ous people in uncultivated society, in order to copy their
> words? Or not far rather by the power of imagination pro-
> ceeding upon the *all in each* of human nature? By *meditation*
> rather than by *observation?* And by the latter in consequence
> only of the former? As eyes, for which the former has prede-
> termined their field of vision, and to which, as to *its* organ, it
> communicates a microscopic power? [*ELC,* p. 88; C's italics]

This image of the imagination as a great microscopic lens, which
determines our intellectual field of vision in seeking the laws of
human behavior, is a long way from the Aeolian harp in the direction of the computer. And it is Coleridge himself who has taken us
there. Thinking of how well his gifts might suit the present age,
we may be tempted to paraphrase his friend and say "Coleridge,
thou shouldst be living at this hour!"—but we need not, for he is
alive and will be, as long as the system of ideas to which he contributed continues to function—as it does in the literary and linguistic theory of structuralism.

B. Ulysses: *A Structuralist Perspective*

"We are still learning to be Joyce's contemporaries." So ran the
opening words of Richard Ellmann's *James Joyce* in 1959—and
they are still appropriate. But in the past decade critics who have
learned the lessons of structuralism have at the same time been

learning how to read Joyce. For the later Joyce in particular—the Joyce of the last chapters of *Ulysses* and of *Finnegans Wake* —was a man who had adopted an essentially structuralist view of the world. The reluctance of some critics to accept the mature work of Joyce can thus be seen as an aspect of a larger reluctance, an unwillingness to accept the implications of structuralism. In a very real sense, some of us do not *want* to become Joyce's contemporaries, and we find the collapse of individuated characterization in the later Joyce as threatening as the loss of our own identities in some dystopian nightmare of the future. But it is precisely this structuralist aspect of Joyce's work that we must learn to accept if we are to come to grips with our own situation and the future of man in the universe. For structuralism, like any other way of understanding things, is a response to particular conditions. To reject its larger implications is a refusal to enter the contemporary situation—which is to succumb to the temptation of withdrawal from the world, a temptation which has never been stronger than it presently is.

The extraordinary differences between Joyce's early and late work are not the results of idiosyncratic stylistic experimentation so much as they are aspects of a radical redefinition of the world itself and man's place in it. This redefinition has been summed up neatly and vigorously in a recent collection of essays by Gregory Bateson called *Steps to an Ecology of Mind* (New York, 1972):

> In the period of the Industrial Revolution, perhaps the most important disaster was the enormous increase of scientific arrogance. We had discovered how to make trains and other machines. . . . Occidental man saw himself as an autocrat with complete power over a universe which was made of physics and chemistry. And the biological phenomena were in the end to be controlled like processes in a test tube. Evolution was the history of how organisms learned more tricks for controlling the environment; and man had better tricks than any other creature.
>
> But that arrogant scientific philosophy is now obsolete, and

in its place there is the discovery that man is only a part of larger systems and that the part can never control the whole. [p. 437]

In short, this redefinition of the world has put something like God back in the universe—but not a God made in man's image, bursting with individualism and subject to temper tantrums when His will is thwarted. But a God who truly "is not mocked" because It *is* the plan of the universe, the master system which sets the pattern for all others. This God cannot intercede for His chosen favorites and suspend the natural law. Nor can He promise comforts in some afterworld for pain endured here. Here is where It is. God is immanent. It offers us only the opportunity to learn Its ways and take pleasure in conforming to them. For certainly there is only frustration in trying to thwart them.

If in some ways this resembles the theology of Dante, then so be it. It would be a strange comment on the ecology of ideas if Catholicism could persist for two millennia without a grain of truth in its theology. The point of this is that Dublin's Dante could work himself into a structuralist position more easily by taking medieval theology as a point of departure than could someone handicapped by conversion to a more "reasonable" world view. The intellectual position Joyce arrived at has much in common with that of Lévi-Strauss, or Piaget, or Bateson. Let us consider Bateson again, with Joyce's later work specifically in mind:

Ecology currently has two faces to it: the face which is called bioenergetics—the economics of energy and materials within a coral reef, a redwood forest, or a city—and, second, an economics of information, of entropy, negentropy, etc. These two do not fit together very well precisely because the units are differently bounded in the two sorts of ecology. In bioenergetics it is natural and appropriate to think of units bounded at the cell membrane, or at the skin; or of units composed of conspecific individuals. These boundaries are then the frontiers at which measurements can be made to determine the additive-subtractive budget of energy for a given unit. In contrast, informational or entropic ecology deals with the budgeting of pathways and probability. The resulting budgets are fractionating (not subtractive). The boundaries must enclose, not cut, the relevant pathways.

Moreover, the very meaning of "survival" becomes different when we stop talking of something bounded by the skin and start to think of the survival of the system of ideas in the circuit. The contents of the skin are randomized at death and the pathways within the skin are randomized. But the ideas, under further transformation, may go on out in the world in books or works of art. Socrates as a bioenergetic individual is dead. But much of him still lives as a component in the ecology of ideas. [p. 461]

It is clear to me that Joyce is one of the few writers of his time, perhaps the only one, who arrived at a concept of fiction which is cybernetic rather than bioenergetic. As his career developed, he accepted less and less willingly the notion of characters bounded by their own skins, and of actions which take place at one location in space-time and then are lost forever. Unlike Lawrence, for instance, who reacted against "the old stable ego of the character" simply by giving us characters with unstable egos, Joyce attacked the ego itself, beginning with his own. But not initially. The cybernetic serenity of his later work was long coming and hard won. For he had a good deal of ego to disperse. Nothing could be sharper than the division between self and others as we find it in his early Epiphanies, with their focus upon the verbal or gestural "vulgarity" of others and the "memorable" phases of his own mental life. This same bioenergetic separation persists through *Stephen Hero, Dubliners,* and *A Portrait.* Though there are hints of it in this latter work, it is only in *Ulysses* that we really find the ego breaking down. I think it is reasonable to say that Stephen Dedalus is Joyce's bioenergetic self-portrait, while Leopold Bloom is his cybernetic self-portrait.

Since Ellmann's biography of Joyce, we have complacently referred to Bloom as well as Stephen as "autobiographical"—but surely we need to distinguish between these two kinds of autobiography. And it is not enough to say that Stephen is a young Joyce and Bloom is a mature Joyce. For Stephen "is" Joyce in a different way from the way Bloom "is" Joyce. Stephen is Joyce in his skin, with all the significant features that would make him recognizable. And with no features that Joyce himself did not possess. Insofar as Joyce could create a "true" self-portrait, Stephen is that portrait (somewhat retouched from book to book). But Bloom contains large elements of Joyce's neural circuitry without being recognizable as Joyce; and at some important levels of experience he is a "truer" representation of Joyce than Stephen. But that cellular integrity which marks Stephen as Joyce himself and not any other person is lacking in Bloom. He is a Joyce interpenetrated with others; with the far-wandering Odysseus and with a pathetic Dubliner that the Joyce family actually knew. (And with other figures from life and art as well.) This characterization of the peripathetic Bloom is remarkable not because it shows Joyce creating a great character who is unautobiographical, but because it shows us an autobiographical characterization without egocentricity.

If Flaubert truly thought of Emma Bovary on occasions as himself ("C'est moi!"), he must have donned her skin with a naturalistic frisson, prompted by his sense of how different it was from his own. But for Joyce in *Ulysses* there is no hint of such *nostalgie de la boue.* He lived *là-bas,* and thus his works lack the delight in slumming which is often one aspect of naturalism. And by the time of *Finnegans Wake* he had come to accept the Homais in himself as Flaubert never could. It might also be well to recall at this point how in the *Wake* Joyce's ego is not only diffused among the whole range of major figures and minor; it has also spread out to include the "inanimate" rivers, rocks, and trees of Dublin and the world. Which ought to remind us that if Beckett is Joyce's heir, he is a model of filial rebellion. For the nausea and alienation he has chronicled so articulately are the very antitheses of the acceptance of the ecosystem that animates *Finnegans Wake.*

Ulysses is a transitional work par excellence—in Joyce's treatment of his own ego and in many other respects as well. This very transitional nature of the book has led one school of critics (call it the Goldberg variation) to see the book as a failed novel, which goes off the novelistic track in the later chapters due to Joyce's self-indulgence in various linguistic capers. It would be just as reasonable to invert this critique and see the early chapters as a false start of somewhat too traditional flavor, corrected by the brilliant new devices of the last part. These views I reject as equally wrong. *Ulysses* is a transitional work for us as well as for Joyce. In reading it we learn how to read it; our comprehension is exercised and stretched. We are led gradually to a method of narration and to a view of man (the two inseparable) different from those found in previous fiction. It is this method and this view that I am calling structuralist.

In testing this thesis against the mass of *Ulysses* in such short space, much will have to be taken for granted. But I will try to look at certain representative aspects of *Ulysses* in the light of a few structuralist notions derived from Saussurean linguistics and the genetic epistemology of Jean Piaget, beginning with Piaget's definition of structure as comprising the idea of *wholeness,* the idea of *transformation,* and the idea of *self-regulation.* This triad leads to a more satisfying aesthetic than the one Joyce called "applied Aquinas," and in fact it is more applicable to Joyce's later work. But before applying it we must elaborate on it a little bit. By *wholeness* Piaget indicates elements arranged according to laws of combination rather than merely lumped together as an aggregate. Such wholeness is a quality of all recognizable literary works. It is, in fact, one way we recognize them. They have the wholeness of all linguistic utterances and the more intense wholeness of discourse specifically literary. Since this is a characteristic of all fiction, it need not be especially remarked in *Ulysses.* By *transformation* Piaget means the ability of parts of a structure to be interchanged or modified according to certain rules, and he specifically cites transformational linguistics as an illustration of such processes. In *Ulysses* the metempsychotic way in which Bloom and Odysseus are related is one notable principle of transformation, and there are other transformational aspects of the book to which we

will return. By *self-regulation* Piaget refers to the "interplay of an-
ticipation and correction (feedback)" in cybernetic systems and to
"the rhythmic mechanisms such as pervade biology and human life
at every level." Self-regulating structures are both "self-maintain-
ing" and "closed." I would like to suggest that in *Ulysses* the Homeric parallels function as a kind of feedback loop, operating to correct imbalance and brake any tendency of the work to run away in
the direction of merely random recitations from Bloom's day. And
there are many other such loops. Each chapter, in fact, is designed
to run down when certain schematic systems are complete and
when a certain temporal segment of the Dublin day has been covered. Whereupon the next Homeric parallel is activitated to provide a diachronic scheme for the following chapter.

This system can be illustrated by a brief consideration of the
much maligned "Oxen of the Sun" chapter. It exhibits all of the
structural properties I have been discussing, and can thus serve to
illustrate their working in some detail. This chapter is basically a
simple narrative segment of the day: Stephen and Bloom happen
to come to the same place, a lying-in hospital where Mrs. Purefoy
is engaged in a long and difficult accouchement. After young Mortimer Edward is born, Stephen and some medical students, accompanied or followed by Bloom, go off to a pub for some superfluous
drinking. This base narrative is transformed according to a complex set of rules. Rule 1: the events must be narrated by a sequence
of voices that illustrate the chronological movement of English
prose from the Middle Ages to contemporary times. Rule 2: each
voice must narrate an appropriate segment of the events taking
place. That is, a Pepysian voice must deal with Pepysian details
and a Carlylean voice with a Carlylean celebration. Which assumes Rule 3: the voices must be pastiches or parodies of clearly
recognizable stylists or stylistic schools.

The purpose of these rules is not merely to show off Joyce's skill
as a parodist and pasticher, which is considerable, but to enrich our
experience of the characters presented and events narrated. And it
is their interaction which gives shape to events that in themselves
are only minimally shapely. In this chapter Joyce operates with

roughly six sets of narrative materials, to be arranged according to these rules. He has Bloom's present words and deeds, plus his thoughts of the past, and the same two sets of present and past for Stephen. He also has the simultaneous actions of the medical students, Haines, and so on, along with a sixth item, the birth itself. The selection of what comes when, in the necessarily linear sequence of prose narrative, is thus the result of a complex interaction among these rules and sets of possibilities. (The Homeric parallel, in this chapter, offered the initial idea, but had less influence on structure than in some other chapters.) In this chapter, the selection of the moment of birth, for instance, is saved from arbitrariness by the appropriateness of the voices of Dickens and Carlyle to celebrate the new arrival. And if *they* are to celebrate him, young Mortimer must appear in the middle of the nineteenth century, the era of phyloprogenitiveness. Similarly, the drunken conversation that closes the chapter functions in a structural way because it is a linguistic transformation of the antistructural randomization of an afterbirth: a mélange of entropic noise. It is what structure prevents *Ulysses* from becoming, though for those who cannot perceive the structure it is precisely what the book seems to be.

This kind of structure, of course, is a function of Joyce's massive unwillingness to get on with it and tell a simple linear tale. And thereby hangs a good deal of critical hostility. In discussing this aspect of *Ulysses* the terminology from linguistics that is discussed in some detail in chapter 2 will be helpful. (The reader is advised to turn back for a moment to pages 18–19.) Extrapolating from the linguistic distinction between syntagmatic and paradigmatic aspects of verbal communication, it is customary in structuralist literary theory to see narrative literature as a transformation by enlargement of our basic sentence structure. Characters are nouns; their situations or attributes are adjectives; and their actions are verbs. (Cf., for instance, Todorov's formulation of narrative "parts of speech" on page 113, above.) And fiction is defined by its emphasis of the syntagmatic or linear (horizontal) dimension of linguistic possibilities, whereas poetry is less concerned with syntagmatic progression and more inclined to play with paradigmatic possibilities.

Joyce, in *Ulysses,* is often very reluctant to speed along the syntagmatic trail like an Agatha Christie. Often, it is as if he cannot bear to part with many of the paradigmatic possibilities that have occurred to him. He will stop and climb up the paradigmatic chain on all sorts of occasions, such as the various lists in "Cyclops," in which displaced possibilities are allowed to sport themselves and form syntagmatic chains of their own. These lists *do become* syntagmatic in themselves, and they further relate to other lists and other parts of the whole narrative in a syntagmatic way. A book as long as *Ulysses* which was really paradigmatic in its emphasis would be virtually impossible to read—as *Ulysses* is for those who do not see its structure. But even the lists in *Ulysses* if examined closely will prove to have both an internal syntagmatic dimension and an external one.

The lists in "Cyclops," for instance, tend to follow some basic comic laws which depend on syntagmatic expectation. For instance, they may establish an innocent pattern, apparently a simple process of repetition, and then violate it while appearing to continue in the same manner—as in this sequence from the opening of the list of ladies attending the "wedding of the grand high chief ranger of the Irish National Foresters with Miss Fir Conifer of Pine Valley. Lady Sylvester Elmshade, Mrs Barbara Lovebirch . . ." and so on (*Ulysses,* New York, 1961, p. 327). We quickly pick up the basic principle of these names—or we think we do. There is to be an appropriateness between the first and last names of these arboreal damsels which makes it amusing to consider them. Such names further down the list as "Miss Timidity Aspenall" or "Miss Grace Poplar" are constructed by animating an attribute of the tree names in the last name and deriving a first name from this attribute. Poplars are graceful and aspens quake. (And by extension, Miss rather than Mrs is appropriate for them too.) In this list, the opening "Fir Conifer" and "Sylvester Elmshade" establish this pattern without being as clever as some of the later combinations—thus allowing for some syntagmatic progression. But this pattern is enriched by some others, which add a different kind of comedy to the list and complicate its syntagmatic relationships. That third name, "Barbara Lovebirch," introduces into this green world the whole motif of sadomasochistic perversion that will culminate in the "Circe" chapter. The name "Lovebirch" not only includes the masochistic idea but refers to the author of the pornographic novel *Fair Tyrants* (James Lovebirch), which Bloom has inspected in "Wandering Rocks" and rejected ("Had it? Yes.") as not so much in Molly's line as *Sweets of Sin.* And of course in "Circe" Mrs Yelverton Barry accuses Bloom of making "improper overtures" to her under the *nom de plume* of James Lovebirch. Among the list of innocent trees the barbaric lovebirch is comically sinister. And once directed this way the reader may well see sexual connotations lurking beneath every bush. Is "Mrs Kitty Dewey-Mosse" innocent? Thus even what appears to be a purely paradigmatic excursion in *Ulysses* proves to have a system of its own and beyond that to exhibit connections of the syntagmatic sort with other events and episodes.

The process illustrated here in little is related to the larger processes of the book. The "Oxen of the Sun" is written as it is not merely to vary our perspective on Stephen and Bloom, showing aspects of them that could only be shown through the styles employed. The chapter also represents an acknowledgment of all the narrative voices that have been displaced by Joyce in uttering *Ulysses.* The whole chapter is a climb up a particular paradigmatic ladder on the level of style. And it serves not only to throw new light on Bloom and Stephen. It also takes Bloom and Stephen and the whole world of *Ulysses* back through the system of English literature and allows this work of 1922 to intermingle with the past. If Carlyle's voice can celebrate Theodore Purefoy in 1922, then Carlyle's cybernetic self still lives through Joyce's agency. And if the "Oxen of the Sun" chapter serves partly to install Bloom and Stephen among the literature of the past, the "Ithaca" chapter serves a similar purpose with respect to science.

The technological and scientific perspectives of "Ithaca" extend Bloom and Stephen to new dimensions without aggrandizing them—and without dwarfing them as is sometimes contended.

The final lesson of the "Ithaca" chapter is one of the most deeply imbedded meanings in the entire book. At the end of the chapter, after a day of anxiety, Bloom rearrives at an equilibrium which is not merely that of a body at rest but that of a self-regulated system operating in harmony with other systems larger than itself. He views his wife's adulterous episode "with more abnegation than jealousy, less envy than equanimity" for a very important reason. Because it is "not more abnormal than all other altered processes of adaptation to altered conditions of existence, resulting in a reciprocal equilibrium between the bodily organism and its attendant circumstances . . ." (p. 733). Blazes Boylan is Molly's adjustment to Bloom's sexual retreat. As she might say herself, "It's only natural." Bloom is homeostatic man, centripetal, his equilibrium achieved. And Stephen is young, therefore centrifugal, and therefore to be forgiven. In time he too will return, like Shakespeare reading the book of himself, and writing it too. Stephen and Bloom and Molly have other roles to play in *Finnegans Wake,* permutations and combinations hardly dreamed of in 1922. And for this total achievement, we may say of Joyce what Bateson said of Socrates. As a bioenergetic individual he is indeed dead. "But much of him still lives in the ecology of ideas."

C. The Vision of Structuralism
in Contemporary Fiction

In the structuralist vision of man, a new awareness of the nature of language and the processes of thought has led to a new awareness of human universality. Structuralism, with its necessary adjunct, transformationalism, has worked against nationalism and against egotism in general. In the sciences, the structuralist imagination has emphasized the universal and systematic at the expense of the individual and idiosyncratic. And it would be a very *un*systematic world indeed if the arts remained oblivious to these new emphases. That writers of fiction, in particular, who deal in the creation of complex systematic wholes, should prove attuned to structuralist ideas and attitudes ought not to surprise us. The resurgence of interest in mythology, among both writers and critics, is an aspect of the general structuralist movement in fiction. But more specific evidence of structuralist awareness can be found in the work of contemporary writers of fiction—as in the two passages I am about to quote from Robert Coover and John Barth. In the Dedication and Prologue of *Pricksongs and Descants,* Coover addresses Miguel de Cervantes on the subject of fictional creation:

> But, *don* Miguel, the optimism, the innocence, the aura of possibility you experienced have been largely drained away, and the universe is closing in on us again. Like you, we, too, seem to be standing at the end of one age and on the threshold of another. We, too, have been brought into a blind alley by the critics and analysts; we, too, suffer from a "literature of exhaustion," though ironically our nonheros are no longer tireless and tiresome Amadises, but hopelessly defeated and bed-ridden Quixotes. We seem to have moved from an open-ended, anthropocentric, humanistic, naturalistic, even—to the extent that man may be thought of as making his own universe—optimistic starting point, to one that is closed, cosmic, eternal, supernatural (in its soberest sense), and pessimistic. The return to Being has returned us to Design, to microcosmic images of the macrocosm, to the creation of Beauty within the confines of cosmic or human necessity, to the use of the fabulous to probe beyond the phenomenological, beyond appearances, beyond randomly perceived events, beyond mere history. [New York, 1969, p. 78]

Coover is obviously not a programmatic structuralist. But in considering the situation of fiction at the present time, he is led to a line of thought that has strong affinities with structuralism. And it is worth noting that despite the difficulties he sees so clearly, his paragraph continues and concludes on a note of life and energy:

> But these probes are above all—like your Knight's sallies —challenges to the assumptions of a dying age, exemplary adventures of the Poetic Imagination, high-minded journeys

toward the New World and never mind that the nag's a pile of bones.

It is precisely on a high-minded journey of the poetic imagination toward the new world that John Barth's character Ebenezer Cooke experiences what we might call a structuralist epiphany—a moment of illumination which echoes (quite unconsciously, I am certain) the experience of Lévi-Strauss among the "sad tropics" of America. The French anthropologist acquired his sense of human universality while living among the primitive tribes of Brazil. Ebenezer learns a similar lesson while facing torture and death at the hands of the escaped slaves and "salvages" of Maryland:

The point in space and time whereto the history of the world had brought him would be nothing perilous were it not for the hostility of the Indians and Negroes. But it was their exploitation by the English colonists that had rendered them hostile; that is to say, by a people whom the accidents of history had made in many ways superior—Ebenezer did not doubt that his captors, if circumstances were reversed, would do just what the English were doing. To the extent, then, that historical movements are expressions of the will of the people engaged in them, Ebenezer was a just object for his captors' wrath, for he belonged, in a deeper sense than McEvoy had intended in his remark of some nights past, to the class of the exploiters; as an educated gentleman of the western world he had shared in the fruits of his culture's power and must therefore share what guilt that power incurred. Nor was this the end of his responsibility: for if it was the accidents of power and position that made the difference between exploiters and exploited, and not some mysterious specialization of each group's psyche, then it was as "human" for the white man to enslave and dispossess as it was "human" for the black and red to slaughter on the basis of color alone; the savage who would put him to the torch anon was no less his brother than was the trader who had once enslaved that savage. In sum, the poet observed, for his secular Original Sin, though he was to atone for it in person, he would exact a kind of Vicarious Retribution; he had committed a grievous crime against himself, and it was himself who soon would punish the malefactor! [*The Sot-Weed Factor,* New York, 1964, p. 579]

For all his Colonial trappings, Ebenezer is of course a quintessentially modern man, especially in such passages as this one, which has its affinities with the zany speculations of McLuhan and the optimistic evangelism of Charles Reich. Structuralist thinking is having a powerful effect on the contemporary novel, which I shall explore in more detail before concluding. But one aspect of this effect has naturally been a decline of fictional individuation of character and a resurgence of typification. And another aspect has been an increase in novels where structure dominates character as it did not in the best fiction of the previous century. But these changes ought not to be seen as either pure loss or pure gain. They are a mixture, of course, for fiction. But the greatest achievements of one mode of narration can never be duplicated by another. The decline of the epic and the rise of the novel complement one another as neatly as the phases of the moon.

The change in the vision of man which we find in contemporary fiction implies a whole new ideology, with implications for every aspect of human existence including the political aspect. A structuralist politics implies in particular a move away from adversary relationships in political processes at every level, to the extent that this is possible: away from combat between countries, between parties, between factions, and above all between man and nature. The ideological implications of structuralism can be seen by contrasting it with another powerful modern ideology: existentialism—especially the existential Marxism that has played such a vigorous role in recent European political thought.

Existentialism has produced an ethic that places freedom and choice at the center of the human condition, and a politics that has combined with Marxism and Freudianism to construct an attractive vision of a future in which all men are free, equal, and fulfilled human beings. The trouble with existential Marxism is that it has put its faith in history and history has betrayed it. The political vision of existentialism has ended in Marcuse's picture of a managed society in which a perceptive elite imposes freedom on the passive masses. And its personal vision has ended in R. D. Laing, who finally advocates madness as the solution to the problem of arriving at a sane existence. Among the few public figures who have been able to maintain the delicate balance required of an existentialist political thinker is the dean of existentialism himself, Jean-Paul Sartre. And Sartre, more and more, has found that a man can be an existentialist only if he abandons his position in a dominant society and plays a role in the revolutionary aspirations of the Third World. In existentialist politics, the revolution cannot be enacted, it can only be re-enacted. To have a good revolution one must first return to the conditions that prevailed in the nineteenth century—or possibly the eighteenth century. One must, in fact, reverse history. Hence the despair of current existentialist thought.

The relationship of structuralism to existentialism can be illustrated in the relationship between Sartre and Claude Lévi-Strauss. Existential Marxism assumes that man is *in history,* moving toward a better future in a progressive way. Structuralism assumes that man is in a system not necessarily arranged for his benefit. Structuralism has accepted the main insights of modern science as existentialism has not. In particular, the structuralist sees the human truth embodied in the physical principle of relativitity. What Einstein demonstrated in the early part of this century was that all measurement is a matter of the frame of reference in which the measurement is made. One and one make two—sometimes. Other times, seen from another standpoint, they add up to one, not two. Translated to human terms by Lévi-Strauss, the relativity principle leads to an attack on the liberal notion of historical truth. For Lévi-Strauss there is not one history but many, and each one, he says, "is the interpretation which philosophers or historians give of their own mythology, and which I would consider as a variant of mythology."

Sartre has replied to this, and accused structuralism of being a trick of the bourgeoisie, an attempt to substitute for the Marxist vision of evolution a closed, inert system where order is privileged at the expense of change. Put simply, Sartre feels that men live in history and seek refuge from it in myth; while Lévi-Strauss feels that men live in myth and seek refuge from it in history. For Lévi-Strauss, history is a myth that men make up for their own satisfaction. But what looks like progress to the historian is only transformation or displacement to the structuralist. Seen from its own perspective, every society has the best values, better than those of any other society. But rightly understood, the values of one society are merely transformations of the values of another.

This intellectual struggle between existentialism and structuralism is closely related to the history of fiction in our time. Most serious novelists of the past few decades have either consciously or unconsciously operated out of an existentialist perspective. And much literary criticism has been distinctly existentialist in its techniques and values. Thus it is highly significant that some of our best novelists have begun their work as existentialists only to move in the direction of structuralism. This movement can be observed with striking clarity in the work of Iris Murdoch, John Fowles, and John Barth.

Iris Murdoch's first book was a study of Jean-Paul Sartre, in which she criticized him for his failure as a novelist.

> Sartre has an impatience with the *stuff* [her italics] of human life. He has, on the one hand, a lively interest, often slightly morbid, in the details of contemporary living, and, on the other a passionate desire to analyse, to build intellectually pleasing schemes and patterns. But the feature which might enable these two talents to fuse into the work of a great novelist is absent, namely an apprehension of the absurd irreducible uniqueness of people and of their relations with each other. [*Sartre, Romantic Rationalist,* New Haven, 1953, p. 118]

This statement and other citations of F. R. Leavis and George Eliot in her book show that, if anything, Iris Murdoch's view of fiction was more traditionally liberal than Sartre's, before she began her own fictional work. And in her first novel, *Under the Net,* she deliberately sought to render concretely her existential sense of human uniqueness and the contingency of human existence. In the dozen or so novels she has written since that time she has returned again and again to the great concerns of formal existentialist philosophy, especially the problem of freedom. But her treatment of these matters has grown increasingly critical of existentialist dogma, and the shape of her fiction, as she has acknowledged, has become more and more deliberately patterned and structured.

In a footnote to her chapter on "Picturing Consciousness" in *Sartre,* she had noted that

> the striking symbol of the petrifying Medusa is interpreted by Freud as a castration fear (*Collected Papers,* vol. v). Sartre of course regards as its basic sense our general fear of being observed (*L'Etre et le Néant,* p. 502). It is interesting to speculate on how one would set about deciding which interpretation was "correct." [p. 97]

When she came to use that very image as the central symbol of her novel *A Severed Head,* she found a meaning in it that neither Freud nor Sartre had considered. In that novel, Alexander Lynch-Gibbon reminds his brother of Freud on Medusa: "The head can represent the female genitals, feared not desired." And Martin replies that any savage likes to collect heads. Later, when Martin falls violently in love with the incestuous anthropologist Honor Klein, who has lived in strange places and done strange deeds, he is told by this frightening lady,

> I am a severed head such as primitive tribes and old alchemists used to use, annointing it with oil and putting a morsel of gold upon its tongue to make it utter prophecies. And who knows but that long acquaintance with a severed head might not lead to strange knowledge. For such knowledge one would have paid enough. [New York, 1966 p. 198]

In the novel, Martin Lynch-Gibbon must accept his Freudian or Sartrean fear of this incarnation of Medusa and make an existential leap beyond the pleasure principle to reach her love. But the novelist herself in this central image is figuring her own leap from Sartrean freedom to Lévi-Straussean order, from contingency to pattern, from existentialism to structuralism. For the severed head represents literature itself, which, unlike philosophy, speaks mantically, like an oracle (as Roland Barthes, following Hegel, has argued in an essay entitled "L'Activité Structuraliste"). If, as I believe, Iris Murdoch is a greater novelist than Sartre, it is not—as she might have hoped—because she has captured the "absurd irreducible uniqueness" of people but because she has illustrated their rational similarity and relatedness. This is why the dominant motif of all her work has been not alienation but its opposite: love.

And here a word needs to be said on the relationship between structuralism and love. In saying this word—and in speaking of structuralism as an ideology at all—I am going beyond what many structuralists would say themselves. Men like Jean Piaget and Roland Barthes insist that structuralism is an activity or a method, not an ideology. But I believe (with the Marxists) that any method implies its ideology, and structuralism is no exception. Furthermore, it is precisely the ideology of structuralism that we need most desperately today. And this is where love comes in. It is in the differentiation of the sexes that we learn our earliest and deepest lessons about sameness and difference. Sexual differentiation is the basis, not only of our social systems, but of our logic as well. If there were three sexes, our computers would not have begun to think in terms of binary oppositions.

Beyond this, it is in the rhythms of sexuality, the various periodicities of sperm production, menstruation, courtship, and coitus, that our sense of narrative structure is itself generated. It is because narrative structures bend time to human will that we delight in them so. Rhythm is man's triumph over mere chronology, his way of making time dance to a human tune. This is nowhere more apparent than in the temporal structures of fiction, in which repetition, periodicity, and climax give shape and meaning to the course of events. In fiction, as in life, the coming together of two human beings in the sexual embrace of love represents the reconciliation of all opposites, the peaceful resolution of all disputes, the melting of all swords into plowshares. In such an embrace, the cyclical dominates the temporal, the lovers are united with all lovers, and we partake of the universal. Marriage is a sacrament of structuralism. It is also precisely the point at which structural ideas and fictional structure are brought into the closest correspondence. From ancient fiction to modern, the structural pattern of courtship and marriage, separation and union, has been one of the most persistent and popular. It has proved capable of the highest development and the most basic appeal. Love stories and allegories of love have gone hand in hand since the "Song of Songs" and even before that. Therefore, it is most natural and fitting that a structuralist fiction should have embraced this most durable of patterns and quickened it with new life.

Like Iris Murdoch, John Fowles has followed the path from existentialism toward structuralism, though not quite so far nor in exactly the same way. The exploration of human freedom has led him to write of the necessity for love. And the investigation of time (which few writers have handled more adroitly) has led him to a view of life that transcends time. This is the vision that emerges from *The French Lieutenant's Woman*—from the novel as a whole and specifically in passages such as this one:

> In a vivid insight, a flash of black lightning, he saw that all life was parallel: that evolution was not vertical, ascending to perfection, but horizontal. Time was the great fallacy; existence was without history, was always now, was always being caught in the same fiendish machine. All those painted screens erected by man to shut out reality—history, religion, duty, social position, all were illusions, mere opium fantasies. [New York, 1970, p. 165]

Because men see things and women see the relationships between things, as one of his characters puts it, total vision depends on men and women uniting in love. And the artist is likely to be himself an Eve-man or herself an Adam-woman. Vision, for Fowles, becomes finally a union between an essentially male, existentialist perspective and an essentially female, structuralist perception. This is why *The Magus* is both a hymn to freedom and an allegory of love. The free man must use his freedom to choose his proper mythic role in the ritual of love.

Like Nicholas Urfe in *The Magus,* the hero of John Barth's structuralist epic, *Giles Goatboy,* is instructed to "See Through Your Ladyship." And it is when literally united to Anastasia in sexual embrace that Giles achieves a structuralist vision of the universe:

> In the sweet place that contained me there was no East, no West, but an entire, seamless campus: Turnstile, Scrapegoat Grate, the Mall, the barns, the awful fires of the Powerhouse, the balmy heights of Founder's Hill—I saw them all; rank jungles of Frumentius, Nickolay's cold fastness, teeming T'ang—all one, and one with me. *Here* lay with *there, tick* clipped *tock, all* serviced *nothing;* I and My Ladyship, all, were one. [New York, 1967, p. 731]

The literary imagination has moved through existentialism and into structuralism in our time. The question remains whether the political imagination can follow. We desperately need a politics of structure (and a politics of love). One can only hope that ecological thinking (which is structural thinking) will help to reeducate us all. Man exists in a system beyond his control but not beyond his power to rearrange. The fall of man is neither a myth from prehistory nor an event at the beginning of human time. It is a process that has been occurring for centuries, and it is not so much a fall into knowledge as into power—the power to work great changes in ourselves and our immediate environment, the power to destroy our planet in various ways, slowly or quickly, or to maintain it and our life upon it for some time. On various levels of activity, man's ability to exert his power in self-destructive ways exceeds the ability of his feedback systems to correct his behavior.

The great failures of our government in recent years have been failures of imagination. What we need in all areas of life is more sensitive and vigorous feedback. The role of a properly structuralist imagination will of necessity be futuristic. It will inform mankind of the consequences of actions not yet taken. But it must not merely inform, it must make us feel the consequences of those actions, feel them in our hearts and our viscera. The structuralist imagination must help us to live in the future so that we can indeed continue to live in the future. And this task, this great task, as it makes itself felt, will work its changes in the system of literature. New forms will arise, must arise, if man is to continue.

If imagination fails us, if we fail ourselves, then structuralism offers its cool comfort. Man is a part of an orderly and intelligible system. Though it was not designed for him nor made by him, it is real, it is there, it is to to some extent knowable. If he cannot continue to adapt to it, it will go on without him. He can study it, love it, and accept its functioning as a thing of beauty which needs no human sanction nor even human existence for its justification.

Bibliographical Appendix

This is not a full listing of all works associated with structuralists or structuralism. It is a select list of significant works in structuralist literary criticism and theory, along with important precursors and related studies. It is, insofar as possible, a list of works in the English language, French titles being included only where there is as yet no English version of a text available. In an effort to make it as useful as possible to those for whom this really is an *introduction* to structuralism, I have provided notes for many entries, indicating the nature and value of the work listed, as I understand it.

I. The Formalists: Studies, Anthologies, and Works by Formalists

Bakhtin, Mikhail. *Rabelais and His World.* Cambridge, Mass.: M.I.T., 1968.

——. *Problems of Dostoevsky's Poetics.* Ann Arbor: Ardis, 1973.

Chklovski, Victor. *Sur la théorie de la prose.* Lausanne: L'Age d'Homme, 1973. This is a major work in narrative theory, first published in Russian in 1929. It should be translated into English in the near future. For Chklovski and Eikhenbaum (below) I use the spellings more current in English-language texts: Shklovsky and Eichenbaum.

Eikhenbaum, Boris. *The Young Tolstoy.* Ann Arbor: Ardis, 1972.

Eisenstein, Sergei. *Film Form.* New York: Harvest Book, 1969.

————. *The Film Sense.* New York: Harvest Book, 1969.

Though Eisenstein was not a member of the formalist group, and in fact was frequently required to repudiate formalist "tendencies," much of his work on film belongs with theirs on literature.

Erlich, Victor. *Russian Formalism.* The Hague: Mouton, 1955. This is still the standard work on the history and doctrine of the formalists.

Jameson, Fredric. (See section II below.)

Lemon, Lee T., and Reis, Marion J., eds. *Russian Formalist Criticism.* Lincoln, Neb.: Bison Books, 1965. Probably the best brief introduction to the formalists, this volume includes four selections from the writings of Shklovsky, Eichenbaum, and Tomashevsky, with useful introductory material and notes.

Matejka, Ladislav, and Pomorska, Krystyna. *Readings in Russian Poetics.* Cambridge, Mass.: M.I.T., 1971. The fullest collection of formalist writing available in English, this volume includes the work of Eichenbaum, Jakobson, Tomashevsky, Tynianov, Bogotyrev, Propp, Brik, Voloshinov, Bakhtin, Trubetskoy, and Shklovsky, as well as informative essays by the editors.

Propp, Vladimir. *Morphology of the Folktale.* Austin: University of Texas, 1970.

Shklovsky, Victor. (See Chklovski.)

Todorov, Tzvetan, trans. and ed. *Théorie de la littérature.* Paris: Seuil, 1965. Much of this material is now available in English in the Lemon and Reis and the Matejka and Pomorska anthologies, but some is not, including Shklovsky's important piece on "The Construction of the Story and the Novel." Selections from Eichenbaum, Jakobson, Vinogradov, Tynianov, Brik, Tomashevsky, and Propp are also included.

II. Structuralist Anthologies and Books about Structuralism

Auzias, Jean-Marie. *Clefs pour le structuralisme.* Paris: Editions Seghers, 1971. Entirely rewritten for this third edition, Auzias's book is a general introduction to the subject of structuralism. In addition to the linguistic background and basic concepts, Auzias devotes chapters to anthropology (from Durkheim to Lévi-Strauss), to Althusser and Marxism, to the "non-structuralism" of Foucault, and to Lacan and psychoanalysis. His treatment of literature is a bit thin, but as a whole the book is bright, lively, and makes a useful introduction to the subject.

Chatman, Seymour, ed. *Approaches to Poetics.* New York: Columbia, 1973. This is a collection of English Institute papers on the subjects of structuralist and stylistic approaches to literature—both pro and con. Like most such volumes, its parts outshine the whole. It includes essays by Victor Erlich on Jakobson, Hugh Davidson on Barthes, and others by Frank Kermode, Richard Ohmann, Stanley Fish, and Tzvetan Todorov.

Culler, Jonathan. *Structuralist Poetics.* London: Routledge and Kegan Paul, 1973. As this bibliography goes to press, Culler's book has not appeared. But judging from his piece in Robey's anthology (see below) and an essay in *Centrum* (see section VII), it should be a thoughtful and judicious piece of work.

DeGeorge, Richard, and DeGeorge, Fernande, eds. *The Structuralists from Marx to Lévi-Strauss.* Garden City: Doubleday Anchor Books, 1972. This is an anthology which includes works by Marx, Freud, Saussure, Jakobson, Barthes, Lévi-Strauss, Althusser, Foucault, and Lacan, as well as a brief but useful introduction by the editors. It differs from similar endeavors by insisting that Marx and Freud are structuralists, because they share with Saussure and others "a conviction that surface events and phenomena are to be explained by structures, data, and phenomena below the surface." Structuralism in literature is represented in this collection only by two essays of Barthes's, but they are important essays.

Ehrmann, Jacques. *Structuralism.* Garden City: Doubleday Anchor Books, 1970. Originally a volume in the Yale French Studies series, the ten essays in this collection treat structural aspects of linguistics, anthropology, art, psychiatry, and literature. The collection is a rather mixed bag of essays by structuralists (Lévi-Strauss, Lacan, and Ehrmann himself) and essays about structuralism and related subjects. The whole collection tends somewhat toward the elliptical and overingenious. It is definitely for the advanced inquirer into structuralist activity, not the beginner. But Geoffrey Hartman's essay on Anglo-American structuralism and Michael Riffaterre's piece on the Jakobson and Lévi-Strauss analysis of Baudelaire's "Les Chats" are important. Bibliographical material is included, but it is both thin and dated.

Gardner, Howard. *The Quest for Mind.* New York: Knopf, 1973. Subtitled "Piaget, Lévi-Strauss, and the Structuralist Movement," this is a very full treatment of two major structuralists and their ideas. Though it virtually ignores the literary and linguistic structuralists, it is a useful introduction to the epistemology of structuralism.

Garvin, Paul L. *A Prague School Reader on Esthetics, Literary Structure, and Style.* Washington: Georgetown, 1964. This is the best available introduction to the writings of the Prague school of structuralists. In particular, it includes four essays by Jan Mukarovsky and a very useful bibliography with annotations.

Gras, Vernon W. *European Literary Theory and Practice.* New York: Delta Book, 1973. Subtitled "From Existential Phenomenology to Structuralism," this carefully selected anthology includes works by Jakobson, Lévi-Strauss, Barthes, Leach, and Butor as well as a somewhat richer selection of materials from existentialist and phenomenological writers. The introduction is informed and intelligent. But aside from an excerpt from Barthes on Racine, all the structuralist literary "practice" is devoted to myth and fairy tale. Genette and Todorov should have been included here.

Jameson, Fredric. *The Prison-House of Language.* Princeton University, 1972. This is a very well informed and shrewdly critical study of formalism and structuralism by a Hegelian critic who concentrates on the limitations of the formalist and structuralist methodologies. It includes a useful bibliography, though English versions of the many foreign works are not cited.

Lane, Michael, ed. *Introduction to Structuralism.* New York: Harper Torchbook, 1972. This is a general anthology which emphasizes linguistic, anthropological, and literary essays. It benefits from an excellent introduction by the editor and an extensive bibliography. On the whole it is a thorough and thoughtful introduction to the subject.

Macksey, Richard, and Donato, Eugenio, eds. *The Languages of Criticism and the Sciences of Man.* Baltimore: Johns Hopkins, 1970. Subtitled "The Structuralist Controversy," this volume includes the proceedings of an important conference held at Johns Hopkins in 1966. It contains position papers by structuralists and anti-structuralists, as well as transcriptions of the ensuing debates. Girard, Poulet, Goldmann, Todorov, Barthes, Lacan, Derrida, and Ruwet are among those represented. The notes on participants are bibliographically useful. This is an important text for the advanced student.

Piaget, Jean. *Structuralism.* New York: Basic Books, 1970. Superbly translated and edited by Chaninah Maschler, this is a crucial document in the philosophy of structuralism. Though Piaget does not discuss literature, his treatment of structuralist concepts in mathematics, logic, physics, biology, psychology, linguistics, anthropology, and philosophy is of great importance for literary students, as is his definition of structure in chapter 1.

Robey, David, ed. *Structuralism: An Introduction.* Oxford: Clarendon, 1973. This is a slim collection of excellent essays on various aspects of structuralism by Jonathan Culler and John Lyons (linguistics), Edmund Leach (anthropology), Umberto Eco (semiotics), Tzvetan Todorov (Henry James), John Mepham (philosophy), and Robin Gandy (mathematics).

Wahl, François, ed. *Qu'est-ce-que le structuralisme?* Paris: Seuil, 1968. Currently under revision, the original version of this work included five substantial essays: Oswold Ducrot on linguistics, Tzvetan Todorov on poetics, Dan Sperber on anthropology, Moustafa Safan on psychoanalysis, and Wahl on philosophy. Todorov's manifesto has been substantially rewritten and is soon to appear as an independent volume.

Wellek, René. *The Literary Theory and Aesthetics of the Prague
School.* Ann Arbor: University of Michigan, 1969. An important monograph on the Prague structuralists, emphasizing the
work of Mukarovsky.

III. Structuralist and Proto-Structuralist Studies in Language and Literature

Barthes, Roland. *On Racine.* New York: Hill and Wang, 1964.
Very much a book on Racine by an individual rather than a representative of some school, this is a better guide to Barthes as a
critic than to structuralism as a subject, but it is a brilliant book,
well translated by Richard Howard.
————. *Writing Degree Zero* and *Elements of Semiology.* Boston: Beacon, 1970. Two of Barthes's monographs are brought
together in this little volume. The *Elements* is the less paradoxi-
cal of the two.
————. *Critical Essays.* Evanston: Northwestern, 1972. Translated by Richard Howard, this is a rich and varied collection,
which includes some of Barthes's most important pieces on literature and criticism.
————. *Mythologies.* New York: Hill and Wang, 1973. These
are mainly short journalistic pieces on popular culture, showing
the practical semiologist at his best.
————. *S/Z.* Paris: Seuil, 1970. As this bibliography goes to
press, Richard Howard's translation has not yet appeared—
and it will not be easy to get this astonishing semiological exe-
gesis of a Balzac story into English.
Benveniste, Emile. *Problems in General Linguistics.* Coral Gables:
University of Miami, 1971. A collection of essays of unusual lu-
cidity, frequently referred to by structuralist literary critics.
Booth, Wayne C. *The Rhetoric of Fiction.* University of Chicago,
1961. Neither formalist nor structuralist, Booth's neo-Aristo-
telian approach to fiction has been influential on the younger
generation of structuralists.
Bovon, François, ed. *Analyse structurale et exégèse biblique.* Neu-
châtel: Delachaux et Niestlé, 1971. This is a collaborative

collection of essays by literary structuralists and traditional exegetes. It includes a discussion of structuralism by the editor and essays in biblical structuralism by Barthes, Martin-Achard, Starobinski, and Leenhardt.

Bremond, Claude. *Logique du récit.* Paris: Seuil, 1973. In the first section of this book Bremond includes important critiques of Bédier, Greimas, and Todorov. The larger second part is devoted to his study of "The Principal Narrative Roles."

Dorfman, Eugene. *The Narreme in the Medieval Romance Epic.* University of Toronto, 1969. Subtitled "An Introduction to Narrative Structures," this is a rather feeble attempt to apply structuralist techniques to *Roland* and the *Cid*.

Frye, Northrop. *Anatomy of Criticism.* Princeton University, 1971. A major document in Anglo-American structuralism.

————. *Fables of Identity.* Harbinger, 1963. A collection of essays, mostly written after the *Anatomy,* which first appeared in 1957.

Genette, Gérard. *Figures.* Paris: Seuil, 1966.

————. *Figures II.* Paris: Seuil, 1969.

————. *Figures III.* Paris: Seuil, 1972.

Genette is one of the two or three most important literary structuralists. His books have yet to appear in English, but a selection from them is presently anticipated from the Johns Hopkins Press.

Goldmann, Lucien. *The Hidden God.* New York: Humanities, 1964. This Marxist/structuralist study of Pascal and Racine is one of the works to which Barthes responded in *On Racine.*

————. *Pour une sociologie du roman.* Paris: Gallimard, 1964. Not yet available in English, this volume includes a long study of the novels of Malraux and three short essays in which Goldmann develops his "genetic structuralism," which seeks to unite a Lukácsian Marxist view of society with a structuralist methodology.

Greimas, A. J. *Semantique structurale.* Paris: Larousse, 1966.

————. *Du sens.* Paris: Seuil, 1970.

Frequently crabbed and cryptic himself, Greimas has been an important influence on the younger generation of structuralists.

Guillén, Claudio. *Literature as System.* Princeton University, 1971. This collection of essays is in no sense programmatically structuralist, but the whole book aims "to support a structural approach toward the fundamental units, terms, and problems of literary history." It is, among other things, an "inner dialogue" with Lévi-Strauss and Saussure. A major document of literary structuralism.

Heller, L. G., and Macris, James. *Toward a Structural Theory of Literary Analysis.* Worcester, Mass.: Institute for Systems Analysis, 1970. This attempt to reduce literary values to a few structural principles is the sort of hard-core structuralism that properly horrifies more traditional literary critics, because it leaves out so much that is important in literary study. On the other hand, it focuses attention on some matters which are frequently overlooked, perhaps because they seem so obvious.

Hendricks, William O. *Essays on Semiolinguistics and Verbal Art.* The Hague: Mouton, forthcoming.

Jakobson, Roman. *Selected Writings.* New York: Humanities, in progress. This six-volume edition will finally bring together the bulk of Jakobson's varied and voluminous writing on language and literature. Volume 3, *The Grammar of Poetry and the Poetry of Grammar,* will be especially important for students of structural poetics. Until it appears, certain crucial essays will be available in English only in collections such as Lane (section II above) and Sebeok (section VI below). See also Jakobson, in section VI.

————. *Questions de poétique.* Paris: Seuil, 1973. An excellent collection of essays compiled under the direction of T. Todorov, this includes most of Jakobson's important essays on poetics, with the notable exception of "Linguistics and Poetics," which can be found in English in Sebeok (section VI).

Jakobson, Roman, and Halle, Morris. *Fundamentals of Language.* The Hague: Janua Linguarum, Mouton, 1956. Part 2 of this work contains Jakobson's celebrated discussion of metaphor and metonymy.

Jolles, André. *Formes simples.* Paris: Seuil, 1972. Translated from

Einfache Formen by Antoine Marie Buguet, this important work of proto-structuralism, dating originally from 1930, may yet appear in English.

Lewin, Jane. "Structural Poetics." Dissertation in progress, Brown University. The long introductory section of this work includes a full discussion of Genette and Todorov.

Metz, Christian. *Language of Film.* New York: Praeger, 1973. This is a major statement on the semiology of film.

Mukarovsky, Jan. *Aesthetic Function, Norm and Value as Social Facts.* Ann Arbor: University of Michigan, 1970. Translated and annotated by Mark E. Suino, this work by a leader of the Prague school originally appeared in 1936. It is an important monograph in its own right and also serves to illustrate the move away from formalism toward a structuralism which investigates social as well as literary data.

Rabkin, Eric. *Narrative Suspense.* Ann Arbor: University of Michigan, 1973. An interesting contribution to generic theory.

Saussure, Ferdinand de. *Course in General Linguistics.* New York: McGraw-Hill, 1966. Translated and annotated by Wade Baskin, this work compiled by Saussure's students in 1915 is still the essential first book in structuralism.

Scholes, Robert, and Kellogg, Robert. *The Nature of Narrative.* New York: Oxford, 1966. This work belongs to the formalist/structuralist tradition because it attempts to treat the evolution of narrative literature primarily in terms of the working of a generic system.

Souriau, Étienne. *Les deux cent mille situations dramatiques.* Paris: Flammarion, 1950. An important work of proto-structuralism dealing with dramatic literature.

Todorov, Tzvetan. *Littérature et signification.* Paris: Larousse, 1967. This is primarily an application of structuralist methodology to *Les liaisons dangereuses.*

———. *Grammaire du Décaméron.* The Hague: Mouton, 1969. In this monograph Todorov systematizes and amplifies the method of Propp in order to describe the structure of Boccaccio's fiction.

————. *Introduction à la littérature fantastique.* Paris: Seuil, 1970. A translation of this by Richard Howard was published by the Case Western Reserve Press in 1973. The book is an important essay in generic theory, as well as a lucid and insightful study of fantastic literature.

————. *Poétique de la prose.* Paris: Seuil, 1971. A major collection of Todorov's structuralist literary criticism, this includes essays on the theory of fiction and on narratives of various kinds from various times and cultures. The Cornell University Press expects to publish a translation by Robert Scholes in 1975.

————. *Poétique.* Paris: Seuil, 1973. This is a revised version of the structuralist manifesto that appeared in Wahl (see section ii above).

One of the two or three major structuralist literary critics, Todorov is as yet insufficiently available in English; therefore I am indicating here the locations of six brief essays that have appeared in translation:

————. "Structural Analysis in Narrative." *Novel: A Forum on Fiction,* Fall 1969. Reprinted in Lipking and Litz, *Modern Literary Criticism.* New York: Atheneum, 1972.

————. "The Discovery of Language: *Les Liaisons Dangereuses* and *Adolphe.*" *Yale French Studies,* 1970.

————. "The Fantastic in Fiction." *Twentieth Century Studies.* May 1970.

————. "Language in Literature." Macksey and Donato (see section ii above).

————. "Meaning in Literature: A Survey." *Poetics,* no. 1. The Hague: Mouton.

————. "The Two Principles of Narrative." *Diacritics,* Fall 1971.

Van Rossum-Guyon, Françoise. *Critique du roman.* Paris: Gallimard, 1970. This is an extended essay in structuralist criticism applied to a single work of fiction: Butor's *La Modification.*

Wollen, Peter. *Signs and Meaning in the Cinema.* Bloomington: Indiana University, 1969. This is a useful introduction to a subject too large to be properly bibliographed here. The last chapter, "The Semiology of the Cinema," is a brisk discussion of the relationship of structuralism to film, which emphasizes the contributions of the neglected American philosopher of language, Charles Sanders Peirce. Unfortunately, the book contains neither notes nor bibliography.

IV. Structuralism in Fields Related to Literature and Language

Obviously this is a catch-all category. And after a certain point its usefulness would diminish in direct proportion to its extensiveness. But here are included the major figures most frequently called structuralists, whose work lies outside the fields of linguistics and literary criticism, along with a few key books not always recognized as "structuralist" but important for presenting essentially structuralist perspectives on human activity.

Althusser, Louis. *For Marx.* New York: Vintage, 1970. Althusser is frequently called a structuralist, perhaps because he insists on treating the works of Marx as a body of "scientific" material, to be tested, developed, and discarded as any other scientific hypotheses might be. This collection of essays on Marx is a critique and elaboration of a Marxian "science of history."

Bateson, Gregory. *Steps to an Ecology of Mind.* New York: Ballantine, 1972. Though Bateson does not use the word, his essays on epistemology, ecology, biology, psychology, and anthropology are important contributions to the philosophy and ideology of structuralism.

Burnham, Jack. *The Structure of Art.* New York: Braziller, 1971. This is a work of programmatic structuralist intent, beginning with brief discussions of Lévi-Strauss, Saussure, Barthes, Chomsky, and Piaget, then continuing with analyses of paintings and other art works from Turner to Duchamp.

Derrida, Jacques. "Structure, Sign, and Play in the Discourse of the Human Sciences." Included in Macksey and Donato (see section II above). Though frequently called a structuralist, Derrida is closer to existentialist phenomenology in his outlook. The essay cited above is a formidable attack on structuralist premises by one who says essentially "you do not go far enough." His two volumes on the nature of language, writing, and thought (*De la grammatologie,* Paris: Minuit, 1967; and *L'Écriture et la différence,* Paris: Seuil, 1967) are being translated but have yet to appear in English.

Foucault, Michel. *Madness and Civilization* [*Histoire de folie*]. New York: New American Library, 1973.

————. *The Order of Things* [*Les mots et les choses*]. New York: Pantheon, 1970.

————. *The Archaeology of Knowledge.* New York: Pantheon, 1970.

Foucault persistently denies that he is a structuralist, but his interest in the patterns of historical process suggests that despite his denials he belongs to the formalist/structuralist tradition. Thus far he has not been especially well served by his American publishers. The name of the translator of *The Order of Things* is nowhere indicated in the volume, and this shyness is understandable in view of the clumsiness of the text's English. In addition to this, the frontispiece of the book, a reproduction of "Las Meninas" by Velasquez which is indispensable for understanding the first chapter, has been omitted from this overpriced volume, despite the fact that it is referred to in the notes. But for the English-language reader, this is what is available. Perhaps the student should begin with the *Archaeology,* especially the conclusion and the appended "Discourse on Language."

Gombrich, E. H. *Art and Illusion.* Princeton University, 1961. Seldom accused of structuralism, Gombrich's brilliant treatment of the system of evolution in the plastic arts links him to the formalist/structuralist tradition.

Köhler, Wolfgang. *The Task of Gestalt Psychology.* Princeton University, 1969. Jean Piaget in *Structuralism* associates the Gestalt psychologists with the beginnings of structuralism in psychology. Köhler's brief and lucid summary is an excellent introduction to the achievement and the doctrine of the Gestaltists.

Kuhn, Thomas S. *The Structure of Scientific Revolutions.* University of Chicago, 1970. By treating scientific thought as an evolving system—much the way Gombrich treats painting or literary critics treat the history of genres—Kuhn has narrowed the gap between science and art. He has also started a great controversy within the ranks of historians of science. An important book.

Lacan, Jacques. *The Language of the Self: The Function of Language in Psychoanalysis.* Baltimore: Johns Hopkins, 1968. This is Lacan's only major work available in English. It includes a full bibliography. Important essays by Lacan may also be found in the works by Ehrmann and by Macksey and Donato listed in section II above.

Piaget, Jean. *Six Psychological Studies.* New York: Vintage, 1968. Piaget has been as productive a scholar in his field of genetic epistemology as Lévi-Strauss in anthropology. The single title listed here is meant to serve as an introduction to the larger body of work, which is extensively available in English. These six studies have been well selected to reveal the range and quality of Piaget's research, and they are accompanied by a good bibliography of French and English titles.

Wiener, Norbert. *The Human Use of Human Beings.* New York: Avon Books, 1967. Subtitled "Cybernetics and Society," this book appeared first in 1950. It is a book about concepts important in contemporary structural thinking without being itself structuralist. Along with Bateson's work cited above, it is a major contribution to structuralist thinking nonetheless.

V. *Works by and about Claude Lévi-Strauss*

The following is an abbreviated listing which omits most of Lévi-Strauss's more specialized anthropological writing.

Charbonnier, Georges. *Conversations with Claude Lévi-Strauss.* London: Cape Editions, 1969. Under Charbonnier's shrewd and humane questioning, Lévi-Strauss expounds and expands his ideas on anthropology and art.

Hayes, E. Nelson, and Hayes, Tanya, eds. *Claude Lévi-Strauss: The Anthropologist as Hero.* Cambridge, Mass.: M.I.T., 1970. This is a collection of essays on Lévi-Strauss and structuralism, ranging from popular journalistic portraits to serious exegeses. It is well selected and includes an extensive bibliography of works in both French and English.

Leach, Edmund. *Claude Lévi-Strauss.* New York: Viking, 1970. This monograph in the "Modern Masters" series is the best possible introduction to Lévi-Strauss. Edmund Leach is the leading British anthropological disciple of the master, but he keeps his exegeses well this side idolatry.

Lévi-Strauss, Claude. *Tristes Tropiques.* New York: Atheneum, 1970. This is a somewhat abridged version of the French text that was first published in 1955. In it, the author describes in a very personal way his first anthropological studies and the questions they raised in his mind.

————. *Structural Anthropology.* Garden City: Anchor Books, 1967. This is a collection of essays on anthropological subjects, first published in France in 1958.

————. *Totemism.* Boston: Beacon Press, 1963.

————. *The Savage Mind.* University of Chicago, 1966.

These latter two works, taken together, constitute a major statement on primitive thought. As such they form a prelude to the four-volume *Mythologiques,* which is now nearing completion.

VI. Stylistics: Anthologies and Major Works

Because contemporary stylistics brings linguistic knowledge to bear on an aspect of literature, it is often confounded with structuralism, which "does the same thing." The thing is similar enough, surely, to deserve some bibliographical notice here, but also different enough to belong in this separate section. This is a basic, unannotated list of works drawn from a very extensive field.

Chatman, Seymour. *A Theory of Meter.* The Hague: Mouton, 1965.

————. *Literary Style: A Symposium.* New York: Oxford, 1971.

————. *The Later Style of Henry James.* New York: Oxford, 1972.

Chatman, Seymour, and Levin, Samuel, eds. *Essays on the Language of Literature.* Boston: Houghton-Mifflin, 1967.

Enkvist, Nils E. *Linguistic Stylistics.* The Hague: Mouton, 1973.

Fowler, Roger, ed. *Essays on Style and Language.* New York: Humanities, 1966.

————, ed. *The Languages of Literature.* New York: Barnes and Noble, 1971.

Freeman, Donald C., ed. *Linguistics and Literary Style.* New York: Holt, 1970.

Jakobson, Roman, and Jones, Lawrence G. *Shakespeare's Verbal Art.* The Hague: Mouton, 1970.

Leech, Geoffrey N. *A Linguistic Guide to English Poetry.* London: Longmans, 1969.

Le Guern, Michel. *Sémantique de la métaphore et de la métonymie.* Paris: Larousse, 1973.

Levin, Samuel. *Linguistic Structures in Poetry.* The Hague: Janua Linguarum, Mouton, 1962.

Love, Glen A., and Payne, Michael, eds. *Contemporary Essays on Style.* Glenview: Scott, Forsman, 1969.

Nowottny, Winifred. *The Language Poets Use.* London: Athlone, 1965.

Sebeok, Thomas A., ed. *Style in Language.* Cambridge, Mass.: M.I.T., 1960.

Uitti, Karl D. *Linguistics and Literary Theory.* Englewood Cliffs: Prentice-Hall, 1969.

VII. Periodicals

This is a highly selective list of periodicals devoted entirely or primarily to structuralist and related studies in language and literature.

Centrum. Published by the Minnesota Center for Advanced Studies
in Language, Style, and Literature, in Minneapolis. Volume 1,
Number 1 appeared in Spring 1973.

Change. Published by Seuil in Paris, this is a series rather than a
journal. Number 3 on "Le Cercle de Prague" and Number 5 on
"Le Dessin du récit" are especially relevant here.

Communications. Published by the École Pratique des Hautes
Études, in Paris, this series has been a major source of structuralist and semiological statements. Number 4 includes important
essays by Bremond, Todorov, Barthes, and Metz. Number 8, devoted entirely to the "Analyse structurale du récit," is the principal manifesto of structuralist narratologists. Numbers 11, 15,
and 16 also contain material important for students of structuralism.

Diacritics. Published four times a year by the Cornell Department
of Romance Languages since 1971, this journal has been very
hospitable to works of structuralist persuasion.

Hypothèses. A series published by Seghers/Laffont in Paris. The
first number (1972) deals with Jakobson, Halle, and Chomsky.

Journal of Literary Semantics. The first number of this series was
published by Mouton in 1972, and included articles by Fowler,
Richards, and Chatman, among others.

Poetics. Published irregularly by Mouton, this series frequently includes works of literary structuralism and stylistics.

Poétique. Published four times a year by Seuil in Paris, this is now
the major journal of the literary structuralists. Genette and Todorov are coeditors, along with Hélène Cixous. Contributors include major structuralists and related critics from both hemi-
spheres.

Semiotica. Published eight times a year by Mouton, this journal
frequently includes studies in literary semiology. Articles appear
in either French or English.

VIII.   Addendum

The four works listed here have come to my attention since the first
printing of this book. Two of them are bibliographical aids of a

complementary nature: one dealing with French Structuralism and the other with Anglo-American stylistics. And two of them are critical studies which happen also to be complementary. One is a work by a Russian who writes in the formalist tradition of low structuralism. The other is by a Frenchman who is close to Lacan and Foucault. The title of Uspensky's book is deceptive; it is a study of point-of-view in narrative.

Deleuze, Gilles. *Proust and Signs.* New York: George Braziller, 1972.

Harari, Josué V. *Structuralists and Structuralisms: A Selected Bibliography of French Contemporary Thought, 1960–1970.* Published by the journal *Diacritics.* Ithaca, 1973.

Kluewer, Jeffery D. "An Annotated Checklist of Writings on Linguistics and Literature in the Sixties." *Bulletin of the New York Public Library* 76 (1972): 36–91. Lists and discusses works written in English and dealing with English and American literature.

Uspensky, Boris. *A Poetics of Composition.* Berkeley: University of California Press, 1973.

Index

Terminology is a major problem for all students of structuralism. Not only do structuralists in general employ an extensive special vocabulary; as individuals, they often vary in their use of certain terms. Thus, in this index I have tried to record all contexts in which this terminology is defined or elaborated through use, as well as the customary list of names and subjects discussed.—*R. S.*